D1614438

C015858625

The Women's Land Army in First World War Britain

The Women's Land Army in First World War Britain

Bonnie White
St Francis Xavier University, Canada

First published 2014 by
PALGRAVE MACMILLAN

Palgrave Macmillan in the UK is an imprint of Macmillan Publishers Limited,
registered in England, company number 785998, of Houndmills, Basingstoke,
Hampshire RG21 6XS.

Palgrave Macmillan in the US is a division of St Martin's Press LLC,
175 Fifth Avenue, New York, NY 10010.

Palgrave Macmillan is the global academic imprint of the above companies
and has companies and representatives throughout the world.

Palgrave® and Macmillan® are registered trademarks in the United States,
the United Kingdom, Europe and other countries.

ISBN 978–1–137–36389–3

This book is printed on paper suitable for recycling and made from fully
managed and sustained forest sources. Logging, pulping and manufacturing
processes are expected to conform to the environmental regulations of the
country of origin.

A catalogue record for this book is available from the British Library.

A catalog record for this book is available from the Library of Congress.

Typeset by MPS Limited, Chennai, India.

Contents

List of Illustrations

Acknowledgments

This project has been the most difficult and rewarding task I have set for myself. Without the support of a number of people and organisations, this book would not have been possible. My interest in the Women's Land Army began with my doctoral research on communities at war. I owe thanks to McMaster University and the Department of History for their support. Thank you to the History and Political Science departments at Saint Francis Xavier University for giving me a place to call home during the completion of this book.

I am also grateful to the archives and libraries where I carried out the research for the project. I would like to thank the staff members of The National Archives, the Women's Library, the Imperial War Museums, the Devon Record Office, and the Museum of English Rural Life for their informed assistance. I would like to extend a special thank you to Caroline Vollans for her work at the Women's Library. Sections of Chapter 3 appeared previously in *The Local Historian*. I would like to thank the British Association for Local History for permission to reproduce that work here. I acknowledge permission to quote from private papers granted by the Trustees of the Imperial War Museum for allowing access to the collections, as well as the British Broadcasting Corporation and Southampton Museums. I am grateful to the copyright holders for allowing me to produce excerpts from the private papers under their authority.

I have been lucky to be surrounded by people who have tolerated by absences, absentmindedness, and moments of panic. I am indebted to Drs Johnathan Pope, Nicholas Mansfield, and Robert Zecker for reading a draft and making suggestions that strengthened the final version. Dr Olaf Janzen gave me the perspective and clarity to find my way. Drs Samuel Kalman and Cory Rushton offered stimulation and motivation – both have been mentors and I am grateful for their advice and support. Dr Bernard Wills reminded me of the adventures that lay beyond the walls of the university. Thank you Marcy Baker – the seventh floor would not be the same without you.

Above all, I would like to thank my families. To my parents, William and Judy White, thank you for your love and support, and to Ruby Thomas for teaching me to 'dream big'. Mary and Howard gave me the peace of mind to direct my attention to this project. Terri, thank you for Sunday

viii   *Acknowledgments*

afternoons. Thank you to Sheila for her support and encouragement and to Olivia whose companionship was invaluable. Jay, patios are meant to be shared – thank you for sharing yours. Jack makes my life wonderful and complete. John has had to endure my restlessness, which at times spun into excessive enthusiasm. Thank you for your patience, confidence, and love. Without Yvonne I would not have completed this book. It is likely I would not have started it. This is for her.

List of Abbreviations

CWAC	County War Agricultural Committee
FPD	Food Production Department
NAL	National Association of Landswomen
NFU	National Farmers' Union
NFWI	National Federation of Women's Institutes
SWLA	Scottish Women's Land Army
WAC	War Agricultural Committee
WFGU	Women's Farm and Garden Union
WLA	Women's Land Army
WNSC	Women's National Service Scheme
WWAC	Women's War Agricultural Committee

Introduction

The role of the Women's Land Army (WLA) in the agricultural history of the First World War has often been overlooked due to the seemingly minor role played by the organisation in maintaining domestic food production between its formation in January 1917 and its demobilisation in October 1919. The WLA, however, marked the first time that a group of women came together in a national organisation for farm work. The creation of the WLA was part of a broader effort to mobilise a domestic force of women workers, but with the specific task of replacing the male agricultural labourers who had enlisted or who had been conscripted into Britain's armed forces. This study argues that although farm work became an imperative patriotic act, valued not just for the food produced, but also through the symbolic act of tending the land, organisers like Meriel Talbot (the Director of the Women's Branch in charge of the WLA) and Edith Lyttelton (Deputy Director) did not envision the organisation simply in patriotic terms. The WLA was formed to help solve the real problem of the dwindling agricultural labour supply, but organisers believed that a national organisation would help convince farmers, potential recruits, and the public of the valuable role women could play in agriculture, not only in wartime, but as a viable employment opportunity beyond the years of the conflict. This organisational history of the Women's Land Army contextualises the work carried out by the Land Army by examining the relationship between organisers, farmers, unions, and Land Girls between 1914 and 1919.

Little work has been done on the organisational history of the Land Army, and existing works fails to include the Scottish experience due to the structural variations between the English and Scottish organisations. Historians have focused on England, the motivations of Land Girls for undertaking agricultural work, and how their experiences fit

1

into the larger narrative of women's war work. While including the voices of Land Girls, this study aims to understand the role of organisers in England, Wales, and Scotland in bringing women to the land. Examining how they envisioned the organisation, what their goals were, and what obstacles they faced allows us to properly contextualise the Land Army's role. Understanding the organisers' motivations and the organisation's goals helps clarify the WLA's successes and failures. On the one hand, the WLA recruited, trained, and placed thousands of women on Britain's farms and made a meaningful contribution to the British war effort. On the other hand, the organisation faced the difficult challenge of making women's employment in a male-dominated industry acceptable and permanent, a goal organisers ultimately failed to achieve. The reasons for the acceptance of women on the land and their departure from it post-1918 was most directly a result of the war and its cessation; however, broader trends in agriculture helped to ensure the brief lifespan of the organisation.

The purpose of this book is not to provide a breakdown of every organisation and organiser involved in the Land Army's operations, but rather to construct a history of the Women's Land Army that is attentive to the variances of – and motivations for – the establishment of the Land Army scheme, how those methods and approaches impacted the operability of the scheme, and why, in spite of the efforts of organisers to validate the Land Girls' contributions on the land, the WLA demobilised in 1919 when the food situation remained uncertain.

The obstacles facing organisers were great. Throughout the nineteenth and twentieth centuries, women's role in agriculture was diminished as changes to agricultural practices created a clearer division of gender roles. As the sharing of work diminished, the separate spheres of home and field were gradually reinforced. The proportion of women engaged in fieldwork varied from region to region, but the loss of women from the land confirmed the common belief that women were unsuited to the work despite the fact that the daily operation of farms tended to rely, to some degree, on women's labour. The First World War presented an opportunity for organisations interested in the advancement of women in the agricultural industry to affect change. The vulnerability of British imports to German U-boats meant that the state would have to adopt new strategies to maintain a population of 36 million, especially considering that half of all of the food consumed in Britain in 1914 was imported.[1]

The Women's Branch, the central organising body for the WLA, set out to restructure the various groups that had advocated for a place for women in the industry prior to the war in England, Wales, and Scotland into a formal national organisation. Talbot's goal was to turn the organisation into a long-term training and promotional group for women's agricultural work. Talbot thus approached the organisation and its management from this perspective. These organisations would become an important part of the Land Army organisation both locally and nationally. The arduous task of managing domestic food production, even just women's involvement, meant that independent groups had to cooperate if the scheme was to be a success. Groups that had eagerly promoted agricultural work for women prior to the war devised plans to replace male agricultural labourers with an army of women workers. The British nation sought victory by many means and the government urged citizens to participate in and support the war in various ways. Beginning in 1915, the 'call to the land' became part of this nationalist experiment and the formation of a women's land army became part of a broader national dialogue about identity, nationalism, gender, and class. Revisionist studies of the war have sought to re-examine how Britons experienced the conflict beyond the national framework. Adrian Gregory's work on British society's response to the Great War moves beyond the national narrative in an effort to avoid over-generalisations about how Britons responded to the outbreak of war in August 1914, but also to examine why people consented to war and continued to support the state throughout the war's duration.[2] While Gregory does not deny patriotism as a real and organic response to the conflict, he carefully dissects 'myths' surrounding Britain's war effort through a cautious examination of the British home front. This study heeds Gregory's warning by challenging the assumed patriotic impulse of the organisation and by expanding our critical engagement with it. Cecilia Gowdy-Wygant argues that although the war 'brought significant change in the relationships women and their governments had with agriculture', our evaluation of that change cannot be confined to weighing material gains for women, nor can it be reduced to a cultural memory of women's patriotic work or wartime nostalgia.[3] Earlier works such as Pamela Horn's study of rural responses to the war asserts that not only was the Land Army a patriotic construct, but that its existence exposed unpatriotic farmers who refused to release their sons for military service.[4] Horn not only imposes a patriotic framework on the Land Army, but also connects female patriotism to the perceived absence of male patriotism in Britain's agricultural districts. Her conclusions dilute the economic, social, and political value of the Women's Land Army and accepts that the culturally constructed image of the

Land Army – broadcast to the public as an organisation that offered women new opportunities during wartime without disrupting accepted pre-war gender codes – was an accurate reflection of the organisation and its responsibilities and duties, rather than examining the politically charged atmosphere within which the Women's Land Army was formed and operated.

This history of the Women's Land Army is therefore positioned at the crossroads of various histories and illustrates the organisation's social, economic, and cultural importance in the shaping of identities in the first quarter of the twentieth century. Over the course of the war the women of the Land Army, and organisers in particular, used the new organisation and its wartime importance to make statements about the way in which women saw their role in agriculture and in the war itself. In turn, the Land Army's interactions with government and the farming community made an equally important impression on the organisation. Land Girls not only provided necessary labour, but the process of promoting women's place and space on the land intersected with both national and local historical interests. The government exercised caution in moving women into wartime industries, characterising their employment as a vital service, rather than as a new employment opportunity and a future model for women in the workforce. Likewise, rural paternalism, the evolution of small specialised labour force, and the declining importance of agriculture as imports increasingly satisfied British dietary needs, meant that farmers had more to lose than just their male labourers.[5] The placement of women on British farms was never simple. This truth serves as a warning that reducing the challenges faced by organisers in the promotion and implementation of the Land Army scheme to simple prejudice on the part of farmers or the public ultimately ignores regional farming practices and devalues local experiences. Yet, the prejudices of farmers were made paramount during the war as the propaganda campaign surrounding women's land service vilified farmers who refused the well-intentioned efforts of women workers. The farmers' self-interests were juxtaposed with propaganda and imagery that focused on the government's attempt to cultivate a national identity based on a willingness among the populace to make the necessary sacrifices and to exercise an unrelenting resolve to nobly bear the burdens of war. The cultivation of the land was essential to victory and the return of women to the land was a character-building exercise that demonstrated many women's eagerness to support the war in any way they could. As such, the Land Army became connected to a national campaign that aimed to reaffirm British identity and the role of women in the nation's future.

The shift from the aesthetics of identity formation to the Land Army's utilitarian purpose forced organisers to reconceptualise the Land Army. Although the WLA sought to redefine femininity through the work the girls performed and through an interrogation of contemporary assumptions about womanhood, the Land Army actually reinforced traditional conceptions of masculinity and femininity. Historians have tended to adopt this framework in their discussions of the women who participated in the WLA. Susan Grayzel's study of women at war uses the popular axiom that women should 'do their bit' for the war effort by entering the labour force to challenge the one-dimensional propaganda narrative of duty-bound women whose contributions were both supportive and limited. While Grayzel's intention is to broaden our understanding of women's work, her attention to the Land Army is limited to the point that she reinforces the limited nature of women's agricultural employment, but without a full examination of the organisation's intentions and purpose. Janet Watson's work on the Land Army reaffirms the patriotic value that middle-class Land Girls placed on their war work, but she also argues that those women who came from the working-classes tended to see their war work as just that – work, and not service. Although Watson offers a new conceptual framework for our understanding of 'middle-class make-up of the Land Army', the exclusion of the organisation's female leadership both nationally and locally, which tended to come from the upper classes, and the lack of discussion surrounding the organisation's attempt to advance the position of women in the industry tends to limit her conclusions. As the educated, middle-class Land Girls gave way to a more diverse group, the need to reinforce the temporary nature of the organisation and to emphasise conventional stereotypes about gender became a primary concern. While the organisation was invested in creating a positive experience for women in farming and aimed to create a new place for women in the industry, the regimentation of life on the land and the hierarchical nature of land service glossed over individual efforts in favour of the group narrative. This is not to suggest that organisers devalued the opinions of Land Girls or that they were uninterested in how the women viewed their wartime roles, but the promotion of a Land Army culture became a solution to the myriad social, economic, and gendered struggles experienced by women during the war.

Although women's labour disturbed the social order, their displacement from farming once the war ended represented the reclamation of the land by men and the return to normalcy after 1919. Women in the nineteenth century had few options in terms of entry into the agricultural industry beyond their employment as temporary or seasonal workers, and although the war did little to increase those options in the post-armistice period, the formation of a national organisation of women workers that laboured to help feed the nation between 1917 and 1919 was a victory for those who made the scheme possible. So although the war did not bring a 'sudden and irreversible advance in the economic and social power' of women workers, it was not necessarily regressive either.[6] Although the patriarchal system remained in place[7] and the Land Army scheme proved to be temporary, the WLA owed its heritage to the efforts of middle-class reformers who drove the movement for expansion of women's role in agriculture forward, leading to the creation of the Women's Land Army. The resumption of the Land Army's duties in the Second World War and the development of new organisations in the inter-war period that aimed to expand employment opportunities for women in industry hints at progress even if the results were not wholly tangible.[8] Even before the outbreak of the Second World War in September 1939 the need to organise women for agricultural work was apparent. The government recognised that women agricultural workers would be a valuable part of the domestic economy and the WLA was reconstituted in June 1939, before the outbreak of hostilities. The advocacy work carried out by Talbot and Lyttelton on behalf of women agricultural workers was invaluable to the speedy deployment of Land Girls post-1939. Unlike in the war of 1914–18, the government did not wait for women to respond to the call to service and instead introduced conscription for single women between the ages of 18 and 32. Understanding the role of women in the First World War requires that we do not separate the years 1914–18 from the larger narrative of the women's lives or from the rest of the twentieth century. These women not only staked their claim on the land through their war work, but also appropriated a place in the nation's victory.

As the war came to an end in late 1918, the British government re-evaluated its priorities. The resumption of foreign importations would take time in order to match pre-war levels, which meant that domestic food production was still in demand. Further, the destruction of European lands by the war meant that home food production in Britain was not only essential to Britain's post-war recovery, but was also a political instrument. With price guarantees still in place in 1919, British farmers hoped to return to pre-war farming practices and readily made room for the returning men. The importance of the industry in the post-war economy gave the Land Army an extra year of life, but the exodus of women from farming and the oversaturation of the labour market meant that the Land Army's services were no longer needed. Public recognition of the Land Army came in several forms, but one way was through the construction of cultural memories about the WLA that served both the individual Land Girls and the state. Land Girls could appropriate the language of essential service to define their work and contributions, and the state not only bore witness to their efforts, but also formed a national body to coordinate the women's work. But the construction of a cultural memory of the Land Army tended to mute the efforts and ambitions of organisers like Meriel Talbot who, in spite of her missteps, saw a future for women in agriculture. The recognition of this fact offers a unique perspective of the Land Army. In an attempt to understand the organisation, its objectives, failings, and successes, this study focuses on the intersection of groups and people who helped inform the Land Army's development and operation. Moving beyond the national image of the Land Army as a patriotic organisation that served the needs of the nation in wartime, this study reclaims that WLA as a tool for understanding broader trends in agriculture, women's work, and women's organisations in the early twentieth century.

Each chapter of this work establishes a link between characterisations of the Land Army and the real problems and challenges experienced by both organisers and Land Girls. It begins with an examination of volunteer groups that pre-dated the WLA. By exploring the challenges faced by the groups that pre-dated the WLA, we can come to a better understanding of the difficulties faced by the Land Army itself. The book then moves on in the second chapter to explore the relationship between the female organisers of the Land Army and the Board of Agriculture, both of whom approached the issue of women's farm labour from different perspectives. While both groups wanted to see women employed on the land, what the women's employment would look like, the longevity of the organisation, and the potential future of women in the industry were perceived and weighted differently. The third chapter looks at the role of propaganda in the marketing of the Land Army, but also at the promotion of women's participation in the war effort generally. Promotion for the Land Army as a patriotic work opportunity served to elevate the attractiveness of land service, but at the same time made it less desirable. The chapter also considers the degree to which intra-organisational divisions about what the Land Army was and what it sought to achieve, hindered recruitment and diminished the organisation's efforts to promote the role of women in agriculture.

The next chapter analyses the impact of the propaganda campaign on Land Girls after they were enlisted, trained, and placed on farms. Rather than focusing on the Land Girls as an independent unit, this chapter recontextualises the Land Army by examining the experiences of Land Girls as a part of the larger agricultural community. Male prejudice toward female workers was only one obstacle faced by Land Girls, and this chapter seeks to understand the inter- and intra-gender conflicts and relationships that affected the experiences of women on the land.

The divergence of women's experiences is explored in the fifth chapter with the inclusion of the Scottish Women's Land Army (SWLA), which differed in its structure and organisation from the English model. This chapter stresses the importance of acknowledging and understanding regional variations, especially under the unifying umbrella of total war, and therefore warrants a separate chapter. Gender roles, rural structures, and government authority and priorities were determined by local attitudes, customs, and expectations, and each had a direct impact on organisers' presumptions regarding how the SWLA should be run. At the local level, the Land Army paradoxically supported and fractured the national image of the organisation. Finally, we turn to the aftermath of the armistice. In the peace that followed, the language of female war service was refashioned in order to return to the pre-war social and political order. The absence of women on the land was the value of victory, asserting that British society had not been destroyed by the war – the retreat of women from the land was as much a symbol of the return to pre-war conditions as was the return of men from the theatres of war. The demobilisation of the Land Army represented the actualisation of the return to normalcy.

The Women's Land Army could be dismissed as a wartime organisation that failed to find relevance beyond the war, and a case could arguably be made that the Land Army was a small and relatively minor addition to the agricultural labour force given that Land Girls numbered only 27,000 of the 250,000 women who worked the land in some capacity during the conflict.[9] Despite its gloomy future after November 1918, organisers proved themselves to be resourceful, and at times outright defiant, and Land Girls were competently adaptable and resilient. Although the women who toiled on the land between 1917 and 1919 did not necessarily understand all of the economic, social, and political forces that were responsible for and resistant to their employment, land work was an exciting new work opportunity. The value of the WLA lay not in the specifics of its day-to-day accomplishments on the land, but in its existence as an organisation that crossed class lines, that simultaneously challenged and reinforced gender expectations, and which was developed and implemented by women both locally and nationally.

1
Answering the Call: The Formation of the Women's Land Army

In the summer of 1915 British women took to the streets of London demanding the right to serve. This 'Call to the Women' of Britain was part of a larger campaign that encouraged women to support the war effort by entering the labour force and relieving men for military service. At the beginning of the war women flocked to factories and urban centres hoping to capitalise on the wartime market, but in the winter of 1916 there were rumours of food shortages in the capital and all groups involved in women's farm labour agreed that a concerted effort was needed to bring more women to the land. While these volunteer organisations did much to encourage enlistment, offer training, and put women to work on British farms, they did not have the support of the Asquith government and lacked central organisation. To coordinate and effectively employ women in agriculture, Lord Selborne, who had been working independently to organise women's farm labour since 1915, established the Women's Branch in December 1916 before retiring from his post as minister of food with the Board of Agriculture. The Women's Land Army was created in 1917 to serve as a central organisation for women's farm labour and was intended to act as an umbrella for those volunteer organisations already in place. The lack of central coordination, the volunteer nature of early farm and horticulture organisations, the absence of government support, and the divergent tactics employed by the various groups involved undermined the success of these organisations and presented a number of obstacles and challenges for the organisers of the Women's Land Army (WLA) after 1917. While the WLA was successful in bringing women to the land and establishing a viable source of labour, its overall efforts were impeded by organisational mismanagement and the unwillingness of central government to abandon its commitment to laissez-faire policies regarding agriculture.

On the eve of the First World War the British government spent an average of £269 million for the purchase of food, tobacco, and drink from overseas markets.[1] Although Britain relied extensively on imports to feed the population, in 1914 the weather was good and the harvest fruitful, labour was not yet in short supply, and it was estimated that home supplies of grain would last for five months.[2] Agriculture anticipated no immediate problems since the war was supposed to be over by Christmas and British imports would remain largely unaffected. This lack of intervention in the early days of the war was partly because initial concerns were not about supply, but rather prices, which reflected the inflationary nature of war finance, the high cost of imports, and rising shipping costs.[3]

While the government under Herbert Asquith was accused of neglecting agriculture, by the end of 1914 the state was directly responsible for buying and shipping the bulk of Britain's imported foodstuffs and was considering the regulation of prices and the distribution of food items. In December 1916 Asquith appointed a Food Controller (Lord Devonport was the first but was not actually appointed until David Lloyd George became Prime Minister) to control food prices, and later civilian rationing. In the same month he also established the Food Production Department to increase home food production. The result of these changes was the control of imports and production, and the sale of much of the nation's food supply. From the perspective of the populace, these changes had the benefit of slowing the rate of inflation on food prices, and they eventually led to the stabilisation of bread prices between 1917 and 1919.[4]

In the first two years of the war, however, a number of merchant ships had been requisitioned to provide essential supplies to Britain's troops on the continent, which decreased the number of ships available for civilian food imports.[5] Volunteerism in the early days and weeks of the war led to a shortage of dockhands to manage Britain's imports, leading to congestion and delays in British ports. In addition, the submarine campaign against Germany meant that shipping had to be diverted to ports away from the English Channel,[6] many of which were not initially equipped to handle the new loads. There was also concern that the U-Boat campaign would intensify as the war progressed, a problem that was compounded by the fact that the Royal Navy was slow to adopt convoy practices until there was no other recourse in 1917.[7] Shipping losses meant higher prices at home, which had already provoked consumer discontent. In order to make up for losses in shipping and imports, Britain's farming community had to increase home food production. The only practical way to increase production was to abandon the livestock regime in favour of cereals and grains. Even under ideal conditions this would have been a tricky undertaking given the nature of British farming. Large landowning estates were in decline, although this did not diminish the role of this group in local politics and recruiting, which they did enthusiastically.[8] Changing from livestock to cereals would have required massive intervention and the implementation of restrictive government controls to manage Britain's farms, which Asquith's Liberal government opposed.

Ultimately, the war's impact on agriculture can be divided into two stages: indirect and direct. In the first stage, August 1914 until May 1916, few changes were made to the agricultural sector and Britain's farmers continued to operate within a laissez-faire framework. Farmers were left to produce what they thought they should and the impact of the war on farming remained indirect. In the second stage – mid 1916 until the end of the war – the rise in demand for farm products clashed with the expansion of the armed forces under the new conscription laws, resulting in a decline in agricultural production. The inability of the farmers to meet quotas forced the government to change its agricultural policies.[9] The formation of the Women's Land Army was one of the changes introduced by the Lloyd George government in January 1917 as part of a larger policy to manage the nation's food supply.

In the meantime, the government encouraged farmers to manage the food situation locally. Upon the outbreak of war the government made several proposals to farmers through the medium of press releases by the Agricultural Consultative Committee. The policy favoured by the Committee was released on 18 August 1914, when it encouraged farmers to increase the production of staple crops by breaking up grasslands.[10] There were no incentives offered to the farmers; instead the Committee was content to offer *suggestions* that it hoped the farmers would implement. The Committee's suggestion to the farmers was part of the broader 'business as usual' approach adopted by the Asquith government at the beginning of the war. Under this plan, Britain would participate in the European war through limited military, industrial, and financial means, and with minimal disruption to the domestic life of the nation.[11]

During the war farmers' unions played a central role in organising and protecting members' rights, but their efforts were initially unsuccessful.[12] Many farmers, whether owner-occupiers or tenant farmers, were reluctant to plough up their fields because they wanted government assurance that prices and demands for their crops could be secured; the issue of price guarantees was an important part of pre-war discussions between the government and the National Farmers' Union (NFU). The union also worried about the requisite labour for such an undertaking. Due to the decline in agricultural production in the second half of the nineteenth century the number of agricultural labourers had declined from 3 million in 1870 to 2.3 million in 1911.[13] Farmers sought improved wages for their labourers in the hopes of preventing further loss of manpower to manufacturing and other industries where wages were higher, an issue that the Land Army would also be forced to deal with during recruiting.[14] This was especially important for those farmers who had limited access to machinery. Ploughing up pastures was a risky undertaking that the farmers, smallholders in particular, were not willing to consider without guarantees. In October 1914 the NFU's organising secretary reported that the Union had 'absolutely failed to get a guarantee' of government support in return for increasing the acreage of grain.[15]

While the Asquith government dithered about the implications of government intervention into the domestic food supply, Lord Selborne, President of the Board of Agriculture, was given the responsibility of managing the nation's food supply. In early 1915 he established the Milner Committee, comprised of three councils for England, Ireland, and Scotland, to consider the NFU's position. The unanimous finding of the English Committee in December 1915 was that a 'plough-up policy' was the only way for England to substantially increase the gross production of food for the 1916 harvest. The committee recommended offering farmers a minimum price for wheat over the next several years, but only if the farmers were successful in increasing the percentage of arable land by ploughing up their fields to plant staple crops. However, the Irish Committee rejected the idea of guaranteeing prices for any longer than one year, and the Scottish Committee was opposed to fixed prices for cereals, believing that the 1916 harvest would be bountiful and price guarantees would be unnecessary.[16] The findings of the Milner Committee eventually formed the basis of the food policy adopted for 1917–18, which included the formation of the Women's Land Army in England, Wales, and Scotland. Until then, however, intervention was rejected.[17]

Nevertheless, Selborne continued to stress the need for increased government action and encouraged the NFU to maintain pressure for government guarantees. Selborne also suggested that farmers offer a token of goodwill by voluntarily planting more potatoes and wheat, which some farmers did by abandoning their normal crop rotations. This was only a temporary solution as the land soon became weedy and infertile and instead of improving the productivity of the country, the move resulted in financial losses and a drop in agricultural production.[18]

Despite Selborne's protests his scheme received little support from the War Committee. Supporters of laissez-faire policies, including Reginald McKenna, Chancellor of the Exchequer, and Arthur Balfour, First Lord of the Admiralty, blocked all recommendations of regulation. Of primary concern was the scope of Selborne's scheme. Both McKenna and Balfour were apprehensive about the intended timeline for the proposal – was this to be a permanent policy or would it be terminated with the cessation of hostilities in Europe? Selborne's plan was to guarantee prices for an indeterminate amount of time, which was unacceptable to all but David Lloyd George, who supported government intervention in terms of price guarantees. The War Committee was also worried that the scheme would require a considerable commitment of personnel, rail lines for the transportation of equipment, horses and supplies, and funds to convert grazing land into arable land. Due to the war the rail lines and the treasury were already over-extended.[19] Despite disapproval from the War Committee, Selborne's programme was intended to reduce maritime shipping needs and negate foreign exchange demands by growing food at home, thereby protecting Britain's food supply from the vulnerability of a wartime market and, later, the German submarine campaign.[20]

Lord Selborne was unhappy with the results of the Milner Committee and felt that the Asquith government was too preoccupied with issues in Ireland, as well as with labour and munitions shortages, to give adequate attention to agriculture. While Selborne resigned from government in 1916 over Ireland,[21] he was committed to government intervention in agriculture, and in the meantime continued to work toward agricultural reforms. In July 1915 Selborne wrote a letter to Asquith imploring him to develop a plan to increase agricultural production at home, which he believed would have to include a plan for the use of alternative labour supplies, and he emphasised that even if the plan were not implemented immediately it would be ready *once* the food situation became less certain. Asquith's cabinet was not convinced that there would be a food shortage and the Prime Minister refuted the charge that immediate action was critical to ensure that home food supplies were secured.[22]

In September 1915 Asquith conveyed to Selborne that the food question was important, but not vital. While the nation had to produce as much food as possible, the pressing matter was the foreign exchange for the purpose of purchase.[23] In response, Selborne developed a plan to stimulate home food production in spite of not having the full support of the Asquith government for futher interference in agriculture. His initial plans involved the establishment of regional committees to coordinate food efforts, a propaganda campaign to appeal to the farmers' patriotism, and to enlist the help of volunteer organisations that were already dedicated to bringing women workers to the land. In 1915 Selborne set out to establish War Agricultural Committees under the Board of Agriculture to assess local farming needs.[24] Most immediately, farmers needed more labour if the plough campaign was to be considered. Selborne understood that asking farmers to increase crop production by ploughing up older fields, largely without the assistance of machinery, with a dwindling labour supply, a shortage of horses, and no government price guarantees, was neither appealing nor likely. David Lloyd George, who had called for a Food Controller to oversee domestic production, believed by November that the food situation was more pressing than previously thought. He was also supportive of a plan to supplement the agricultural labour force with women workers. Selborne's efforts to affect change with regard to domestic production, and Lloyd Geroge's support, matured after the Royal Commission on the Wheat Supply, headed by Lord Crawford, Selborne's eventual successor at the Board of Agriculture, reported that the food situation was uncertain, due in part to shipping losses, but also due to the uncertainty of domestic outputs.[25]

Selborne believed that the War Agricultural Committees (WAC) were a critical first step in increasing home food production, but these committees varied in their activity and efficiency. The cause of inconsistency was that the WACs were not uniformly introduced across the country, meaning that the structure of each committee reflected county, not local, needs and interests. Each county was required to appoint a WAC, but the County Councils determined the structure of the committee. Therefore, the WAC could consist of an existing committee or sub-committee of the County Council with co-opted members, or it could be a newly formed committee constituted for the express purpose of meeting food needs in wartime. While each committee was to be fully representative of all agricultural interests in the county, including landowners, farmers, and labourers, as well as educational authorities and unions, the interests of all groups were not necessarily represented equally.[26] The WAC was to appoint a local committee for each Rural District in the county and for each Urban District that contained a considerable amount of agricultural land.[27] The districts, however, were not of equal size and since labour needs would be decided by committee, the fear among some farmers was that smaller districts would lose out to the districts with greater yields or to ones where estate owners exercised more political clout. The Board of Agriculture only stipulated that all interests were to be represented, but did not indicate how 'representative' the committees should be. Considering that decisions and recommendations would be determined by vote, the distinction could be critical.

Since the WACs were to coordinate not only with the County Councils and the Board of Agriculture, but also with the Centre for Higher Agricultural Education and the National Farmers' Union, small holders feared that their interests would not be represented and many failed to respond to the government's request for cooperation. Although surveys were distributed in the counties most farmers refused to return questionnaires or circulars[28] commissioned by government. Thousands of circulars were sent to farmers throughout the country, but only a fraction received replies. In Herefordshire 2,220 circulars were issued with only 80 responses from farmers, and in Lincolnshire 8,000 circulars were distributed but the Board of Agriculture received only 499 replies.[29] It took some time for the WACs to be established in the counties and in the meantime Walter Runciman, President of the Board of Trade, decided it was best to work through the county councils.

The councils had the ability to reach every person in their area and possessed the administrative machinery to coordinate local efforts, and it was believed that by working through the county councils and various other organisations, including the Labour Exchanges, labour needs could be reasonably quantified. Reliance on the Labour Exchanges to assess labour needs was not without problems. Labour Exchanges did not exist in all areas and because they served as a register where prospective employers could find workers, farmers did not often utilise them. Most farms in Britain were small and irregular in shape, especially in the south-west. Changes to the land, changes in tenancy and holdings, and outmigration of the rural workforce meant that farmers relied on a small pool of labourers, most of whom were skilled. Because skilled agriculturalists were in short supply, they generally had no need to register with the Labour Exchanges to find work. As such, most farmers did not look for workers through this method. What the Labour Exchanges did offer was a list of men and women willing to work in agriculture, but these were generally unskilled and therefore less desirable.[30]

Selborne recognised that there were thousands of available men and women to work the land, but most were unskilled and had no knowledge of farm work. Prisoners of war (POWs) offered a possible solution, but they could only be used in limited numbers and only in *safe* areas. Early in the war POWs were most effectively used in farming districts where there was a negligible distance between the prison and the work site. In this way small gangs could be deployed under guard and returned to the prison at the end of the workday.[31] Outside of these limited parameters, the use of POWs did not prove to be fruitful. In the spring of 1915 talks between County Councils and the Education Authorities for the release of school-aged boys for agricultural work began, but progressed slowly.[32] Although the employment of children was regulated, farmers paid fines incurred by parents who allowed their boys to work beyond the hours permitted.[33] Attempts were also made to use interned aliens but they were not permitted to work in coastal areas or in close proximity to military camps.[34] The most complete failure was the use of conscientious objectors, due to the strength of public hostility.[35]

While the County Councils negotiated with the educational and military authorities and appointed committees to coordinate local efforts, Selborne recommended that women would not only be useful, but would be willing to answer the call and enlist for work in agriculture. He also believed that farmers would overcome initial prejudices and come to see the value in women land workers. What Selborne had in mind was a national campaign to bring women to the land. Selborne was careful to note, however, that unless the Asquith government fully committed to agriculture (which he stated had to be placed on an equal footing with the nation's military needs), either by offering concessions or devising a strategy to find suitable replacement labour, they were not likely to convince farmers to change their farming practices.[36] Selborne, therefore, tied the issue of women's labour to the issue of domestic production. Only with the assistance of women could the British war front remain productive, making their employment a vital part of the British war effort.

In November 1915 Sydney Olivier, Permanent Secretary to the Board of Agriculture, presented Selborne's case to the County War Agricultural Committees. Selborne's circular encouraged the Committees to acquaint themselves with the work of women in agriculture so that they would be in a better position to instruct farmers on the value of women workers. The Departmental Committee on the Home Production of Food recommended in their Final Report that women in rural areas should offer their services to local farmers. County Committees could assist in bringing women and farmers together by collecting the names and addresses of interested women. From there the Committees could work with the Labour Exchanges or, where none existed, another local body. This effort would require county-wide canvasses to determine the number of women willing to undertake agricultural work in each district. The Committee would also be responsible to assess the women's qualifications. Olivier stressed that the Committees should also impress upon women that there 'is a serious shortage of skilled farm workers and that their services would be greatly appreciated'.[37] The farmers must then offer fair wages as it would be difficult to retain women for agriculture otherwise. Part of the problem in convincing farmers to increase wages for women was that the various groups had little information regarding pay rates for women in agriculture. Wages fluctuated widely from county to county and from farm to farm.[38] As per Lord Milner's recommendations, the County Committees would then make provisions to have the women trained. This would not require an extensive training programme, but at this stage something along the lines of educational training would suffice. In counties where training was undertaken, Selborne believed that the best results came from short training sessions that ran for two to three weeks. The objective was for women to assist in farming.[39]

The training schemes adopted by each Committee would depend on a number of factors. The establishment of training schools or the extension of training courses for pre-existing agricultural colleges would be conditional on the farmers' cooperation, a sufficient number of interested women, the patriotic efforts of the members of the County Committees, and the available funding under the Board's regulations. If only a small number of women and farmers showed interest in the scheme, then it would be more fruitful and cost effective to train women locally. The farmer would have to ask one of his regular workers to act as an instructor and a nominal fee of 6d would be offered to the instructor from county funds. This would limit the involvement of the County Committees, but also discourage local resistance to the women's training and subsequent employment. The problem with this approach was that it removed one skilled worker from his regular duties to oversee the training of a few women. In the long term this approach might produce well-trained women workers, but they would be few in number.[40] In the end, the decision had to be made by the County Committees. Once a decision was made, however, Selborne recommended that all activities be carried out in conjunction with the Women's Committees, Labour Exchanges, and Educational Authorities. Although this meant that there was a considerable amount of oversight for the training/ placement scheme, there was no centralised authority.

For the time being a national programme with government support was unlikely, but Selborne knew that alternative labour was the way

forward and that the farmers would have to be convinced if home
production of food was to increase in 1916. Moved by the images of
French women pulling ploughs (Figure 1.1) that were strapped to their
shoulders while the men and horses were off at war, Selborne believed
that a similar campaign would be effective at home.[41] The propaganda
campaign would not only have to appeal to farmers to make sacrifices
for the good of the nation, but offer a practical solution to the labour
shortage. In Britain, women who wanted to serve had already put their
names on a list, the National Register for War Service, beginning in
March 1915. As the government was slow to organise women for farm
labour, Selborne encouraged women's clubs with interest in agriculture
to take up the cause.

One of the first to offer support was the Women's Farm and Garden
Union (WFGU). Established in 1899 as the Women's International
Agricultural and Horticultural Union, this group organised women
workers in London, primarily from the gentry, who were interested in
farm work to train at the few agricultural colleges in the country that
were open to women. The main goal of this group was to train women

Figure 1.1   French women pulling a plough, First World War
© akg-images / Alamy.

who were interested in a career in agriculture and to unite professional land workers through a central organisation that would offer advice and support for women in agriculture. In addition, it sought to change public attitudes toward female farmers and agricultural labourers. With just over thirty members at the outbreak of the war, the group hoped to expand when it launched the Women's National Land Service Corps to replace men lost from agriculture to the front. With the creation of an Education Committee in 1910 the WFGU sought to overcome farmer's prejudice toward female workers with proper education and regularly scheduled exams that would demonstrate the women's knowledge of farm work.[42] Together with a national propaganda campaign, the Union believed that women could offer a practical and viable solution to a looming labour crisis. Selborne agreed, and in 1916 the group was recognised by the Board for its work and allocated land for the construction of an agricultural training college. Selborne saw the organisation and the future college as a positive step toward a more comprehensive solution to the existing labour shortage and continued shortages in the future.[43]

The Agricultural Section of the Women's Legion and the University Association of Land Workers also came forward and promoted women replacing men on the land. The Women's Legion received an annual stipend from the Board of Agriculture for training purposes, but the results were limited and do not appear to have made a meaningful contribution to agriculture.[44] In 1915, all three organisations released press statements announcing schemes to organise and train women for work on the land. Funds were also established by the Board of Agriculture to help offset the initial cost of training for the women. While these organisations were willing and eager to do their part to bring women workers to Britain's farms, the lack of coordination between the groups created a number of challenges for Selborne and did little to impress farmers to employ women or the Asquith government to give much needed support to the scheme. The approaches taken by these organisations varied considerably and because there was no clear exchange of information, their efforts often overlapped. The Women's Legion established both Horticultural and Agricultural Sections and maintained separate training facilities for the two groups. Whereas the Horticultural Section appealed to women interested in the 'picturesque revival of herb growing' and encouraged women to take up selling plants on the streets of London for the successful growth of plants in home gardens, the Agricultural Section encouraged patriotic women to undergo a six-week training programme to teach women the basics of farming, but offered little practical experience.[45] Only thirty women could train at one time, making training both costly and inefficient.

Likewise, the WFGU had experimental training programmes to educate women about work on the land. Training lasted for twelve weeks and covered different kinds of farm work. Women had to pay for their own lodgings and daily living costs, but training was paid for by the Union.[46] The Board of Agriculture also had its own programme for educating and training women. Of the 218 women who completed the training course, 199 found agricultural employment. The Board established scholarships for milkers and general farm labourers, but these courses only lasted two weeks and even after they were extended to four weeks they were still considered to be inadequate by agriculturalists.[47] Most women completed courses in milking and of the 199 who found employment in agriculture the majority were either milkers or assisted the farmers' wives and daughters with domestic chores.[48] Some of the training programmes offered through the National Political League lasted up to two years, while other programmes ran for only three to four weeks. Alternately, some women were placed on farms without any training at all.

The Board of Agriculture's training options, much like those of the Women's Legion and the WFGU, endeavoured to demonstrate that women *could* be trained for agricultural work, not necessarily to actually train them. Likewise, the NPL was more of an information centre than a training organisation. Its initiative was to make men and women aware of the need for labour in agriculture and to educate them about work opportunities and the different classes of workers under the NPL. It also worked to match workers with farmers, but training was secondary and the League did not cover training costs. These programmes did not coordinate their training efforts or procedures, so the length of training, and in what areas the women were trained, varied from organisation to organisation.

It was only after February 1916 that the Board began to organise volunteer efforts into a comprehensive labour programme. In 1916 the Women's Farm and Garden Union was largely folded into the Women's National Land Service Corps (WNLSC). While the former groups remained operational throughout the war, the WNLSC represented the first step toward a change in direction away from the former volunteer organisations and toward the official launch of the Women's Land Army. In October 1916 the County Councils, Women's Agricultural Committees, Women's Legion/WNLSCs, and any other group that received grants from the Board were asked to present training schemes.

This was the earliest effort by the Board to begin integrating volunteer efforts into a national strategy to deal with the labour shortages in agriculture. The Board also took aim at the farmers who it believed expected too much from initial attempts to supply alternative labourers. The Board recognised that farmers were frustrated and disappointed, but argued that success was only possible if all groups involved lowered their expectations. Additionally, the Board took the opportunity to impress upon farmers that if they insisted on a certain degree of training, the best chance of success would come from self-training and the self-selection of candidates.[49] The Board of Agriculture under Selborne's leadership put the onus on farmers to make the scheme successful and made the farmers responsible for the persistence of labour shortages on their farms.

If initial training proved to be inadequate to convince farmers of the value of women agricultural workers, the propaganda campaigns initiated by the various groups and the Board of Agriculture proved to be equally problematic. The propaganda campaign surrounding women's work in agriculture will be discussed in detail in Chapter 3, but a few comments are required here to provide necessary context regarding the relationship between promoters of women on the land and the farmers. In the early stages the propaganda campaign surrounding women's agricultural work was uncoordinated, but featured two key themes: publicly shaming farmers for their lack of cooperation, and planting a seed in the public consciousness that women *could* offer a viable solution to the nation's labour issues. In a letter to the *Standard*, Philip Cambray for the Association to Promote the Employment of Women in Agriculture blamed farmers' unwillingness to cooperate with local authorities and the Labour Exchange for the dismal number of women placed on farms up to mid-1915. He stated that the farmers' prejudices, especially evident among farmers in the Midlands and West Country, had to be overcome and that farmers had to be more willing to work with local organisations to arrange replacement labour. While Cambray indicated that only women seriously interested in farm work should apply through the Labour Exchange, he also indicated that neither he, nor the Exchange, was responsible for arrangements made between farmers and employees.[50] This is an interesting propaganda strategy: first, he told the farmers that they were responsible for shortages, and second, he told them that they were entirely on their own to deal with the unskilled, untrained replacement labour that they did not want, but were publicly chastised for not accepting.

How to match the needs of farmers with appropriate workers was a growing source of concern and confusion for Selborne, the Board of

Agriculture, and other participating bodies. On 31 December 1916 a letter placed in the *Sunday Times* by Margaret M. Farquharson of the National Political League indicated, 'There is no work on a farm that strong, properly trained women cannot undertake'. Farquharson's intention was clearly to demonstrate that women were capable of all sorts of farm work and that women could and should be used to assist farmers, but that it was the farmers' responsibility to give the women a chance to prove their value. The letter also states, however, that 'The treasure is the highly-educated girl of gentle birth, between the ages of, say, 18–30. This girl needs no training' and is very little trouble for the farmer.[51] Here we see that a certain type of woman is of interest to advocates, but the desirable candidate has no training in farm work, and apparently does not require training. In terms of trouble for the farmer, the letter makes the point that these women are of good character, but notes the problem of housing is pressing and prevents many women from being placed. In this regard, it is the farmer's prejudice that is primarily to blame, the logistical issue of housing comes a distant second, and the lack of training is never indicated as a problem.

On the same day a letter appeared in the *Western Independent* from Bernard N. Wale, Principal of Seale-Hayne College, announcing an arrangement between the Board of Agriculture and the College to train women at no charge. The course was to last one month, but would only offer courses in the 'lighter branches of farm work'. Further, admission was restricted to women from Devon, Dorset, Cornwall, Gloucester, and Somerset, but open to all women in these counties between the ages of 18 and 35. The letter ends with an appeal to women of all classes who wish to take part in work of national importance.[52]

In general, before the formation of the Women's Land Army in 1917 training colleges and local farm courses were aimed at offering focused instruction for a short period of time to emergency and temporary workers. The WFGU and WNLSC had limited success and provided fewer than 3,500 workers between the start of the war and the end of 1916. Furthermore, the training colleges were not as effective as Selborne had hoped. In 1916, 376 scholarships were provided by the Board, but with only 233 placements as of October.[53] Yet, the training colleges were the most effective means of attracting women to agriculture and getting them trained. Take, for example, a second scheme introduced in early 1916 for training courses to be organised by the County Councils. The same report in 1916 indicated that this scheme was believed to have been a complete failure. Not only did few women register, but only half of those enrolled completed basic training courses in milking or hoeing, and of those who completed the course there was the problem of placement. Women felt that because their numbers were limited and the need great that they could negotiate their employment terms. Such difficulties deterred farmers from employing women from this group.

In addition to organised groups, local women took up the charge of devising their own schemes. In Herefordshire, local women worked in gangs of twelve between the hours of 9 a.m.–1 p.m. and 2 p.m.–6 p.m. and were paid 3d per hour. While the organiser professed the scheme worked very well, numbers were limited and the group was relatively unknown.[54] In Chepstow the women took it upon themselves to meet three days a week on an informal basis. The women stayed as long as they could and work hours were flexible. On the best day Mrs Thorno, the woman in charge of the ad-hoc scheme, placed 21 women on local farms, but only 16 of these were regulars. The women were paid 3d per hour for 6 hours a day and Thorno was in charge of keeping track of the time sheets and paying the women.[55] The Board of Agriculture received a few dozen similar reports of local efforts, but the lack of coordination meant that the work was ineffectual in terms of meeting national needs.

In the absence of a national organisation and government support, volunteers were forced to gloss over problems such as the lack of training, variable and uncoordinated training schemes, and unfocused recruiting campaigns.[56] To help overcome these problems, in November 1915 Lord Selborne arranged for the formation of Women's County Agricultural Committees to work in conjunction with the WACs, County Councils, and Labour Exchanges.[57] In February 1916 Selborne recommended that the WCCs be brought under the authority of the Board of Agriculture and that circulars be distributed to recruit the best women organisers to oversee the work of these committees. From these committees advisors would be appointed to a Joint Committee under the Board in an effort to coordinate efforts and to ensure the training and placement of women workers.[58]

Problems were experienced almost immediately. The WACs argued that given the number of cooperating bodies already in place, adding another would only cause further delays and complications. These criticisms stemmed from the fact that while the WCCs were supposed to corral volunteer organisations at the county level, some organisations refused to relinquish control and in some counties the WACs actually worked to block the formation of WCCs by refusing to work with organisers. Initially no WCCs were formed in Devon, West Sussex, Kesteven, the Isle of Ely, or Salop. In Huntingdonshire, Bedfordshire, and Berkshire WCCs were formed, but there was no communication between the committee and the WACs. In areas where the Board experienced difficulties in establishing WCCs it was recommended that the WAC appoint a female representative to their committee to represent the interests of women agricultural workers. Even this proved difficult with several WACs, including Staffordshire and North Hampshire, refusing to accept female representatives.[59]

Selborne was determined to make improvements to the organisation and implementation of women agricultural workers and while the staff at the Board of Trade worked with the WCCs, Selborne worked on plans to establish a centralised committee to deal with women in agriculture. Throughout 1915 the question of how to organise women workers was paramount and it was determined that two categories of workers were required: (1) women in villages who were willing to work close to home and (2) women workers willing to travel to areas in need. Local scholarships and training programmes would serve the first group and ensure that farmers had local women to do lighter farm work. The second group would become the focal point of Selborne's scheme to train, relocate, and place women interested in farm labour. In order to help coordinate the expansion of earlier volunteer organisations into a national scheme, the Board of Trade (later transferred to the Board of Agriculture) established Women's War Agricultural Committees (WWAC) in late 1915 and in January 1916 appointed a woman's inspector, Meriel Talbot, to work with women's groups on behalf of the Board of Agriculture. The WWACs were not responsible to the Board and could not be compelled to act in a particular way; rather, the WWACs were sub-committees of the War Agricultural Committees and their duties and responsibilities were determined, to a large extent, by the parent committee.[60] The central role of the WWAC in 1915–16 was to establish a register of women interested in working in agriculture. Under this scheme the WWACs would receive financial support from the WACs through the Board of Agriculture, forcing these groups into closer communication. Other women's groups requesting financial support would now have to work with the WACs and WWACs and be in contact with the Board of Agriculture through the woman's inspector.

Here again, however, the success of these committees varied. Numbers were highest in Cornwall with 6,051 women registered and 4,373 working with the highest proportion in Bedfordshire with 680 women registered and 580 working. While Herefordshire registered 1,500 women only 500 were working and in Montgomeryshire there were 250 women registered with no reported figures for the number of women undertaking agricultural work. Montgomeryshire was representative of the counties' participation – over half of the counties either only reported registered numbers, or no numbers at all. In total there were 57,497 women registered, but only 28,767 working.[61] While Peter Dewey acknowledges that organisers did increase the number of women working in agriculture between 1914 and 1916, he argues that their attempts were ultimately unsuccessful before the formation of the Women's Land Army in 1917. Dewey's argument is based on two factors: first, that the labour shortage was not as severe as farmers suggested, and second, that female replacement labour had a negligible impact on farm productivity. Regarding replacement labour, Dewey argues labour declined by approximately 6 per cent in 1915 and 9 per cent in 1916 and rather than hiring replacement labourers, farmers simply worked with what they had.[62]

Evaluating the effectiveness of early schemes, however, is not straightforward and cannot be reduced to raw numbers. Given the missing numbers, as well as the importance of the number of women registered, but not working, the picture is incomplete. Women registered but not working could mean that the women were still in training colleges. It is also likely that many women may have agreed to place their names on registers when women recruiters arrived at their doors, but may not have been willing to undertake agricultural work with a specific organisation when called upon to do so or they simply may not have been asked. Given the pressures placed on the County Committees and farmers to find and use replacement labour, the number of women on the registrars was inflated both intentionally and accidentally. By Meriel Talbot's own admission, the number of women registered did not honestly reflect the number of women interested in working in agriculture or at least not through one of the above organisations.[63] In addition, the 'lists' were continually changing hands and new lists were compiled. Sometimes lists were combined and at times not all names made the transfer (the reason for this may have been human effort or the withdrawal of a name). Many women also preferred to find employment with a local farmer outside of agricultural organisations or the Labour Exchanges. Given that organisations like the Women's Farm and Garden Union (WFGU) were relatively unknown in rural communities, it is plausible that women did not think to register.[64]

The variation in numbers of registered versus working women reflected problems in organising the various groups. A report from October 1916 provides some clarification of the challenges these committees faced. The purpose of the report was to request a transfer of responsibility for the WCCs away from the WAC and to the Board of Agriculture. Although the WWACs operated under the Board of Agriculture already, they were not subject to mandates by the Board. The request for further oversight by the Board was to bring the WWACs under the administrative control of the Board of Agriculture. As the WCCs were sub-committees to the WACs, much of the work they undertook was in support of the broader efforts of the WACs – the work focused on the issues affecting agriculture generally, and not the application of female labour specifically. Considering that the WACs had limited power to deal with women's labour issues in the counties, the request that the Board of Agriculture assume responsibility for overseeing women's employment in agriculture is not surprising.

The formation of the WWACs and the coordination of various groups and committees under the Board of Agriculture through Talbot was in part about redistributing scarce resources and reducing competition between organisations, and in part about sorting out county and borough registers. With so many volunteer organisations and county committees in place to deal with the women's work, the Board of Agriculture had no clear indication of how many women were interested in agricultural work or even how many women worked in agriculture. Each group submitted figures for the total number of women in their areas willing to undertake agricultural work. In some counties the numbers were broken down further with separate lists for those already employed, those awaiting placement, those in training, and those who had simply registered but had not gone any further in the process. As each group (whether the WFGU, Labour Exchanges, or another organisation) had representatives in various parts of the country, the numbers often overlapped so that the women counted on one list were also counted on other lists without a clear indication of how many names were repeated.[65]

A far more contentious problem was that the registration numbers were being used at local tribunals against farmers. The lists were presented to tribunals and military representatives as incentives to remove men from agriculture, which the women representatives presented on behalf of the Board of Agriculture without Selborne's or Talbot's knowledge. One report from Mr Somerville, local representative of the military tribunal at Bath, indicated the lists provided were somewhat disingenuous in that they did not clearly indicate most of the women were part-time.[66] Selborne was clearly irritated that this practice had been used to further the women's cause, but also recognised it infuriated farmers and provided some clarity as to why the farmers had been cautious in working with the Board on labour issues. Selborne cautioned the WWACs that no further communication was to take place between the women's committees and the military tribunals. While Selborne recognised the farmers' hesitation to employ women pre-dated the mischievous actions of the women's committees, he also noted the situation had certainly been made worse by the lack of discretion on the part of the WWACs.[67]

Throughout 1915 there was some uncertainty about the nature of the relationship between the Board of Trade, its officers, and the various women's organisations. It was decided the Board would no longer work directly with the Women's County Committees, which also meant any request for the Board to assume greater responsibility for the WWACs was denied; instead, the WCCs would deal with officers on employment matters only, which came under the purview of the Board of Trade. By August 1916 it was determined that a further division of powers was required in order to properly distinguish between the duties of the Board of Agriculture and the Board of Trade. Issues of labour supply would be left to the Board of Trade and its Labour Exchanges, while all questions regarding women in agriculture would be left to the Board of Agriculture. The Board of Agriculture would appoint a permanent Woman Inspector with appropriate staff to organise women's labour under the Board. Talbot's new position meant she would no longer be responsible for the WWACs and instead would help to provide oversight nationally, which Selborne hoped would begin the process of coordinating local and national efforts.[68] This work would be carried out with the cooperation of the Labour Exchanges, which would provide a link between the two Boards.[69]

By 1917 the nature of the war had changed. Unrestricted submarine warfare in 1916 doubled cargo losses and organisations like the Women's National Land Service Corps could no longer keep up with demand. When David Lloyd George became Prime Minister in December 1916 he committed to dealing with the 'food problem' by appointing Rowland Prothero, an agricultural expert, as President of the Board of Agriculture. While Lloyd George had been sympathetic to the needs of farmers and Selborne's attempts to deal with growing food shortages, Prothero convinced him the WACs were simply too large to be effective and the WWACs did not possess the power to effectively manage women's employment. Under Prothero, 61 executive sub-committees were set up and granted additional powers with regard to policy formation and compulsory action. In addition, the Corn Production Act was introduced in 1917 guaranteeing a minimum price for wheat and oats and a minimum wage for agricultural labourers.[70] The powers of the Board of Agriculture were extended, and managing the agricultural labour supply became a priority. As part of the new powers granted to the Board, a Women's Branch was created in January 1917 and was responsible for increasing the number of women workers in agriculture. The Women's Branch was the culmination of Selborne's hard work and the volunteer organisations that had assisted in bringing women to the land now agreed to work under the Women's Branch. In March the Women's Branch was transferred to the authority of the Food Production Department and a mobile but permanent force of women agricultural workers was formed. Talbot's position as Director of the Women's Branch was finalised, and the staff put in place by Selborne to oversee the operations of the WWACs was transferred to the new organisation.

A patriotic organisation thousands strong, disciplined, organised, and trained, the WLA was to provide a partial solution to the labour problem and assist Britain's farmers in 'answering the call' to service and feeding the nation. Rather than emerging as a new centrally organised group, the WLA was a patchwork of the organisations that came before it and inherited many of the bureaucratic problems that came with stitching together a collection of disparate groups. Although a national organisation, it continued to work with the WWACs, WACs, county councils, the Labour Exchanges, and farmer's unions, and the WNLSC continued to serve as a feeder group for the Land Army. The newly formed WLA faced many of the same propaganda challenges as its predecessors. Convincing farmers who felt they had been treaty unfairly by earlier organisations to work with and trust the efforts of the WLA was not an easy task. Central to gaining the farmers' trust was proper training, but the WLA struggled to find the right balance between sufficient training and immediate need.[71] Connected to this point was the question of who would bear the cost of training and, once trained, where the women would live since the issue of housing was still pressing and unresolved.

From the outside the WLA looked like Lloyd George's effort to solve the food problem. Where Asquith had failed, Lloyd George abandoned the laissez-faire approach of Asquithian liberals and committed to managing domestic food production. The WLA, however, was the result of Selborne's efforts and the efforts of volunteer organisations to find a practical solution to the food problem. These early organisations laid the foundation for the future success of the WLA, but they also foreshadowed the organisational challenges of restructuring British agriculture, while simultaneously trying to both reaffirm and reimagine women's work under wartime conditions.

2
Female Preparedness, Male Authority: Organisers and the Board of Agriculture

The Women's Land Army, formed in January 1917, was not a stand-alone organisation. Consequently, the Land Army did not have a wholly independent structure. At its core, the primary organisational relationship was between the WLA and the Women's Branch. The Women's Branch was responsible for the Land Army's operations and the employment of women in agriculture generally. Meriel Talbot, Director of the Women's Branch, saw the Land Army as a way to promote women's involvement in agriculture generally, not just in a wartime economy. Talbot, however, worked under the Food Production Department, which was itself a division of the Board of Agriculture and Fisheries and whose primary goal was to increase domestic food production during the war. Although the desired result was the same for both the Women's Branch and the Board of Agriculture – to see women employed in agriculture – their methods, motivations, and goals were different. Additionally, the relationship between the organisers of the Land Army and the Board of Agriculture mirrored the relationship between Land Girls and their farmer employers. At both levels, competing motives and ideas about the Land Army's/Land Girls' functionality complicated the pursuit of the same immediate goal.

Lords Selbone and Prothero argued that the largely unsuccessful work of other organisations necessitated government action and the formation of a central committee to oversee women's work. To avoid past mistakes, Prothero insisted that the work of committees could only be successful if they were properly integrated into a broader organisational structure – the Food Production Department.[1] On 1 January 1917 the Food Production Department (FPD) was created as a department within the Board of Agriculture.[2] The FPD's objective was to maximise food production by coordinating the use and supply of land with available labour, raw materials, and machinery. The department did not act alone and was guided on policy decisions by an Advisory Committee on Food Production.[3] The Food Production Department served as an information centre that relied on the work of the Executive Committees to issue reports on everything from labour to fertiliser. Essentially, the Executive Committees carried out the executive functions of the Food Production Department at the local level. The Executive Committees were made up of members appointed by the President of the Board of Agriculture and representatives of the County War Agricultural Committees (CWAC). There were more than 600 committees operating under the Executive Committees, each with specific tasks to accomplish.[4] The Women's War Agricultural Committees (WWAC) were part of this advisory network, but with the specific task of handling matters related to the employment of women in agriculture.

The Women's Branch originally functioned as a subsidiary group within the broader framework of the Board of Agriculture, but in March 1917 it was brought under the authority of the Food Production Department so that it could coordinate the mobilisation of women's agricultural labour and oversee the operation of the Women's Land Army.[5] The Women's Branch functioned under the directorship of Meriel Talbot (Director) and Edith Lyttelton (Deputy Director). Both women had experience in organising women's work. A champion of women's capabilities in the male-dominated world of the early twentieth century, Talbot worked as secretary of the Victoria League and in 1915 served on an advisory committee for the repatriation of enemy aliens.[6] She was the first woman inspector for the Board of Agriculture, a position she held until she became director of the Women's Branch. As director, Talbot was in charge of the enrolment and management of the WLA. Edith Lyttelton was a novelist and activist who advocated reform to British labour laws. Lyttelton was one of the founders of the Victoria League in 1901 and also served as Honorary Secretary of the Women's Tariff Reform League.[7] In addition, Lyttelton served on the Executive of the National Union of Women Workers and was a co-founder of the War Refugee Committee.[8]

Under the leadership of Talbot and Lyttelton, the Women's Branch was responsible for increasing the number of part-time village workers on the land and to make their work more productive. Their second responsibility was to recruit, train, and equip a large number of land workers and make them available for dedicated full-time agricultural work for the duration of the war. The difficulty was that the Land Army did not have exact numbers to work with in terms of how many women they had to recruit, train, and provide uniforms for. What was known was that the 90,000 women employed in British agriculture before the war were not enough to replace the men who had enlisted or who were conscripted into military service. The first task of the Women's Branch was to ascertain where the 90,000 women were living and employed in 1917 and whether or not that number had increased or decreased since the 1911 census. Talbot and Lyttelton requested assistance with this initial task from the Ministry of Labour, but the records for the number of women employed in agriculture between 1911 and 1917 were incomplete. Statistics of employment in agriculture had not been calculated since the census and even then, the number of women employed in the industry could not be exact since it excluded wives and daughters. The task of sorting out the labour supply was tedious, but it was a necessary precondition for meeting agricultural labour needs.[9]

With the creation of the Women's Branch, the Women's Land Army came into existence, at least on paper. In January 1917, however, a land army of capable workers still had to be realised. In order to create a land army quickly, the Women's Branch had to work through the agricultural and employment machineries already in place in the counties. Under the WLA, the Women's County Committees were responsible to coordinate county efforts in terms of women's labour, but also to provide an organisational network, thus creating a corporate atmosphere within the organisation. Each county was divided into districts, and the Village Registrars in the area elected the District Committees. The District Committees in turn elected representatives for the Agricultural Executive Committee. This meant that under the Women's Branch the efforts to coordinate women's labour reached every district in the country, at least in theory.[10]

It was the cooperation of these bodies that largely accounted for the success of the nation's food programme and of the Women's Land Army; however, this interconnectedness created multiple levels of oversight and authority that diminished the power of the Women's Branch and led to confusion within the organisation both locally and nationally. Decentralisation has been a source of debate for historians working in the area of British agriculture in the First World War. Andrew Cooper concludes that the decentralisation of agriculture under the Asquith government was not forceful enough and went too far by leaving the operation of farms to individual landlords. While the Executive Committees were able to offer guidance and direction to farmers, Cooper argues that inducements were not enough – pressure or even compulsion were necessary, and coercion was not part of the Milner

Committee's plan.[11] Contrary to Cooper's assessment, Mancur Olson argues that the extent of agricultural decline in the decades prior to the war, the liberal government's dedication to free trade and laissez-faire economics helped to prevent an unmanageable food crisis in Britain.[12] By the end of 1916 both Liberals and Conservatives accepted decentralisation as a necessary consequence of pre-war trends in agriculture. The task of managing domestic food production was simply too big for one committee or department to handle and required the integrated efforts of various organisations at all levels. The Board of Agriculture did not have the same powers of intervention as the Ministry of Labour had in the munitions industry. Rather, the Board had to contend with the individual and collective interests of more than four thousand farmers/landowners and, in addition, had to manage the various organisations that operated under its direction. Of course, the necessity of decentralisation was also the nagging problem that plagued agricultural management, and in particular the coordination of various groups under the Women's Branch.[13]

The early weeks of January 1917 were a blur for organisers of the Women's Land Army. The vast majority of female workers under the Food Production Department were village women who had some previous experience in agriculture. With regard to women already working on the land, the goal was to make them more efficient, which was done with the introduction of Group Leaders in 1917. Group Leaders were educated women and members of the Land Army who were responsible for organising village women across England and Wales, hopefully encouraging them to join the Land Army as well.[14] This would place educated women in leadership roles and reduce the amount of educational training required for women to work successfully on the land. The work of Group Leaders also helped to elevate the Land Army's status to that of a professional wartime organisation and it was hoped that more educated women would consider the Land Army an attractive work opportunity. As the organisation of village women continued in the early months of 1917, Group Leaders were drawn solely from the educated classes, thereby creating new categories of women agricultural workers. Those who were better educated or more skilled worked as forewomen of gangs and arranged time sheets for farmers, paid the workers, and helped match workers to jobs.[15]

The Women's War Agricultural Committees managed the work of the Group Leaders and forewomen, and worked with the Village Registrars (responsible for compiling lists of available women for work) and the Women's Section of the National Service Department (responsible for recruiting). The relationship between the Women's War Agricultural Committees and the Village Registrars could be tumultuous at times. The issue was the lack of clearly defined roles. In the early stages of the war the Village Registrars and Employment Exchanges had assisted the County Councils in organising local labour by providing lists of women willing to undertake agricultural work.[16] It was the responsibility of the Women's War Agricultural Committees to provide an organisational framework for the scheme by coordinating several groups to match women workers with farmers.[17] Initially, the relationship worked fine: the Village Registrars and Labour Exchanges collected names and the WWACs arranged placements.

The formation of a national organisation – the Women's Land Army – gradually complicated the relationship between the Women's War Agricultural Committees and the Food Production Department by way of the Ministry of Labour.[18] The Ministry of Labour and Food Production Department worked in close cooperation, as more food was likely to mean more workers. Like Talbot, however, many local organis-ers believed the WLA could be more than a labour supply service and the Land Army was seen as an opportunity to advance the role of women in the industry. In pursuit of this goal, local organisers sought greater cooperation with the Village Registrars and the Labour Exchanges.[19] The WWACs were tasked with interviewing recruits and allocating them either to training centres or, if experienced, to farms. Valuable assistance was provided through the Ministry of Labour's Employment Exchanges, but the WWACs wanted the women to be screened in order to weed out those not suited to the work and to streamline the interview process.[20] Ultimately, the Ministry of Labour objected to these added responsibili-ties, as did the Board of Agriculture.[21]

Unfortunately, WWACs did not exist in every county and its numerous responsibilities overburdened the small staffs in the counties where they did exist.[22] If the Labour Exchanges provided organisational support, it would have relieved some of the pressure on the WWACs and allowed these committees to carry out their second mandated task more effi-ciently: to organise training centres, either on farms or in colleges, and to provide a depot where the women could be sent between the completion of their training and employment, and during times of unemployment. This responsibility strained relations between the WWACs, the Food Production Department, and Ministry of Labour. 'Training' was used rather liberally by the Food Production Department and the WWACs argued that 'training' was impossible in so short a time as four weeks. All that could be hoped for was some 'toning' and a 'less than familiar acquaintance with animals and the use of tools'.[23] Miss MacDonald, the Organising Secretary for Essex, protested that sending women to the land 'whom had hardly been trained' sent the wrong message to both Land Girls and farmers. Miss Hepburn of Devon also insisted it was pointless to send untrained women into the fields where they would 'demonstrate little value to already sceptical farmers'.[24] Miss Pullar, the District Organiser of the Land Army in Hertfordshire, noted that throughout the county farmers were refusing to employ gangs of village women because they were untrained and even when it came to the employment of Land Girls, farmers wanted a clear demonstration of their skills before agreeing to employ them.[25] Dorothea Ward, who was the Village Registrar in Aldbury, informed the Gang Leader that farmers were not interested in employing women because the women did not want to work. Even when women could be recruited, they wanted to put in a few hours of light work and go home.[26] Yet, the National Service Department, which was responsible for recruiting, continued to advertise 'trained women on the land', despite the arguably disingenuous nature of such claims.

Rather than changing the training to make it more comprehensive, the Board of Agriculture, with the assistance of its advisory committees, arranged for training tests to be administered at the end of each training period. The purpose of the training tests was not to establish efficiency, but rather to assist those responsible for placements so that they could rate the qualifications of the students in certain types of farm work. The tests were suited to those who undertook courses in milking, carting, ploughing, threshing, planting, horse-managements, and ditch digging, but could not be used effectively to test general farm knowledge. The percentage of marks gained was high, but it was not based on individual scores. Students were graded on a curve – judged against the group that they were tested with, not against an objective standard outside the group.[27] Miss Biddle, the Organising Secretary for Kent East, informed Talbot that the 'training tests are not very helpful' and that they 'tend to confuse the trainers who are responsible to rate the girl's efficiency'.[28] Miss Baker of Surrey cautioned that 'if tests continued to be administered in this way, potential employers must be informed so as to not assume they are hiring one type of worker only to receive another'.[29] These problems fell back on the WWACs since they were responsible for training and the placement of Land Girls locally.

Talbot recognised that the training available to Land Girls and village women varied greatly between counties because the WWACs were told to consider the needs of local farmers when training women workers and also because the type of training offered depended on the training facility.[30] Although the Land Army was a national organisation, central authority through the Women's Branch was compromised by the decentralisation of the organisation. While decentralisation was in many ways a benefit to the organisation, when it came to training, the lack of coordination and a core training programme led to confusion and varied standards in the counties. The Women's Land Army could not afford to establish new training facilities for Land Girls, which meant that it had limited control over the type of training the women received. Initially the question of training a land army was debatable.[31] Organisers had to consider whether or not it was practical or even necessary to train an entire 'army' of women workers. In the opinions of farmers training was an absolute must, even if they doubted that it would do much good in the long term. The questions confronting Talbot, Lyttelton, and the WWACs seemed to go around in an endless circle: who would train the women? How would they respond to the training? If they could not complete basic training courses, would they be capable of farm work? This of course led back to the inevitable question of whether or not women were even suited to farm work in the first place. If appropriate training facilities could be acquired, how much training was enough and how would the Women's Branch pay to train, and potentially house, thousands of Land Girls?

Based in part on the farmers' criticism and the fact that the Land Army was promoted as a trained organisation, Talbot knew that the women had to be trained. Patriotic pleas were dispatched for a number of agricultural colleges to offer short courses for Group Leaders. Mrs Jones, the Organising Secretary for Cardigan and Fembroke, worked out of the Education Office in Haverfordwest and believed that training Group Leaders alone would not be enough to convince the farmers to employ more women and feared that the Land Army would find itself in a similar position as the WFGU or the Agricultural Section of the Women's Legion if more care was not taken to educate and train Land Girls.[32] If the training colleges would agree to a basic training programme, Talbot believed that the colleges would successfully assist the National Service Department in promoting the Land Army as an organisation of skilled and educated workers.[33] The Board of Agriculture agreed and pressed for training programmes to be initiated straightaway and for monthly reports to be sent to the Food Production Department and Ministry of Labour on the women's progress, both in terms of organising training programmes and on the women's developing skills once training was underway. Such oversight was necessitated by the fact that although the Women's Branch was responsible for the Women's

Land Army, the Board of Agriculture was ultimately accountable for all Land Girls employed through the Women's Branch.

While the colleges provided Land Girls with an agricultural education and the basics of gardening and goat keeping, the WWACs felt that the training programmes did not best reflect the needs of farmers. With no authority to influence college curriculum, the WWACs looked for alternative training options.[34] The WWACs came up with a scheme for farm training courses. The idea of training farm workers on a working farm was not new, but it was a good way to provide practical training for Land Girls, while at the same time demonstrating to the farmers that women were capable of farm work. The Board of Agriculture provided funding and the training period was extended from four to six weeks. The training centres in England and Wales operated on a grant of £25 per week per trainee and each Land Girl was given a maintenance allowance of 15s or 16s per week. Office furniture was also budgeted for at a rate of 6s 10d per trainee. All training centres had to be approved by the Board of Agriculture before training could begin. The training centres operated by having skilled men teach Land Girls basic skills in gardening, milking, hoeing, ploughing, and thatching on working farms. At training centres where a number of women were training simultaneously, an instructress was hired and paid by the farmer at a rate of 25s to 30s per week depending on the region. Instructresses served as a role model for Land Girls by stressing the value of training and hard work, and also suggested the possibility of upward mobility for those Land Girls who excelled in their work. Practical knowledge and experience were offered together and the men who were responsible for training were able to encourage a more positive atmosphere on local farms and throughout the farming community by offering verification of the women's abilities. In turn, this helped to improve relations between local farmers and the Board of Agriculture.[35] The WWACs found that word of mouth provided not only validation for the Land Girls' work, but promoted the Land Army in a way that a national propaganda campaign could not.

When this relationship worked, it worked very well.[36] But when relations between the WWACs and farmers were strained, the scheme struggled. Reports from the Women's Branch indicate that there was considerable variation in the willingness of farmers to offer their farms for the purposes of training. In Leicestershire more than sixty farmers came forward to provide training for women, but in Devon not a single farmer offered his farm. Further, the number of women the farmers were willing to train varied from region to region. In Sussex farmers were willing to take on a greater number of women thereby increasing the instructor-student ratio, but in Lontgomery farmers wanted one woman per available farm hand and no instructresses. In Sussex the issue for the WWACs was that the high instructor-student ratio decreased the effectiveness of the teaching and in Lontgomery the problem was the low output of trained Land Girls. Other counties failed to file reports regarding training centres due to a lack of interest on the part of farmers. The farmers who were willing to provide training facilities and instruction did not do so at a personal loss. In exchange, farmers requested a maintenance allowance. The maintenance allowance was to pay partial wages for the men employed to train Land Girls. Farmers in Devon, Somerset, and Westmorland, among others, refused to consider the possibility of training farms until the government made a formal offer of monetary assistance. Compounding the problem was that in Liddlesex farmers refused to offer training unless a maintenance fee was paid for each Land Girl and living accommodations were secured by the WWACs.[37] Once a training maintenance fee was thought to be feasible, most farmers requested some degree of government support thereby increasing the outlay of money for the Land Army scheme and furthering government intervention in the industry.

What the Board of Agriculture described as a natural prejudice by farmers against the employment of women was only one challenge organisers faced in getting the Land Army off the ground.[38] Prothero understood the farmers' hesitations, but he also believed that the WWACs and Women's Branch had to do a better job of placing women for farm work. All groups involved recognised that the choices made by organisers in terms of which women were placed on the land were crucial to the success of the Land Army.[39] On the one hand, Prothero wanted suitable women placed to help combat the farmers' prejudices. On the other hand, the Board of Agriculture faced its own challenges from the Ministry of Labour and the needs of the military. Certainly it was better to choose the right women, but there was little time to sift through the applicants and weigh the virtues of each individual case. In the end, Prothero needed the Land Army to be successful. Prothero had been critical of Asquith's handling of domestic food production, encouraging greater government interference in agriculture before the fall of the Asquith government in late 1916.[40] The year 1917 not only brought hope for women's war work in agriculture and the opportunity for the Land Army to prove itself, but it also brought hope that the Lloyd George administration could settle domestic labour problems and win the war, two areas where the Asquith government was perceived to have failed. Prothero vacillated between demands for more women on the land and only suitable women on the land, leading to much confusion for the Women's Branch and the Women's Section of the National Service Department.[41]

When the first appeals for recruits went out in February and March 1917 the response was encouraging. Thousands upon thousands signed up for agricultural work until the numbers belaboured the more than 200 Selection and Allocation Committees that had been appointed to handle women's agricultural employment. The WWACs were overwhelmed, as was the Women's Branch, and each scrambled to come up with a workable system of administration. With more than 45 Instruction and Depot Committees, 67 storerooms for the administrating of clothing, and more than 70 Volunteer Superintendents appointed, the Women's Branch could not maintain administrative control in the counties. The instructions issued to the counties were too broad and poorly defined to be successful – what type of woman did the Land Army require was the most difficult question to answer. Like Prothero, Talbot recognised that the need was great and Selection Committees typically met three or four times a week to sort through the piles of applications. In major urban areas the Selection Committees met daily. Of the first 47,144 who enrolled, three-quarters were rejected for various reasons or failed to come forward when called upon (see Chapter 3). Despite reviewing more than 50,000 applications, the Land Army only placed 7,000 women in its first year.[42]

Talbot was disappointed by the results and decided the structure of the Land Army had to be simplified. Rather than the Women's Branch organising all efforts locally and nationally, Organising Secretaries were put in place in the counties to help coordinate local and national efforts and provide an effective and efficient communication network between the counties and the Women's Branch. Circulars and memorandums initiated by the Women's Branch concerning the Women's Land Army were issued to the Organising Secretaries and then disseminated to the relevant bodies. Concerns from the counties would in turn be sent through the Organising Secretaries to the Women's Branch.[43]

Correspondence was not always swift, but Talbot felt it was more efficient than trying to manage communication between the various committees (which continued to happen anyway). Talbot also stressed the need for greater cooperation locally. The WWACs had to send representatives into the villages to recruit women and to talk to farmers and convince them of the value of the Land Army. For Talbot, this important work could not be left up to the Village Registrars.[44] The

WWACs were saddled with more, rather than less, responsibility as their jobs now extended beyond an administrative role. More responsibility was also placed on the Labour Exchanges to make sure that applicants interested in farm service were aware of the terms of service and that the farmers who sought to employ women workers completed the proper paperwork. Incomplete applications would not be considered, thereby eliminating the need for committees to search for the missing information before assessing the applications.[45]

The restructuring and selection process took time and the Food Production Department was increasingly concerned that the number of women working on farms did not reflect the national effort to bring women to the land.[46] Organisers and the Board of Agriculture remained uncertain as to the real demand for women's labour in agriculture. One week the depots were overflowing with recruits and partially trained Land Girls stood about with nothing to do. The next week the WWACs could not keep up with requests for workers and the demand quickly outpaced the supply.[47] The Board of Agriculture and Ministry of Labour sought to discover why so many Land Girls were trained but not placed, and if their efforts were not needed, why the Women's Branch continued to press for the extension of the training scheme.[48] To help improve results, the Board of Agriculture instituted Clearing Sheets – Land Girls were to be placed on farms, not held in hostels. It was the primary task of the Women's Branch to match workers with employers, and it was to this order of business that the Board of Agriculture and Ministry of Labour were most insistent in their instructions to organisers.[49] The blame for such irregularities could not reasonably be placed on organisers or farmers. The benefit of employing village women was that when they were not needed, they did not have to be housed, nor did they sit idle in training depots waiting for work. On the local level, employment on farms was more organic, responding to the ebb and flow of demands for labour, whereas the organisers were attempting to impose structure on an organic system. Both responses were circumstantial and both had the potential to succeed, but the creation of the Women's Land Army and the training of Land Girls told farmers that there was a new hierarchy among female agricultural workers: those who were trained were superior and more desirable than those who were not. Yet, there were not always enough Land Girls to meet demand and some farmers refused to employ unskilled village women when the promise of a trained army of women workers had been so aggressively promoted. The effort to find a solution meant that organisers were largely unprepared for high demand and low demand for labour – there were not enough women when they were needed most, and those women that they did have were left idle when the work slowed. The Board of Agriculture wanted to be able to meet the labour needs of British agriculture, but did not want to create a large, permanent, trained labour force that would be unemployed during the down times because labour was in such short supply elsewhere on the home front. In contrast, the Board of Agriculture needed numbers and the resultant productivity to rationalise and justify its investment in the scheme, because that is what it had promoted as the solution to the food problem. For her part, Talbot preferred a smaller, more effective and well-trained group of women rather than tens of thousands of bodies to be thrown at the problem. There was no easy solution to the operational challenges the Land Army faced. Certainly at times the war justified the Land Army's existence, but at other times it revealed the enduring impact of the industry's neglect. The need was not simply for more women, but rather for more skilled, educated, and experienced women. But slowing the enlistment of women into the Land Army and reducing the number of women in training depots would work against the Board of Agriculture's desire to see tangible results.[50]

Connected to the issue of training was the problem of finding suitable accommodations for Land Girls once they were trained. The WWACs were responsible for placements and for finding suitable housing. The Women's Branch and WWACs preferred for Land Girls to live in barrack-style housing with a matron, but the housing shortage in England and Wales meant that such accommodations were not always available. Instead, most Land Girls lived in hostels during their training period or in cottages during work placements. The WWACs had to contend with numerous problems related to the suitability of the cottages. Drafty cottages, lumpy mattresses, and the unwanted houseguests (mice) made for cranky workers, which displeased farmers and made organisers anxious.[51] The WWACs complained to the County War Agricultural Committees and the Women's Branch that congestion had to be relieved at one end or the other: either the screening process had to be further improved or more money had to be found in the operational budget of the Food Production Department to pay for better accommodations. The Board of Agriculture chose neither. Some repairs were made to existing cottages and the Girls' Friendly Society provided rooms in their lodges for Land Girls who were briefly unemployed due to work shortages or illness.[52] Matrons were appointed to larger cottages or in areas where a few cottages were grouped together and Welfare Officers were hired to oversee work conditions and report on the girls' productivity. The number of women enrolled in the WLA determined the number of Welfare Officers employed by the Land Army, and each officer oversaw up to 200 women. The payment of salaries was not to exceed £3 per week for officers who had the maximum number of women under their care.

In terms of operational costs, the greatest source of conflict between the Women's Branch and the Board of Agriculture was with regard to accommodations.[53] The establishment of hostels for working Land Girls was an expense that the Board of Agriculture argued should be the responsibility of Land Girls, not of the government. The Land Girls worked for private employers and therefore the costs associated with their employment were their responsibility. The Women's Branch countered that Land Girls could not pay for hostels and because the number of Land Girls in need of accommodations were always uncertain, the operational efficiency of the hostels would always be in question. In areas where cottages were insufficient or inappropriate for women workers, the Board agreed to the outlay of money for improvements; however, the Women's Branch sought the cooperation of patriotic Britons willing to rent out houses at a reduced rate. The Land Girls would pay rent, thus negating much of the cost of refurbishing existing dwellings. In some remote areas accommodations could not always be found. The Board had the option of either not placing a significant number of Land Girls in those areas or bearing the cost of caravans.[54] Procuring these accommodations was the Board's responsibility, but the Land Girls still paid rent to cover the day-to-day costs. The issue with regard to the payment of rents by Land Girls was that often there was a waiting period between the end of training and the beginning of a work placement, and in this period the Land Girls were expected to pay rents even though they had no income. Talbot argued the cost of room and board for a short period of time was worth the positive message it sent to Land Girls – that their service was valued and that their work was important.[55]

In the absence of a solution to the housing problem, the Women's Branch focused on securing the right social conditions for Land Girls. In order to make the system work, the Land Army had to not only recruit women into its ranks, but also retain the women it recruited. This was especially important once the women had received training. Much correspondence was exchanged between the various committees regarding the outlay of money for training recruits who never worked a day on a farm.[56] It was important that all women workers on the land felt valued, but it was especially important for Land Girls to believe that they had a good support network because they were often employed away from home and did not have a family support system. The formation of the National Federation of Women's Institutes (NFWI) in 1915 encouraged women to become active in rural life and promoted the growing and preservation of food. Since the NFWI aimed to improve the lives of rural women it was not tied to one organisation; rather, the NFWI was a non-partisan popular movement that aimed to serve the various needs of groups connected to the land and rural life.

The NFWI had monthly meetings and a broad agenda with regards to country life, but the most important element of the NFWI for the Land Army were the social functions and entertainment it provided. Although the Women's Institutes had trouble filling a meeting hall, they had no trouble attracting rural workers to dances and village socials.[57] Talbot saw an opportunity to promote the Land Army, and the role of women in agriculture generally, through the popularisation of the 'back to the land movement' exemplified by the NFWI.[58] Talbot encouraged the Organising Secretaries and WWACs to cooperate with the NFWI in 'any way possible', but to leave the propaganda campaign for the WLA and NFWI separate. Talbot's rationale was that the Board of Agriculture financed both organisations, but the NFWI would, by nature of the organisation, promote the WLA as a wartime organisation devoted to the employment of women in agriculture.[59] In 1916–17 the NFWI focused their efforts on public demonstrations of fruit bottling and canning, cheese making, market gardening, and even toy making.[60] The association of the NFWI with domestic food production encouraged public support for women's efforts in this area, without compromising gender expectations.[61] Whereas the Women's Institutes were not a subsidiary of the WLA, the operational budget of the NFWI could enhance the operational budget of the WLA but not detract from it. There was no need for the WLA to promote the NFWI, but the Women's Branch of the Food Production Department was responsible for increasing the membership to both organisations. The NFWI also served in an advisory role to the Women's Branch and therefore provided an additional perspective regarding rural needs. In particular, the NFWI was able to identify areas where training centres for the Land Army could be fruitful and promoted the training of women locally.[62] As for the Land Army, the NFWI provided another outlet for the Land Girls' frustrations and feelings of isolation. Even if Land Girls chose not to participate in NFWI events, the opportunity was there and proved to be a worthwhile promotional tool for the WLA.[63]

In addition to social networks provided by the NFWI, the Village Registrars were encouraged to befriend all Land Girls, as well as the village women. This meant keeping track of all the women in their districts and visiting them periodically to 'keep in touch'.[64] The role of the Village Registrars and Welfare Officers was not as simple as making the Land Girls comfortable.[65] Both groups interacted directly with farmers, Land Girls, and the WWACs. If a Land Girl was unhappy with her employment or living situation, this became a potential source of conflict between the employer and the organising body.[66] While Welfare Officers did not generally discuss the terms of work with farmers, they did report to the WWACs if a problem arose.[67] Welfare Officers, therefore, served in a surveillance capacity and contumacious farmers actively resisted their presence.[68] The presence of Welfare Officers was not always received negatively as their participation in agricultural affairs meant a greater opportunity for assistance and reciprocity between the WLA and farmers that had the potential to improve the positions of both Land Girls and the agricultural industry. The relationship between Welfare Officers and Land Girls is discussed in Chapter 4, but from an organisational perspective the position of Welfare Officers speaks to the problems of authority and responsibility within the Women's Land Army and the Food Production Department.[69] The WWACs were responsible for the training and placement of Land Girls and Welfare Officers were accountable for the Land Girls' well-being once placed, but the farmer determined the terms and conditions of work.[70]

This complicated relationship was central to the Land Army's operations, and conflict resulted from the difficulties in determining authority. Farmers were aware of their role in the Land Army's success and not only had the ability to influence the level of success the WLA claimed, but also asserted the right to exercise some power over its members. The authority farmers exercised over Land Girls did not come from clearly defined rules laid out in an employment contract, or even an agreement with government.[71] Rather, it came from long-established customs and social structures. Yet, the Land Army interrupted the traditional relationship between farmers and labourers. Rural life was traditionally insular. The nature of the work meant that labourers worked long hours before returning to their families in the evening. Although that relationship had changed with the growth of towns and urban centres and improvements in transportation, the countryside remained disconnected from urban centres. The presence of Welfare Officers and the connections that were maintained between Land Girls and the various subsections and committees of the FPD challenged this relationship and led to greater government involvement in the industry than many farmers were comfortable with.

Farmers' concerns for their economic well-being also created problems in trying to establish authority over land workers. The presumption that female land workers were less useful to employers was a belief that was not easily overcome, even when employers agreed to hire Land Girls.[72] For some farmers, the women's work did not justify equal pay and the patriotic impetus of their new jobs was approached with caution, curiosity, and scepticism.[73] It was not an uncommon belief in the early twentieth century that female labourers' value was determined by social and economic circumstances. As a reserve labour force, women could be called upon in times of great need, but otherwise the separate sphere mentality continued to permeate labour-intensive industries.[74] The presence of Welfare Officers gave weight to the farmers' concerns that women were generally unsuited to farm work, thereby necessitating continued oversight through the Women's Branch. The demand for greater authority over Land Girls was one way farmers could justify the Land Girls' social and economic inferiority, even if they came to respect the work they did and their role in the war effort.

Prothero refused to give way to the farmers' demands for greater authority over the employment of Land Girls. From its inception, the Land Army was envisioned and presented as a government organisation that brought patriotic women to the land to help solve the looming food crisis. In an attempt to ease public anxieties and assist in the success of the scheme, the Board determined that the role of Welfare Officers had to be improved to ensure that Land Girls were treated fairly[75] and that the agreed-upon wages were paid. In turn, Welfare Officers and the WWACs ensured that the Land Girls carried out the work they were contracted to perform, that they were well mannered and deferred to the farmer's authority, and that they upheld the good name of the Women's Land Army, the Women's Branch, and the Board of Agriculture.[76]

The role of the WWACs in coordinating activities at the county level afforded committee members a great deal of responsibility. At the county level the WWACs contrasted with the visibly male County Executive Committees.[77] Most organisers were connected to the land in some way, either from a landowning family by marriage or birth or through their work on other committees, and the agricultural committees as a whole reflected the deferential and paternalistic nature of rural society in this period. Although the formation of the WLA, and other organisations like it, suggested the participation of all Britons through the national war effort, the county organisers indicated that the social levelling expected from the exigencies of total war and the mass participation of the populace were less complete in the countryside.[78] The role of women in organising efforts in agriculture was minimal compared to the role played by men, as women's participation was often restricted to sub-committees or organising secretaries. Most of the women who participated in the Land Army organisation were either middle or upper class, but were nevertheless expected to have a working understanding of country life. Knowledge of who wielded power locally, the character of rural communities, the structure of the traditional workforce, and the nature of land ownership in the late decades of the nineteenth century and early decades of the twentieth century was central to functioning within local systems. Locally, the agricultural industry was a face-to-face enterprise existing within face-to-face communities. Farming practices were not necessarily based on rational efficiency, but rather practices that were passed down from generation to generation. With those practices came expectations of how farms worked, how to keep them working, and how to make them profitable.[79] While WWAC members may have had exceptional knowledge of the workings of country paternalism, they were still women promoting the intrusion of a non-traditional labour force into pre-existing structures, and the farming community tended to work within self-affirming groups. The reality was that the rural hierarchy remained in place during the war and the WWACs had to work within this existing framework.[80] At the county level social conflicts permeated the WWACs and the WLA.[81]

It is perhaps understandable that the work of the WWACs and the desire of members to make the Land Army a feasible and permanent source of employment for women meant that some organisers were overzealous in their work, while others sought to subvert the traditional male hierarchy. It was unusual for the women who served on the WWACs to have recorded employment information; in fact, it was not common for representatives of the Land Army serving on any sub-committee to be listed as having had an occupation. Many patrician women who volunteered with the Land Army were able to devote much of their energy and time to the war effort, but also to the promotion of women in wartime industries. This position was coterminous with the position of the agricultural community. Their actions were not necessarily remonstrative because both sides sought to promote the health and wellness of the agricultural industry and agricultural life, yet their efforts were distinguishable by the intentness each group assigned to the use of and need for substitute labour for agricultural work. The WWACs did not always carry sufficient weight locally to handle matters that arose, and the Executive Committees and the NFU regularly worked together to maintain positive working relations with the farmers.[82] Farmworkers' unions, which were growing after 1915, were hostile toward women in the industry and did not recruit women workers because they opposed the employment of women in the industry out of fear that women workers would diminish men's wages. Conflicts that emerged between employers and Land Girls left the WWACs with little room to manoeuvre. Britain was never really close to starvation during the war, so it seems that the committees did their work well, at least nationally. The creation of county committees and the Land Army itself made sense within the context of national needs, and national policy decisions made sense for the purpose of increasing domestic food production. Trying to convince farmers that government interference from national boards to local committees was in their best interests was much more difficult. Enforced change at the local and county levels engendered a mixture of acceptance, uncertainty, and social discord.

Similarly, the Women's Branch functioned as a subsection of the Food Production Department. The Women's Branch, therefore, occupied a position between the transparently male FPD and the publically female Women's Land Army. Apart from recruiting, equipping, and training a large number of women for agricultural work, the Women's Branch was responsible for managing expectations – Land Girls', farmers', and the Food Production Departments', as well as managing the Land Army scheme. Talbot and Lyttelton were distanced from the day-to-day operational challenges at the county level and also largely distanced from national policy decisions, working somewhere between the two. While in charge of policy for the Land Army, Talbot had to work within the parameters established by the FPD, but also within the limitations of the WWACs and Organising Secretaries. In addition, although the Women's Branch was responsible for the functions of the Land Army, government directives issued by the Board of Agriculture, National Service Department, and the Ministry of Labour restricted its operational prerogative. The interplay between the Women's Branch and the Board of Agriculture nationally reflected the interplay between Land Girls and farmers locally.

The relationship between the various groups was never so tense as to threaten the overall operability of the Land Army scheme. It did, however, force organisers to carefully manage all aspects of the scheme from its operational organs, to the behaviours of Land Girls and their employers. As each component of the structure worked to carry out its duties, conflicts inevitably arose as areas of jurisdictional authority became conflated. In order to avoid redundancy and to prevent conflict, the Land Army's operations were further systematised. Jurisdictional controls were enforced, paperwork filtered upward through stages of approval, and conferences were held to bring the various parts of the Women's Branch, and the WLA, together. The most exacting duties, aside from those performed by Talbot and Lyttleton, lay with the WWACs and the Organising Secretaries. By the autumn of 1918 the operational problems of the organisation were largely resolved.[83]

These engagements between the Women's Branch and the FPD regarding operational plans and costs were characteristic of the often conflicting approaches taken by the two groups with regard to the WLA. The Food Production Department had a job to do – increase the domestic food supply – and the Women's Branch was tasked to assist in this undertaking. The FPD, however, was concerned with the cost effectiveness and operational efficiency of the scheme, whereas Talbot was concerned to ensure that the system ran smoothly and with the potential for future value. The Board of Agriculture's oversight and austerity measures were not unreasonable given the challenges and costs of the war, but its strategy of making support dependent on the success of the scheme in many ways prevented the scheme's expansion. One group requiring proof of the other's capabilities and success was characteristic of both the relationship between the Women's Branch and the Board of Agriculture, as well as the relationship between Land Girls and farmers.[84] Although generally committed to the same goal, all sides approached the issue of women's employment in agriculture with desires and motivations that were not always compatible. Conflicts among organisers and between the various groups associated with the Land Army not only reduced the organisation's operational efficiency, but sent confusing messages to potential recruits and farmers and muddied the public image of the Land Army.

3
Gender, Service, Patriotism: Promoting the Land Army in Wartime Britain

Efforts to recruit women for agricultural employment worked within the boundaries of a patriotic calling that provided a vital service to the nation. Early attempts to bring women to the land were unfocused, targeting both women of status and education, and any woman able and willing. The creation of a national organisation was intended to overcome the shortfalls of an indistinct and ineffective propaganda campaign that did little to reassure farmers that their labour demands would be met, and even less to convince women that they were urgently needed for work on the land. The Women's Land Army had to satisfy farmers, reassure women, and placate the public. The term 'Land Army' was used to convince farmers that the women would be disciplined, hardworking, and well trained, in the same way that posters of the motherly Land Girl tending to animals in a bonnet-style hat and long-waisted coat aimed to assure farmers and the public alike that the ladies of the Land Army would not be masculinised. Targeting the middle classes, recruiters and propagandists urged women to 'do your bit' for the war effort, a slogan that became not only the maxim of the Women's Land Army, but a successful advertising strategy for organisers. Retaining the premise that the Land Girls worked in service to the state, the Land Army quickly encountered its own marketing challenges. With a limited number of ideal candidates and a growing demand for better wages and terms of service, the WLA had to open its ranks in order to meet labour needs. The mixing of economic and social classes that came to characterise the WLA's ranks and the growing importance of women's work, which gave women more employment options, led to problems with discipline and retention. Yet, the Land Army marketed itself as a middle-class organisation of trained, dedicated, and disciplined women. Stopping short of implementing military style discipline or an official code of conduct for members, an enormous amount of time and effort was dedicated to moulding the Land Girls to fit the propagandistic image sold to the public. The difficulty of work and life on the land combined with the prejudices of farmers – and of the women themselves – meant that the propaganda image created by the Land Army organisers could not be easily maintained in practice.

Women were hardly new members of the agricultural labour force when the Women's Land Army was formed in 1917. Farming was, however, a traditionally male enterprise and women's work was largely confined to the house or garden, or the tending of animals.[1] Early volunteer groups were aware of the divisiveness of agricultural work and public expectations regarding women's involvement in farming. Organisers of the Women's Land Army, therefore, had two options: they could try to change public attitudes, or they could bypass them by urging women to undertake work of national importance in a time of great need, while stressing that women would assist farmers in a supportive role and that their work terms would be temporary. Rather than attempting to change public attitudes, organisers chose the latter option.

How the WLA marketed itself was directly related to the challenges faced by other organisations. The call for women agricultural workers began at the outset of the war, but was intensified in the early months of 1915 when the war had not ended by Christmas and the potential for labour shortages became more apparent. While the Board of Trade issued a call for women to undertake work of national importance by registering through the Labour Exchanges, the overwhelming majority registered for clerical or secretarial duty, or for the making of war munitions.[2] Very few registered for agricultural work. The absence of a positive response necessitated a special appeal. The Board of Trade issued a public plea throughout the country for women to come forward to undertake agricultural work in England, Wales, and Scotland. The Board of Trade sought women from all classes and backgrounds who wanted the opportunity to help revitalise the invaluable role of women in the rural life of the country. While the Board of Trade recognised publicly that the role of women in rural life had largely been relegated to the past 'to which all undesirable things are cosigned', the war had forced the state to turn to women and ask them not to relinquish the 'better-sphere' that had been accorded to them by 'education and the freedom of life which we live', but to reclaim the past (land) and to transform it (the land and rural life) in service to the nation. The National Service Department called on Women to 'Enrol for Service on the Land: Help to Win a Victorious Peace'.[3] As an incentive, the Board of Trade offered to cover the costs of training for the first month for any woman willing to come forward.

Many women heeded the national call, but the stigma of farm work was difficult to overcome. Harkening back to an idyllic past, the mythical and romanticised ideal of rural life became a useful propaganda tool to encourage Britons to defend hearth and home.[4] The ideal of a country girl's innocence, sheltered from the sexual adventures of the city, reinforced both traditional femininity – with childlike undertones – and an image of a nation worthy of sacrifice. The man in uniform served a similar function by reinforcing masculinity in the face of war and death, by adding to their sexual appeal as defenders of the home. The press propagated the idea that the WLA was part of a larger process of reconnecting with England's rural past. Britain's women participated in the war effort by providing 'raspberry jam for the fighting forces' and 'feeding hay to gentle horses' – their work was domestic and patriotic.[5] While the Land Girl's experience was based on actual work, the connection to the land encouraged the belief that the women, even those capable of hard manual labour, needed saving. There was juxtaposition between the propaganda image of women on the land and the organisation's avowal that the work could actually be empowering.

To make the best of the situation, the Board of Trade highlighted the progress and training of the first groups of women who came forward, dubbing them Government Students. Most were ladies of birth and education. They were not countrywomen, but rather had attended schools in France and Russia and were recruited to help change the perception that only a certain type of woman, rural and uneducated, *would* seek employment in agriculture. When questioned about their motivations the women promptly replied 'the war' but noted that such work was of vital importance whether in times of war or in times of peace. Unlike volunteer efforts that focused on recruiting from the upper middle class in early 1915, the Land Army was guilty of mixing the classes, which was one of the key hindrances of its recruiting campaign; the WLA relied on the evocation of patriotic duty to overcome this unnatural, and unwanted, mixing of social groups.

In the immediate term, the Board of Trade's intended outcome was to solve the problem of dwindling labour supplies, not to make suppositions about the potential role of women after the war was over or the nature of the class structure in Britain.[6] Neither the Board of Trade nor the Board of Agriculture wished to offend pre-existing expectations concerning the place of women in British society, but they did wish to encourage the public to see such transgressions for what they were – vital and temporary.[7] This attitude toward women's work in agriculture reflected popular attitudes of the pre-war period and fits into a broader tradition of limiting roles for women outside of the home,[8] or at least limiting their roles in jobs that had not been 'feminised'.[9] Through its promotion of the Land Army as a temporary, patriotic diversion for women of the upper and middle classes, the Boards of Agriculture and Trade gave weight to the assumption that these women were temporarily passing the time with war work, which they only took on out of a sense of duty.[10] The press played its part, and middle-class volunteers were accused of 'amusing oneself at work' – the perception being that these women knew their jobs were temporary, which was part of the appeal.[11] While women were drawn to the forefront of agricultural work, men remained present in the background waiting to reclaim the positions temporarily filled by women.

But women are not men. Rehearsed repeatedly throughout the war, volunteer groups were forced to contend with this general truth. The Board of Trade's offer to pay for a month's training did not negate the fact that the training provided and the conditions in training facilities did not match the reality of life on the land. The staffs of training colleges stood in *loco parentis* to the recruits, a position that no farmer would occupy. The regimentation of farm life and long exhausting workdays meant that fewer than half of the recruits that entered the training facilities actually completed the training programme.[12] Appeals to patriotism only worked to get the women to come forward, but did not ensure that they would make a meaningful contribution in solving the labour shortage.

In the autumn of 1915 the Board of Agriculture launched a national propaganda campaign to bring more women to the land.[13] Many requests were made for women to undertake milking, dairying, and domestic farm service, work that was acceptably done by women. There was also need for women who were capable of weeding, nursery work, and hoeing, but the pay was only 5s to 6s a week for educated workers, up from 4s the year before.[14] Most readily employed were women with agricultural college training who were hired as gardeners or for work with poultry. Unskilled women were able to secure temporary work, normally in the hayfields or later in the season as fruit pickers. Without proper training, farmers argued that they could not offer steady work throughout the season. In the meantime, the Public Schools Association and the Boy Scouts filled labour shortages and carried out much of the unskilled work.[15]

It seemed to the WWACs that the issue was not entirely a lack of willingness on the part of women or the farmers, but a genuine question of training inadequacies and the calibre of worker being offered. While initially calls for recruits were general, taking any woman who was willing, organisers increasingly focused on recruiting able-bodied women who had some experience in agriculture. The problem with this approach, as organisers quickly discovered, was that women who had agricultural experience were already employed in farm work or had made the decision to leave the land. This approach was not likely to drastically increase the number of women working in agriculture, which was the intended goal of the campaign. Recognising that the war was expected to be long in duration and that more men would be called for military service, the potential pool of experienced women would quickly be exhausted. With this is mind, the WWACs acknowledged the need to broaden their focus, but not to the point of diminishing the quality of workers recruited. The focus on training would also assist in recruiting middle-class women in urban areas who could see the training as a possible stepping-stone for a career in agriculture and not just as a wartime diversion.[16] Organisers reasoned, however, that encouraging women to undertake training and to endure the hardships of agricultural life for an unspecified period of time with no possibility for long-term success was counterproductive. Regardless of post-war prospects, for women looking for longer-term stability there was little reason to provide discouragement at the present time. The WWACs were encouraged to look for young, strong, healthy, educated women who could see the potential in outdoor work. Recruits were selected and trained to demonstrate women's aptitudes and to leave a favourable impression on the farming community. Success stories printed in the press focused squarely on the middle classes, highlighting the progress made by the vicar's daughter, the doctor's daughter, or the daughter of a local businessman. The purpose of these success stories was to demonstrate to the public and prospective recruits that the workload was manageable.[17]

The other central problem of the marketing campaign for women's war work was in effectively reaching farmers. Organisers had some success in reaching out to farmers by way of press releases, but this put the impetus on the farmer to contact the Labour Exchanges and register their needs. Similarly, hundreds of postcards were sent to farmers alerting them to upcoming agricultural shows where women would be featured and inviting them to visit training sites where they could bear firsthand witness to the women's training. Again, the obligation was on the farmer to take action, who likely had to travel to see the women working. With a lack of personal investment for either side, these methods proved to be ineffective. Close contact with the farmers personally and individually was key to improving their receptiveness to women workers. Agents from the WWACs and Labour Exchanges were sent out on 'missionary' tours of agricultural districts to put the matter to the farmers in a clear and encouraging light. In the north of England these 'missionaries' had some success and were able to talk with farmers personally about their needs and hesitations. In this regard, the WWACs focused their marketing efforts on the south of England where women working in agriculture was considered undignified. In areas where farmers were especially unreceptive to the employment of women, tactful agents would visit their farms. The initial meeting was to make contact and talk about what women could do and in what ways they could be helpful. It also allowed the agents to assess the farmers' needs in order to prepare for a subsequent visit. The second visit followed along the same lines of the first with no expectation of commitment on the farmer's part. The reason for a follow-up visit was to signify to the farmer that the WWACs took the concerns of the farming community seriously and establish a rapport for future interactions.[18]

Establishing a relationship with local farmers was vital to the success of the scheme and the WWACs in England were encouraged to follow the model adopted in Cornwall where the scheme had achieved considerable success. A Women's Committee was formed in each parish and members were responsible to carry out local canvasses of women willing to work on the land. In addition, the Women's Committees encouraged farmers to bring capable women from their districts to participate in training exercises. In this way, the women could help instruct new recruits on specific farming techniques and the farmers could be assured they would get suitable workers. The act of selecting and transporting capable women also created a spirit of competition among farmers and districts. If the farmer was satisfied with what he saw, he would encourage other farmers in his area to visit the training sites to observe the women working. This approach worked very well and Cornwall's scheme was the most successful among the counties in the West Country. Women trained other women, costs were kept low, farmers could observe for themselves what the women were capable of, and the farmers made recommendations based on their experiences. The only pitfall was that this scheme required a considerable amount of assistance from local farmers and village women. If neither participated, the scheme failed, which is precisely what happened in Devon and Somerset.[19]

Organisers realised that local variations in farming and labour practices necessitated the implementation of marketing strategies that were attuned to regional needs. Publicity meetings were held in Scotland, for example, in an attempt to bring women and farmers together. Local speakers were asked to talk about agricultural work, but were encouraged to specifically address the women's concerns regarding housing, pay, and work expectations. Posters and handbills were also used in Scotland, but mostly to advertise the meetings and not as a recruiting strategy on their own. Pictures of women engaged in farm work were effective for farmers, but not effective in eliciting the preferred response from women. In Scotland the challenge was not convincing farmers to employ women because women had traditionally been employed in larger numbers in Scottish agriculture; rather, it was to convince women to undertake agricultural work. Images of women labouring on the land did not appeal to many Scottish women. Outmigration from the land in nineteenth-century Scotland had depleted the female agricultural labour force and many labourers' wives rejected the solitude and sluggishness of rural life in favour of urban living. Publicity meetings and public rallies were held in rural areas in an attempt to exhibit the vibrancy of rural life and to convince the women that today's farms were not necessarily as isolated as they were in times past.[20]

In Wales, the National Service Committee reached out to bishops in an attempt to ascertain farmers' needs and to encourage them to employ more women on their farms. Bishops played their part in circularising the clergy, a strategy that proved successful in recruiting clerical workers a few months earlier. In addition, the Women's Temperance Association and Cooperative Societies were mobilised to assist the press campaign. While the clergy targeted farmers, the other groups were mobilised to meet with women throughout Wales to promote the physical and psychological benefits of agricultural work and life. To this end it was also recommended that North Wales have its own sub-commissioner to provide a more thorough canvass of northern communities, thereby growing the number of recruits in Wales.[21] While the sub-commissioner for Wales was not approved, the attentiveness of organisers to regional variations helped to increase the number of women entering training facilities, especially in remote areas that had been neglected by promoters who focused their attention on the Home Counties and the south-west in the early stages of the war. The work of local committees allowed organisers to pay more attention to the distribution of women workers. Localised efforts reduced transportation costs and the difficulties associated with utilising the services of women located at a great distance from the farms in need.[22]

While the WWACs were optimistic that the growing number of recruits would result in an increasing number of women employed, in

1916 the Board of Agriculture reported that the deficiencies in training facilities worked to undermine the efforts of recruiters and organisers. A report from Nottingham indicated that local farmers were willing to employ and train women, but only if suitable training facilities were made available. A promotional training farm was established in Nottingham to train a number of young women in milking, hoeing, and gardening. These specific tasks were needed most by farmers in southern England and the Midlands, and women's work in these areas was likely not to offend conservative farmers. As part of the promotion of the training facility, competitions would be held at the facility in order to encourage farmers from surrounding counties, including Devon, Dorset, and Somerset, to participate in the programme. The women selected were from urban and semi-urban districts and had no previous agricultural experience. In total, 218 women passed through the training facility and 199 were employed and working satisfactorily. These numbers are based on an operational time for the facility of 25 weeks, based on a two-week training period.[23] The promotional scheme was a success, despite the fact that a few unsuitable women had been selected and the two-week training period proved to be inadequate. In the West Country the number of women employed on the land increased late in 1916 and early 1917.[24] It is difficult to assess whether or not the increasing number of women working on the land was due to the training programmes, or to the further loss of men from the land and the intensification of farming after the introduction of conscription. It is probable that the demonstrations came at a key time when labour supplies were diminished and the need for alternative labour was both great and readily apparent.

Recruiting and training women, however, was only half of the equation. Farmers had to not only employ the women, but had to agree to a fair and competitive wage. Understanding that there were other more attractive employment options available to women, Lord Milner and Lord Selborne determined that a fair wage was crucial to the ultimate success of the scheme. Lord Milner cautioned the WWACs that some farmers would view the persistence of the propaganda campaign as an opportunity to acquire cheap labour, thereby increasing their profit margins. While he expected that most farmers would not seek to take advantage of the scheme in such a miserly manner, there were reports of such occurrences.[25] Wages varied from 5s to 10s weekly when board and lodgings were provided, or 14s to 20s weekly when the women covered these expenses. Selborne stressed that if farmers were to utilise women's labour 'they must adapt themselves to the particular conditions of women's labour; they must make it easy for them, and not hard' and they must make it worth their while.[26] The central problem facing the Land Army was the substitution of patriotism for wages, or even a meaningful work experience. Selborne's assertion that women should be offered a fair wage was in some way contravened by the earlier assertion that women worked for the good of the nation, not for themselves. The land would be worked, the farmers would lose little in the transaction, and the nation would reap all of the benefits.[27] And yet, the sight of women labouring on the land continued to be looked upon as a spectacle and there was still no assurance from farmers, as a group, that women would be productively employed even if a national organisation were formed.[28]

In many ways the war itself dictated the pace of measures adopted by the Boards of Trade and Agriculture. Despite hesitations from women and the disinclination of some farmers to use women in agriculture, early volunteerism and the introduction of conscription in 1916 meant that the need for women labourers was growing as the war progressed. The WLA was established in January 1917 to provide a trained permanent source of labour.[29] 'Doing one's bit' was the clarion call of the WLA and the government relied on the spirit of volunteerism to bring women to the land.[30] Early in the new year the Women's Branch sent out its first call 'TO THE WOMEN OF THE NATION'. In bold letters the women of Britain were asked, 'Our Soldiers Must have Food. Will YOU do this?', accompanied by a picture of two women tending to calves; 'Our Soldiers Must have Hay. Will YOU do this?', next to a picture of a woman bailing hay in the field; 'Our Sailors need Wood for their Ships. Will YOU do this?', beside a picture of women cutting down trees. The bottom of the poster read, 'Will you respond to the call of the Land and join the Women's Land Army?'[31] On 14 April 1917 the Women's Selection National Service and the Women's Branch placed an advertisement in the *Times* calling for 10,000 strong, healthy women to work as milkmaids on farms in England, Wales, and Scotland (Figure 3.1).[32] In Devon, Alice Mildmay began a promotional campaign for the WLA and in April 1917 placed the following article in the *Salcombe Gazette*:

> A large and daily increasing number of women in Devon are enrolling for the duration of the war as National Service Volunteers, in the Women's Land Army ... I firmly believe that women will realise the immense opportunity ...open to them on the land and will rise to the emergency and if agriculturists will equally patriotically come forward with offers to train them, then agriculture will come

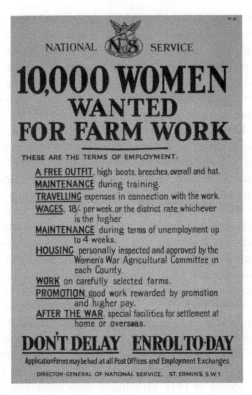

Figure 3.1 'Women Wanted for Farm Work'
Source: The National Archives, NATS 1/109.

triumphantly out of the crisis in which it finds itself at present and the increased production of food which is absolutely vital to the attainment of ultimate and complete victory in this supreme struggle for right and humanity will be ensured.[33]

Posters and leaflets also appealed to women by offering a good wage, proper training, housing and maintenance allowance, opportunity for promotion, and the potential for work once the war ended. A recruiting poster from the National Service Department called for '10,000 Women Wanted For Farm Work' with the potential for land settlement at home or overseas.[34] Other recruitment leaflets read 'When you have signed YOUR Application Form, hand this leaflet to your neighbour and ask her to do the same', thereby placing recruitment in the hands of individual women. The hope was that women would feel peer pressure, patriotism, or even a sense of camaraderie and join the Land Army.[35]

No training was promised, but the women often received instruction. Initially the programme allowed for a wage of 15s a week, a uniform, and a free rail ticket. There was a rush to join in the spring of 1917 with some 30,000 women responding to the call, but in the autumn and winter the number of enlistees dropped considerably.[36] Gill Clarke argues that during the initial surge women were responding to the patriotic call of the Land Army.[37] It is difficult to quantify why so many women came forward in the spring of 1917 and although 30,000 seems like an impressive number, it merits further consideration. The figure is derived from the number of women who filled out applications and returned them to post offices and Employment Exchanges. It does not mean that 30,000 women actually joined the WLA. In fact, by the end of July 1917 only 2,000 additional women had been placed on farms, with another 2,200 in training centres.[38] In October 1917 the Women's Branch indicated concern that the Land Army was unable to compete with the Women's Army Auxiliary Corps, which enjoyed considerable popularity during the war and had already absorbed a large number of potential recruits, particularly from the middle classes.[39] Susan Grayzel notes that since the WLA generally attracted single women from the middle classes, many had to be persuaded of the need for their employment.[40]

To determine the extent of opposition to or support for the Land Army, in the spring of 1917 agricultural demonstrations were held to show how effective women could be on the land. Agricultural demonstrations had been used earlier in the war, but the expectation was that the Land Girls would perform better due to superior organisation and training, and would thus showcase their potential to farmers more effectively. Agricultural demonstrations were held on Saturdays at locations around the country and were intended to exhibit women's abilities in non-traditional areas of work, including spreading manure and driving horses. Earlier demonstrations focused on work traditionally done by women. These demonstrations were more labour-intensive and reflected the urgency with which the Women's Branch and FPD approached the food problem and labour shortages. In Cornwall, the first county in England to hold agricultural demonstrations for women, demonstrations were held in Truro, St Austell, and Helston in April, May, and June, and competitions were held in ploughing, harrowing, harnessing horses and driving wagons, spreading manure, hand hoeing of roots, preparing of seed beds, cutting wood, paring hedges, and a number of other areas. The demonstrations were very popular and attracted thousands of spectators. Following the competition, there was demand for the services of the women and the event was declared a glowing success.[41] In Biddenham a demonstration organised by the County War Agricultural Committee, the Agricultural Society, the Chamber of Agriculture, and the National Farmers' Union for Bedfordshire under-took competitions in harrowing, weeding, cutting clover, and harness-ing a team of horses for women, along with competitions in horse and cattle work for men. Tea was served and 'most of the on-lookers were women of the right class, and they showed the liveliest interest in the proceedings'.[42]

Organisers reported that although few women placed their names on the register for land service, there was considerable interest expressed by both men and women. In Herefordshire, Mrs Whittaker brought five women to a local agricultural fair to demonstrate their ability in milking. Farmers were quite impressed and inquiries were made regarding the employment of three of the women.[43] Land Girls were welcomed by the Lord Mayor of London to demonstrate their skills at an agricultural fair. After a procession in vehicles laden with agricultural produce, the Lord Mayor greeted the girls, introduced them as members of the Women's Land Army, and sent the girls to demonstrate the skills they had acquired after just one month of training. In front of a crowd of onlookers, the women expressed enthusiasm at their new employment opportunity.[44] In Exeter the Women's War Service Committee, the Board of Agriculture, and the Devon War Agricultural Committee put on competitions. Women's agricultural demonstrations had not been especially popular in Devon, so there was increased pressure to make a good showing. Hundreds of people journeyed to the scene to watch the demonstrations and organisers noted that the male-inspired garments worn by the women impressed attendees. With the Lord Lieutenant and his wife in attendance, the protracted programme of ten competitions was described as a 'pleasant way to spend a day in the country'.[45]

While thousands of people journeyed to see the competitions, and the number of women employed in agriculture rose, the response from women was not encouraging. The Exeter competitions were deemed a success by organisers and spectators were generally impressed by the women's abilities, but few women came forward.[46] Unfortunately, the response in Devon was not atypical. In Worcestershire Miss Willan noted that in the country village there were not many women willing to come forward to join the Land Army. Many were impressed by the work of women on the land, but felt it was not work suited to them specifically. Miss Willan indicated that many women in the villages felt they were too delicate for farm work. Accounts from the County Councils revealed similar trends. In Huntingdon some women were willing to assist with agricultural work, but not to be employed full-time as farm labourers. In Cheshire and Lancashire Mrs Cross indicated that due to low enrolments it might be wise to limit wages in munitions in order to facilitate a more positive response to agricultural work.[47] Reports from across the country reflected earlier concerns that women were not suited to farm work. A meeting at the Middlesex Town Hall revealed most women in the town believed that they were not strong enough to work on the land and that perhaps it would be best if those women who wanted to help tended to the children of the women who were more physically capable. They also inquired about whether or not young women would be chaperoned, as some parents wanted guarantees their daughters would be cared for and someone would be responsible for their well-being. In one instance an army doctor inquired about who would hold an umbrella over his daughter's head when it rained and who would bring her tea.[48] In Hampshire Kathleen Macleod surmised that 'Every woman is anxious to help her country at this crisis, but every woman's physique will not stand the exposure demanded, and before any terrible blunders are made by people who have never faced country life at its worst, the whole subject should be very carefully considered.'[49]

The presumption that women might not be aware of the nature of farm work points to more than just the male/female division of labour, but also an awareness of power relations between the sexes. While some women were willing to fight for a woman's right to work the land, others were more ambivalent or accepting of male authority. The problem in looking at politics and power in women's farming movements is the lack of source material. Because women were not admitted to the National Agricultural Labourers and Rural Workers Union, women's involvement in farm labouring movements in the late nineteenth and early twentieth century has been concealed. Yet, women's work through the Women's Protection and Provident League elucidates their activism and points to awareness of power structures with regards to paternalism and women's agricultural work.[50] Of importance here is the relationship between women and labouring men, but also the complex relationship between labouring and non-labouring women. What was viewed as harmless action (farm work) by one group, was viewed as a contentious issue surrounding the lack of awareness of work conditions on farms and the unsuitability of the work for women by another group. For the latter, women's farm work not only posed a potential threat to men, but to some categories of women, as well.

Many women were also not impressed by the expectations of service with the Land Army. Terms of work for the Land Army indicated a mandatory training period of four to six weeks for women who had little to no agricultural experience, and once trained, women had to commit to six months of working the land, but it was preferable if the women signed on to a service period of one year, and could not leave their post without the consent of the Village Registrar or the WWAC.[51] Rather than committing to joining the WLA, they enlisted with the National Service Department as part-time workers to assist local farmers. In reality, there was little change from the pre-war employment structure. The only change was that the names of women interested in part-time work were left with the Village Registrar and their work placement was overseen by the WWACs. The problem was that the registers were only a first step. From the WLA's perspective, it was important to induce women to work and to press for formal registration with the WLA.

Although farmers generally accepted the patriotic presentation of the WLA, their acceptance of patriotism as a motivating factor was not uncritical and farmers' unions across the country expressed concerns about the Land Army's call to patriotic service. When Alice Mildmay spoke at the Totnes farmers' meeting in 1916, she assured farmers that 'If a woman went to work on a farm it would be more for patriotism than because it was necessary to do so to earn a living.'[52] Mildmay's assurances to the farmers that women were motivated by a sense of duty to their nation fits nicely with our existing understanding of the WLA. While farmers appreciated the organisers' dedication and the women's willingness to come forward, the difficulty was that organisers understood little about the business of farming.[53] A farmer from Stoke Fleming was convinced women 'would not even be able to hoe potatoes for dinner, and to expect a woman to use a plough is ridiculous', and at the Dartmouth meeting one farmer was stubborn in his belief that one 12-year-old boy was the equivalent of two women workers. While women workers could be helpful, the Dartmouth and District Farmers' Union petitioned the Education Authorities to allow children over the age of 12 to leave school for the duration of the war, rather than employ women, or at the very least, to employ women only in conjunction with school-age boys.[54]

In Norfolk the farmers' union expressed its concern that a willingness to work was not all that was required. Taking a historical perspective, farmers argued that the conditions of country life were daunting, even for the most experienced men. The loss of men from the land in recent years was proof of the difficulties of country life. While patriotism may have been seen as an adequate reward for joining the Land Army, the concern was it would not keep most women going once the real work began. This is not to say that Norfolk farmers were unappreciative of the women's efforts, but rather that agricultural work required a certain degree of acceptance that the work was the work and that it would not change. Farmers also did not readily admit that, their conservatism aside regarding the employment of women for farm work, they refused to pay labourers, men or women, a living wage, which aided in the disappearance of workers from the countryside. Proof of the women's lack of dedication was unintentionally presented at the agricultural demonstrations. Demonstrations conducted by St Augustine's College in May 1917 revealed that women were quite capable of undertaking work traditionally done by women, but the heavier lifting and the difficulty of horse work persuaded both men and women that even trained women were not up to the task. When working with horses one woman required the assistance of a male trainer to complete the task, while another simply gave up.[55] Farmers wanted less propagandising, and more practical results. For the WLA this would be difficult to achieve. The agricultural demonstrations were intended to showcase the women's skills and their potential to be useful workers with additional training. But the calls to service focused on the act of enlisting and tended not to stress the actual work experience.[56]

The agricultural demonstrations did not achieve the results hoped for by the WWACs, the Women's Branch, and the Board of Agriculture and in response organisers decided on a more controversial approach. If the women's patriotism was not in question, perhaps the farmers' should be. Farmers were divided into two groups: the patriotic farmer who accepted the labour offered by the Land Army, and the unpatriotic farmer who refused to accept the service of Land Girls. Organisers had to be careful not to overemphasise this division. The purpose was to cajole those farmers who had thus far been resistant to female labourers, not to further alienate them. Rather than making the press campaign negative, they opted for a positive approach by highlighting the good work done by patriotic farmers and their Land Girls.[57] Organisers promoted the Land Army by connecting the Land Girls' war service, and the patriotic farmers' war service, to the revitalisation of the land. Keeping the Norfolk farmers' reluctance in mind, the revitalisation campaign was essential. If the concern for some farmers was the depletion of the agricultural labour force and the decline of the agricultural industry, then the Land Army could be seen as a vehicle for positive change. The Women's Land Army drew national attention to the needs of agriculture, placed it at the forefront of government discussions and decisions, and called for public support for changes in British food production. While the Land Army did not accomplish all of this on its own, it provided a platform for such discussions.

The Land Army acknowledged that employing women in agriculture was not easy, nor was the farmers' reluctance purely prejudicial. But, for farmers who took a risk, that farmer was now 'taking stock of his new helpers', and while he was not accustomed to employing women and was of the belief that they would not 'stick it or would shirk the rough and dirty work', the important thing was that 'Seeing is believing. He knows better now.'[58] David Lloyd George further valorised the part played by the WLA in the war by acknowledging that women (and farmers by association) had 'already served the Allies by their splendid work upon the farms', but the army was in need of more men to fight in France. The Prime Minister explained that he had 'watched with great interest and admiration the splendid work already done. Never have British women and girls shown more majority or more pluck.' But more women must come forward, as German submarines 'are trying to starve us by sinking the ships that used to carry to our shores the abundant harvests of other lands'.[59] Earlier in the war Selborne said that the war should have provided adequate motivation for women to come forward, but it would only work if the message reached those women who were capable and actuated to do so. Selborne reasoned that the women who had already come forward did so because they had 'learned and absorbed the lesson that England was living in a moment of national crisis, and they have learned that the solution of that crisis depended upon their personal sacrifice, and their own individual effort. They have come because they have learned that England needed them, and because their imagination has been touched.'[60] Selborne believed that women did not respond to the early calls for land workers because they did not fully understand the need, despite the government's pleas for more workers. Selborne informed the County Committees that:

> If you put an empty shell in front of a woman and tell her that if she fills that shell she will be contributing to the victory of her country and to the safety of her men folk in the trenches, she understands that readily. But she does not quite so easily understand that she will be doing exactly the same service – not less, but equal – if she simply goes over a neighbouring hedge and hoes turnips for a farmer with whom, perhaps, she has never been on great terms of personal friendliness. That is what you have to teach them.[61]

To do this required effort on the part of every county in England, Wales, and Scotland, as well as educated and organised women to 'meet their humbler sisters' and teach them what the call of King and Country meant in a time of war. Keeping with Selborne's earlier plea, Rowland Prothero encouraged all those working on the land to continue their work, as 'it is vital to our national existence'. He offered encouragement to the pioneering women of the Land Army, 'who have been what the first Seven Divisions were to the men'. He reminded Britons that the Land Girls were 'helping to hold the home front as the men are holding the lines by sea and land. I hope that in doing so they may learn the full truth of Whitman's words: "Now I see the secret of the making of the best persons,/It is to grow in the open air, and to eat and sleep with the earth."'[62] Prothero's comments assert that the Women's Land Army was not an unnatural solution to a wartime problem. Getting back to the land was a noble character-building exercise beyond patriotism, the resumption of an ideal and natural state of being. An article in the *Landswoman* entitled 'Land Lasses in Wonderland' told the story of land lasses in Britain dating back to the Middle Ages. Certainly her clothes, tools, and method of travel would have been different, but 'her work would be pretty much the same. After all it is the same earth, and they are the same cattle!' Unfortunately, the advances made in agriculture did not necessarily reflect similar advances in public attitudes. But the Land Girls should not fear, nor be persuaded away from agricultural work. Citing Sir Anthony Fitzherbert's *Book of Husbandry* (1523),[63] the article concludes:

> It is a wyues [wife's] occupation to wynowe all manner of cornes, to make malte, to wash and wrynge, to make heye, shere corne, and, in time of need, to helpe her husbande to fyll the mucke wayne or dounge carte, Dryue the plough, to loode heye, corne, and suche other, and to go or ride to the market to sel butter, chese, mylke, egges, chekyns, capons, hennes, pygges, gese and all manner of cornes.

The 'Land Lasses in Wonderland' implies that public opinion would progress and come to truly value the service of Britain's twentieth-century 'land lasses'.[64] Venturing beyond the earlier patriotic appeals for women to undertake work of national importance, Lloyd George and Prothero connected women's service on the land to the military service of Britain's men. Propagandists focused on making women understand that their war work was not simply a matter of personal preference – it was a matter of national survival.[65]

Womanhood became the symbolic lifeline of national survival and Meriel Talbot, described as the 'chief' of the Land Army, both encouraged the revivalist crusade and epitomised the revivalist spirit of Land Girls. She described the efforts of women on the land as a reformation and opined that 'Left to men, the village would have gone from one stage of dullness and dreariness to another, rotting under the eye of heaven for lack, not of a tax on corn, but of a little imagination.' She tackled the question of women's role in agriculture head-on stating agricultural employment was better than most other forms of employment for women. If women were to undertake agricultural work permanently and continue to work together, 'it is reasonably certain that we shall have a new English Arcady'.[66] Talbot herself was a central part of the fighting spirit of the Land Army. A lady of 'middle-age, with a good masculine voice, large humorous eyes, and a quietly decisive manner', Talbot was an exemplary leader for this pioneering organisation. One might say that she gave 'the impression that she has just got off a ship after a tremendous hammering on the high seas, and is feeling all the better for that shaking up, and doesn't care a button if her hair is a little disarranged and her garments anyhow'. Talbot was 'an intellectual, unfashionable, original, and a worker', and none of these characteristics contradicted her womanliness or her central role in replenishing the agricultural labour supply with capable and productive women.[67] Talbot fashioned herself a Land Girl, wore the uniform for most public appearances, and served as a public symbol of the Land Army's mandate.

Yet, in spite of her efforts to promote the Land Army, a 1917 article in the *Daily Chronicle* notes that the women of the Land Army had not yet come to the full attention of the press, with the notable exception of the caricaturist. The Land Army has been neglected, even though 'it is most gallantly fighting the U-boat'.[68] Organisers, however, could not simply present the WLA as an unrecognised service for women in wartime or as a natural part of England's past. Farm work was strenuous and the suggestion that one's contributions might not be acknowledged was not the way to fill the Land Army's ranks. Building on the limited success of the agricultural demonstrations, the Land Army held rallies and parades to encourage women to become part of a group, thereby staving off criticisms and concerns regarding the isolation of rural life. The use of parades (Figure 3.2) was not only a useful recruiting tool, but also allowed Land Girls to experience firsthand the impact of their work. Observed by waiting crowds and passers-by the parades stirred the patriotic impulse of both participants and spectators.[69] Two hundred girls participated in the Great Rally in London in April 1918 where after

Figure 3.2   Members of the Women's Land Army on parade on the Brighton sea front during the First World War
© Imperial War Museums (Q 54600).

lunch and a speech by Talbot, Queen Mary inspected the Land Girls at Buckingham Palace.[70] In West Riding, Land Girls marched through the streets in full farm kit accompanied by the band of the West Riding Volunteer Regiment. At the end of the parade the girls made their way to Victoria Square where the Lady Mayoress presented them with badges. In East Suffolk a rally was held at Ipswich where after ten minutes of drills, 60 members of the Land Army marched to the Council Chamber. Badges were presented by Meriel Talbot as the women marched two-by-two 'with military precision' to receive their service stripes. The Hertfordshire Land Girls held their reunion in London where a concert was held in honour of their service. Speeches were made by Talbot and Admiral Fawkes and at the end of the proceedings the Land Girls made a New Year's resolution to each bring one new woman into the Land Army in the coming year.[71]

While the spectacle of rallies and parades improved the marketability of the Land Army, why women pursued agricultural work was of significant interest to recruiters and organisers during the war. If they wanted to increase the number of volunteers, they had to understand what factors motivated women to choose the WLA. Reports from the WWAC allowed the Women's Branch to adequately gauge attitudes throughout the country and revealed that in spite of the 'success' of the agricultural demonstrations and Land Army rallies, women had to be offered incentives beyond patriotism. To help the Land Army better compete for recruits, several of the WWACs indicated that changes were needed in three areas: the recruiting and selection process, training and work expectations, and the strict code of behaviour that was to be enforced by the WWACs and Welfare Officers. By the end of 1917, the Women's Branch recognised that its recruitment criteria were too restrictive and that some added inducements were required to bring women to the land. Among the new incentives were better housing, higher wages, and opportunities for advancement; greater access to entertainment and leisure activities were considered to be equally important in keeping women on the land. The promotion of the Land Army as a 'Jolly Sisterhood' illustrated the point that 'laughter, song and strenuous work can go together, and the former tends to help one forget that the latter is "hard"'.[72] At the end of the day the Land Girls made their way to the dinner table where they ate like men, but sang, laughed, and danced like women.

The promotion of Women's Institutes and recreational and leisure activities for Land Girls further helped to promote the image of the Land Army as an organisation that offered more than just a new employment opportunity for women; it also sought to improve the women's emotional well-being.[73] Dances were promoted as an occasion for the girls to come together away from the farmers' fields and provided the opportunity for the women to meet eligible young men, under supervision from Group Leaders. In the early stages of the Land Army's existence dances were uncommon, although a few did take place in larger centres. By early 1918 the importance of dances and other social events were deemed necessary for the women's mental health.[74] Increasingly, dances took place on Saturday evenings and garden parties took place on Sunday afternoons. There were also clubs for women interested in hand crafts and cooking.[75] Trips to the cinema were encouraged and lantern shows were put on for Land Girls through the National Service Department.[76] The propaganda surrounding the Land Army suggested that while the hard work reconditioned their bodies, the enjoyment of one another's company and the pride they took in their work invigorated the women's hearts and minds. Such representations served to comfort potential recruits that rural life was not as isolated as it had been in the past and at the same time worked to reassure the public that despite the masculine nature of the work, Land Girls had not sacrificed their girlish qualities.[77] For organisers, dances and garden parties provided what they perceived as much needed socialisation for the Land Girls in an environment where a high degree of supervision ensured that the women adhered to traditional social conventions.

Presenting the Land Army as a joyous work opportunity that provided the occasion for pleasurable interaction as part of a budding sisterhood was part of the general approach taken by organisers in order to make agricultural work more palatable for women; however, the limits and potential drawbacks of this approach was the cause of much debate among organisers. Songs and dance provided much needed relaxation after a laborious day's work, but the image of Land Girls singing while they carried out their chores was, in most cases, a disingenuous portrayal of a day in the life of a Land Girl.[78] Some organisers feared that such a depiction of the Land Army created unrealistic expectations of agricultural life and had to be properly juxtaposed with the realities of farm living and the expectations of the Women's Land Army.[79]

The fact was that the Land Army was a regimented organisation with high expectations regarding the women's work and character. Land Girls were expected to wear a uniform, which was to be treated with respect at all times. A visual symbol of the organisation and the women's participation in the war, the uniform was emblematic of the group overall, diminishing the role of the individual in favour of the collective. The importance placed on the uniform by organisers reflected the uniform's value as a unifying, protective garment.[80] Conferring legitimacy and prestige (so long as its wearers accepted and respected the uniform), the uniform could also help to deflect public criticisms; ideally, criticisms were directed at the uniform and not the women. The uniform was a garment intended to be removed; the woman's identity was preserved beneath the clothes she wore. Promoters of women's work had to tread carefully – women were not incapable of hard work, but extensive labour could compromise a woman's childbearing function.[81] The women's physical ability was thus promoted in a way that did not jeopardise their reproductive potential.[82] The desire to safeguard the maternal role can be seen with regard to women's work attire. In the early months of the campaign many farmers mocked organisers and recruiters by challenging that women could not work in skirts and feathered hats.[83] It was, of course, never assumed that the women would work in such attire, but the public mockery required a calculated response. Rather than chiding the farmers for their facetiousness, the adaptability of women's dress was used synonymously to advocate the adaptability of the women themselves. Concerns about the maternal body meant that propagandists had to be careful in their presentation of women land workers. Women's caring and nurturing ways could be transferred from the home to the land. Sustaining the population was the woman's mandate and posters appealed to women as care givers, noting 'We must have – Milk for the babies, Bread for our children, food for the sailors and soldiers.'[84]

It all came down to appearances. Recruits were encouraged to look 'workmanlike' but not to wear jewelry or lace or other frivolous accessories. As the women were doing men's work, they were expected to be 'dressed rather like a man'.[85] The emphasis was on making sure the women behaved in an acceptable way. The suggestion was not that they *were* men; rather, they were women who should not act like men except in the valuable work they performed. The uniform was a safe option that refused to challenge the myth of traditional womanhood; while including breeches, the uniform was actually quite feminine – a hat reminiscent of a sunbonnet was worn, the long smocks/coats vaguely resembled a dress, and the synched waist accentuated the Land Girls' female features and served to highlight their femininity.[86] The uniform was conservative, modest, yet masculine, but was feminised by its hosts (Figure 3.3). Smiling women of the Land Army bore the additional responsibilities the war demanded, but they were also protected by an entrenched agricultural system that defined women's role in relation to men's. Organisers reasoned that if a simple change of attire (the WLA did not wear military-style uniforms) could produce a more visually acceptable worker, then the campaign to bring women to the land could garner success along similar lines. Patriotism and femininity were not necessarily in conflict.[87]

The objective, therefore, was to warrant against any radical behaviour that would upset public sensibilities and negatively affect the public image of the Land Army.[88] Women were not to wear their uniforms if entering the bar of a public house or while smoking. Land Girls were to keep themselves fit and presentable. Eight hours of sleep was required, as Land Girls were expected to work between ten and eleven hours each day. They were not to be out late and the Land Army enforced a curfew of eight o'clock. All women were to behave in a quiet manner and avoid any activity that would lead to misjudgment. Women were also encouraged not to take days off unless it was absolutely necessary. While the WLA was non-denominational, Land Girls were encouraged to attend public worship, but were discouraged from wearing their uniforms to church. The Land Army badge bearing the letters L.A.A.S was to be worn

Figure 3.3 A full-length portrait of a member of the Women's Agricultural Section of the Land Army
© Imperial War Museums (Q 30352).

with pride, but was also intended to serve as a reminder. While the letters stood for Land Army Agricultural Section, they also stood for loyalty, ability, ardour, and service: members of the Land Army were loyal to the farmer, showed ability in their work, ardour in completing their tasks, and owed service to their country. The reality was that the dances and activities promoted in the advertising of the Land Army were aimed at potential recruits and those in the training centres, although all Land Girls were welcome to attend.

One aspect of women's employment in agriculture that has received little attention from scholars is the code of behaviour that was enforced throughout the war. Welfare Officers and representatives of the WWACs closely supervised the women's conduct, both at work and during their leisure time. The purpose was not to restrict the women, but rather to stave off public criticisms regarding the unfeminine behaviour of female industrial workers.[89] Meriel Talbot wanted to ensure that recruits upheld the good name of the Land Army, but there was no single set of guidelines that could be applied routinely and consistently across the country. Instead, each county was responsible to determine its own procedures. The counties were not permitted to establish their own written 'codes of conduct', or even to enforce penalties for disobedience – that was the role of Welfare Officers who reported to the Women's Branch – but several did so without permission and felt that clear and enforceable guidelines were necessary for the proper functioning of the Land Army. In Hertfordshire, the Women's War Agricultural Committee believed that a more stringent code of conduct was needed. The Hertfordshire committee had one hundred girls in its service in Waltham Cross and with more than one or two girls to a farm in that area, work ethic and obedience to the farmers had diminished. Although Mrs Puller had promulgated a handbook indicating 'Guides to Conduct' for Hertfordshire, the Hertfordshire WWAC felt it was time for a uniform set of rules to be instituted by the Women's Branch for the entire organisation. Organisers in Hertfordshire complained that the Board of Agriculture's guidelines for conduct were 'too indefinite' and that it 'would be fatal and lead to much confusion to have both the Board's Guides and a set of County Rules in any given county'. The problem the Hertfordshire committee recognised was that although counties did enforce their own rules, doing so could be detrimental because Land Girls could complain about the rules to Group Leaders and ask to be relocated to another county where the rules were 'less definite'. While the badge bearing the letters L.A.A.S established general expectations for Land Girls, the increasing number of behaviour infractions by Land Girls meant that penalties had to be issued and supported by the Land Army organisation and the Board of Agriculture.[90]

The Hertfordshire committee was not alone in voicing a desire for more stringent rules and regulations and for a formal statement of penalties to be applied for misconduct. As in Hertfordshire, the Devon WWAC instituted its own 'Code of Behaviour' that included proper uniform maintenance, working the hours indicated by the farmer, keeping living quarters in good condition, performing the tasks requested without complaint, respecting curfews, and 'general good behaviour'.[91] Most infractions consisted of breaking curfew, refusing to perform certain tasks, and showing up late for work. In a few instances farmers complained that the girls could not be controlled and that their conduct was inappropriate. The problem was that some women joined the

WLA to escape the watchful eyes of their parents. The Land Army likely seemed a natural solution since it called women to the open country-side where they could improve their health and general well-being.[92] E. A. Campbell joined the WLA to spite her mother who wanted her to remain at home to help take care of the younger children. Stationed in northern Devon, however, Campbell struggled with the solitude of farm work and the demands of farm life. On several occasions the farmer in charge reported Campbell to the WWAC for breaking curfew, tardiness, and general disobedience. After several reprimands by the WWAC for unacceptable conduct, the Deputy Controller for Devon determined that she was not suited for farm work and released her from her contract.[93]

Cases such as Campbell's diverged from the propaganda material for the WLA that presented an image of happy, healthy Land Girls surrounded by children and young animals, singing and dancing as they carried out their work on the sunstricken fields of England.[94] The issue was that once the Land Army offered incentives beyond service to the nation and once recruiting expanded beyond the ideal candi-dates of early 1917, individual motives for joining the WLA and the image presented to the public began to conflict. This can most clearly be seen in the increased number of reports relating to reprimands for misconduct between the County Executives and the Women's Branch throughout 1918. Inspectors were sent out to farms in England, Wales, and Scotland to inquire about what could be done to resolve discipline problems and encourage a better work ethic among Land Girls. In sev-eral counties farmers expressed their opinions that increased authority on the part of Welfare Officers and the WWACs would not be enough to turn 'a possible slacker into a willing worker'.[95] While farmers gener-ally accepted that a clearer statement of the rules was advisable from the organisation's perspective, they preferred to take in Land Girls on a trial basis. Those who did not wish to work would be sent home or back to the training depots, and those who were up to the challenge of farm life would be kept on. The farmers believed that this was the only way to circumvent the challenge of employing women who enlisted for agricultural work, but had no intentions of working. Several farmers requested disciplinary powers and to avoid further conflicts with the WWAC, to cease farm inspections entirely.[96]

A meeting of the WWACs, the Women's Branch, and the Board of Agriculture in June 1918 indicated there was 'much anxiety' among members the Women's War Agricultural Committees in policing the behaviours of Land Girls. Representatives across the country stressed the need for 'greater control over members of the Land Army and the power to punish wrong doing'.[97] The problem was that enforcing the code of behaviour could only really be done while the women were in training. Once they left the training centres they worked for a private employer. Yet, they wore Land Army uniforms and served as members of the Women's Land Army organisation. Good conduct badges were used to encourage the women to abide by the rules, but this was no guarantee, and the County Committees were saddled with reports from unhappy farmers.[98] The Land Army promised women of good quality and reputation and this is what farmers expected when they agreed to hire Land Girls. Devon farmers were not alone in expressing their need for greater control over employees. In Hertfordshire the County Committee indicated a desire to either adopt a uniform set of rules, or to allow the farmers full disciplinary powers. The Hertfordshire County War Agricultural Committee argued that the Board of Agriculture and Women's Branch could not have it both ways: that a uniform code of behaviour could not be enforced once the women left the training centres; and although the women were employed by a private employer, the employer was not granted disciplinary powers.[99]

In July 1918 the Food Production Department issued a circular regarding the welfare of Land Girls and charges of misconduct. Indicated in several reports from the WWACs was a desire to impose military-style discipline on the WLA. When the Board of Agriculture announced the parturition of the Women's Land Army in January 1917, the *Daily Express* publicised the event with an article entitled 'Army of Women on a Military Basis', suggesting the Land Army would be structured along military guidelines. This new army of land workers was established to 'supplement the corps of "sedentaries" who will replace farm hands' and would be 'Paid, Billeted, and Uniformed'.[100] At its unveiling, the language of military service was a central feature of the Land Army's public image. Organisers sought to convince the public the WLA was an army of qualified and efficient workers, who worked in service to the state and the national war effort. The Land Army as a military scheme, however, was quickly given up because Talbot believed that it sent the wrong message to potential recruits – the Land Army wished to recruit women of a particular social class so military-style discipline and organisation would not be necessary. Janet Watson argues that after two years of war the integration of women into industries produced a more favourable attitude toward women workers (and the wearing of military-style uniforms) in the press, but it did little to alleviate public anxiety.[101] Even the government's assertion that the war required the mobilisation of all Britons did little to encourage public support for women's organisations that adopted a military structure. Talbot herself was uncomfortable with the public presentation of the WLA as a military organisation and sought to avoid creating a link between military servicemen and the Land Girls.[102]

In spite of Talbot's objections, the connection was not easily broken. The symbol of loyalty to the organisation and the national cause involved wearing the Land Army armlet, the reception of a distinguished service award, or placement on the 'Roll of Honour'. Both the armlet and the distinguished service award were symbols of the Land Girls' service, indicating length of service and commitment to the task at hand.[103] Even the certificate of service was intended to equate, on some level, the service of men and women, Land Girls and soldiers. The certificate was emblazoned with the royal coat of arms and while not indicative of individual accomplishments, it was a sign of patriotic service. Likewise, the Roll of Honour that recorded the deaths of Land Girls who died during the course of their employment evoked military comparisons.[104] The press presented these women as brave and enduring and while they met with a tragic end like the soldiers and sailors who died in battle, their deaths were not in vain. Their work contributed to Britain's war effort and in the end would be justified by Britain's victory.

Although the FPD determined that implementing military-style conduct, or even the adoption of a 'code of conduct' was impractical and undesirable, the decision did not put an end to calls for greater control over members and the military symbolism remained in place. Nevertheless, the FPD explained the expansion of the Land Army in 1918 meant that 'young women of all classes and occupations' were 'attracted to the work in various ways – some by the call of their country to service – some by the desire for fresh air and country conditions – some from the spirit of adventure – and some again from restlessness and a vague desire for change'. Although called an 'army', workers were employed by private individuals, not the state, and worked singularly, not as a cohesive unit.[105] In this way, the WLA could not meaningfully be compared to other organisations like the Women's Army Auxiliary Corps and imposing militaristic discipline would seek only to usurp the image organisers worked so hard to maintain. As an organising body the FPD had two primary responsibilities (aside from food production), the first of which was to ensure the welfare of the women who joined the Land Army, a responsibility it was not willing to turn over entirely to farmers. The FPD's second, and quite separate, responsibility was to the public 'in securing the right behaviours' from workers. Rather than military discipline, Land Girls had to be enticed to follow the rules and the proper incentives, which now included Welfare Officers befriending the women and establishing a relationship of trust, were to ensure that the hard work and service expected from the Land Army was delivered.[106]

Recruiters and organisers recognised the complexities of women's motivations for seeking work in agriculture and made changes to recruiting strategies based on the women's personal experiences and expectations. To avoid competition for women workers an agreement was made to combine the Forage Department of the War Office, the Timber Supply Department of the Board of Trade, and the Forestry Department of the Board of Agriculture into one Land Army.[107] This new provision also meant women could escape the monotony of farm work by supplementing it with work elsewhere during the winter months. The new marketing campaign stressed that women could move between the various sections to find work that suited them best, suggesting the Women's Land Army was aware and sympathetic to the fact that some women would not take to specific jobs, but that the organisation was keen to support the women by allowing them to make changes to the employment contracts in an effort to make their experience more enjoyable. These changes were intended to improve work conditions and hopefully attract respectable workers to the Land Army. Reducing waiting times, shortening the application process, and adding incentives to attract women to the Land Army does not negate the women's patriotism, but it does suggest that patriotism offers only a partial explanation for why women chose the Land Army above other wartime work.

The marketing campaign adopted by the Women's Land Army was successful in getting women into the training centres and onto Britain's farms. Some women chose the Land Army because of the new work opportunity it afforded them. Others were attracted by the suggestion that they would enjoy a lovely stay in the countryside where they could revitalise their minds and bodies, while also doing work of national importance. One source of concern for organisers was the pretext that the Land Army offered fewer restrictions, in terms of access to and the navigation of physical space, than other forms of employment. This perception meant that the WLA increasingly attracted women from domestic service. For domestic servants, restrictions and confinement bred a desire for release, which helps to explain why an increasing number of women from this group joined the Land Army after 1917.[108] Rallies, parades, and dances (and the potential to meet soldiers and sailors recovering in country estates) gave the impression there could be many potential benefits to working on the land besides the actual work and pay. This expectation was not surprising given that posters distributed by the Food Production Department appealed to 'a girl's love of animals and the outdoors' and training focused on the proper use of farm instruments, the care of young animals, and horse work. In fact, many girls cited working with animals as their main reason for joining the WLA (Figure 3.4).

Once placed on the farms, however, animal care was often only one of many tasks the women were expected to perform and in many cases men continued to do horse work.[109] In addition, access to public space was limited by long workdays and physical exhaustion. Some Land Girls complained the work was not what they expected and either wanted to be transferred to another division, or to be released from the Land Army altogether so they could find other employment.[110]

Recruiting and promotion aside, the continued success of the Land Army meant that women entering agricultural employment had to be fully informed of work expectations and conditions. In the summer

Figure 3.4 Members of the Women's Land Army feeding pigs and calves
© Imperial War Museums (Q 30662).

and autumn of 1917 enrolment declined and the number of women awaiting placement was fewer than in earlier months. The reduction in the number of Land Girls can partly be explained by a change in farming practices. The switch from livestock to crops, known as the plough campaign, was mandated by the Board of Agriculture in 1916 and intensified the workloads of agricultural workers.[111] An article produced by the Women's Branch appeared in the *Journal of the Board of Agriculture* and acknowledged that there were simply some jobs that women were unable to perform effectively, regardless of their training. While women were particularly skilled at milking and caring for young animals and many showed skill in thatching and tractor driving, the heavy, manual work 'without variety or change, tends to weary her physically and mentally' and may have accounted for some of the trouble faced by the Land Army.[112] Also of importance was that once trained, the women were dependent on the farmers for employment and this could take a substantial amount of time because even if a woman was accepted as a farm labourer there remained the question of billeting, which was in short supply. Billets were intended to meet the basic need of providing shelter, not to replicate the comforts of home, and in many instances the accommodations were less than satisfactory for the girls. The logistics of accommodations slowed down the placement process and in the meantime some women found employment elsewhere. It is also possible that the initial excitement of women working in a traditionally male industry, or just the opportunity to leave home and get away from parents and family that made working in the countryside an appealing option, was not enough to counter the difficulties of farm work and the isolation of rural life. Many recruiters and organisers stressed that while the Land Army made many promises about the physical and mental benefits of farm work, the reality was a disheartening obstacle for many women to overcome.[113]

The Women's Land Army was beset by an image crisis. Organisers had a clear sense of what they wanted the Land Army to be in theory: middle class, trained, educated, disciplined, and permanent. In addition, these women would confirm their value through demonstration of their abilities and in turn would receive proper compensation in wages and attractive work terms. The value of women's work would be recognised and their 'return to the land' made permanent. In reality, the Land Army was a blend of women from diverse social, economic, and educational backgrounds who received varied degrees of training and who were not a permanent work force. The claim that Land Girls worked out of patriotic service to the state and the ideal that the work was its own reward, was counterbalanced by the simultaneous promotion that the Land Army was a women's organisation that offered a fair wage and the chance for a future on the land. Although the Land Army was able to partially, and in many ways effectively, bypass public disapproval of women working in a traditionally male industry, such attitudes were never fully usurped, which made the disciplinary problems encountered by organisers, the County Committees, and Welfare Inspectors all the more disconcerting and made recruitment much more challenging. This is not to suggest the recruitment campaign for the Land Army was unsuccessful. Thousands of women came to enjoy agricultural work and stayed for the duration of the war. The challenge was in managing the women's expectations while also meeting their personal needs and the needs of individual farmers.

4
'The Lasses Are Massing': The Land Army in England and Wales

Throughout the twentieth century there was a significant decline in the number of women employed in agriculture in Britain and although the WLA temporarily replenished their numbers, the transitory nature of the organisation was part of a larger trend in agriculture that both preceded and followed the war. The loss of women from the countryside in the late nineteenth and early twentieth centuries was the result of the undervaluation of women in the farming industry and the belief that women could find better employment opportunities in the towns and cities.[1] The loss of women from the land was especially prevalent in areas where primogeniture persisted.[2] The decreasing number of women employed in farming does not mean that women ceased to play an integral part in farm life. In the early twentieth century family farms were labour intensive, and with a shrinking domestic market and agricultural labour force, hiring outsiders was unprofitable. With decreased hiring of both men and women, the farmer's female relatives were called upon to fill the labour gap.[3] Their work, however, was constrained to a narrow range of jobs, including feeding animals, caring for the household and children, and operating some machinery that had traditionally been operated by men. While the work of female relatives expanded in the early twentieth century, it typically remained within the realm of female domestic duties. Women did not wear trousers, they did not climb trees, and few ventured alone to the market to sell the family's wares. Wives assisted their husbands and while the gender division of labour on farms was lessening, it remained securely in place at the outset of the First World War. During the war the declining trend of women in agriculture was temporarily reversed. Working alongside the farmers' wives and daughters, Land Girls, many of whom were encouraged by new ideas about women's value as workers, challenged the gender division of labour without toppling the firmly entrenched gender hierarchy.

The nature of relations between Land Girls and the farming community dictated the relative value of the Land Army. When discussing the Land Army historians have most recently been interested in assessing women's attitudes toward their war work and service. What compelled young women to pursue agricultural work or their feelings about their treatment by farmers are central questions in interpreting how Land Girls understood their wartime experiences.[4] Such evaluations have tended toward an understanding that Land Girls were compelled by patriotism and that outright hostility from farmers at the beginning the war turned to grudging acceptance and finally a mutually beneficial relationship by war's end. While these assessments are not wrong, they are incomplete. Neither Land Girls nor farmers worked independently of the larger communities they were part of, and understanding the role played by the Land Army in wartime requires a wider assessment of both groups. The relationship between the Land Army and the farming community contributed to the success or failure of individual women on the land, as well as the Land Army organisation nationally.

With suntanned faces and toned bodies the women of the Land Army were a notable presence on the land. Working long hours for low wages, Britain's Land Girls had answered the 'call to service'.[5] Certainly the 'language of essential service was used to outweigh the stolid work associations of heavy farm labour' for both working- and middle-class women, but not all women identified with the war effort in the same way.[6] Women's motivations were as varied as the men's reasons for enlisting, but regardless of their reasons for joining, the decision to either stay and work on the land or leave came down to a personal choice for each Land Girl.[7] Rosa Freedman was the eldest of ten children and even as a child was used to hard work. She worked with her father on an allotment and after leaving school at the age of 13 went to work as a domestic servant on an estate in the New Forest. Freedman left domestic service during the war, and although she found agricultural work to be physically exhausting, she also found it to be liberating and rewarding and chose to stay with the Land Army until the end of the war.[8] For Mary Bale, the Women's Land Army was her chance to make a meaningful contribution to the war effort. Although Bale complained about the rate of pay and the long hours, she felt pride in her work.[9] Vera Raymond also grew up on a family farm and enjoyed country life. She was a self-described 'natural' and took to the work quickly. Unlike many Land Girls, Raymond liked the regimentation of daily life and although the training was strict, she became the first female trapper in Cornwall. She was also a skilled ploughwoman and entered district competitions, although it is unclear if she ever won. She liked the work and felt that her male co-workers accepted her and respected the work she did. Just before the armistice her father died in battle and Raymond left the Land Army to return to her family home.[10]

With the outbreak of war in August 1914 Edith Airey had just completed her schooling. Her three brothers had enlisted in the army and her older sister decided to join the WLA after returning from London. While she offers the explanation that she, like her sister, wanted to 'do her bit' for the war, her true motivations lay in her childhood memories of life on the land in Suffolk. Airey was the youngest of six children. Her father worked for the Duke of a large estate and the family lived in a cottage close to the Duke's manor. From her cottage overlooking the gardens, Airey came to love country life. She described herself as a tomboy, playing outdoors with the village boys, climbing trees and scaling walls, with little interest in education or 'womanly' pursuits. Knowing something of Airey's childhood helps us to understand her motivations for joining the WLA, but also her decision to leave agriculture after the first winter. Airey was knowledgeable about the daily workings of a farm and expected there to be little time for fun or relaxation. She was young and strong, and believed she was well suited to work on the land. After suffering through unkind treatment from the Scottish foreman, the handling of frozen beets that gave the girls chilblained hands, and the slinging of heavy mud, too heavy for a woman, Airey dropped her tools and went home. For Airey her childhood memories of life in the countryside contrasted with the drudgery of the work, even though she had lived on the land with her family. The difference for Airey was the work expectations for women. She anticipated that she would be required to perform womanly tasks, such as tending to animals, milking, or even a bit of hoeing, but quickly determined that the work asked of her was simply too much for even a strong, healthy woman to undertake. Airey's experience on the land was not unique. Mary Lees was one of the first women to work on the land in Devon, but after nine months she had had enough: 'I was there to work, not to dilly dally. But the work was hard and the farmers needed more men. Farm labour was absolute hell and in the end the money wasn't enough, so I went home.'[11]

The importance of Airey's and Bale's stories is twofold: it adds a new layer of understanding to the 'public' perception of women's work in male industries, and it complicates the image of the patriotic Land Girl.

Studies of the Land Army tend to reinforce the view that it was the British public that expressed certain hesitations regarding the employment of women in agriculture and Land Girls continually had to rebuff such assertions. While this may certainly have been true, Airey herself was ultimately unconvinced that any woman could have or should have been successful under such conditions. Her failure was not the result of physical weakness, but rather the unrealistic expectations placed on women.[12]

The purpose here is not to suggest that women were incapable of farm work; rather, these experiences speak to the larger issue of the insularity of the farming community and the idiosyncrasies of each farm. It has never been seriously debated that women, on average, tend to be physically weaker than men. The Food Production Department and the Women's Branch expected that instances would arise where Land Girls would be asked to perform tasks that were simply too physically demanding. The assumption was that farmers and foremen were also aware of such limitations and would work around them. Yet, some male workers were determined to prove the point that agriculture was a male industry. In addition to other factors such as housing, work terms, leave time, and personal freedoms, the success of the Land Army was dependent on the relationship between individual Land Girls and the farmers who employed them. Success or failure depended as much on the Land Girls' individual disposition as it did on her day-to-day relationship with the foreman, farmer, and other workers on the farm. In addition, the relationships between women – Land Girls and the farmers' female relatives, and Land Girls and Group Leaders/Welfare Officers – were mediated by concepts of power, authority, and tradition. The central source of tension, and in some cases comfort, between these women was less about the work performed by the various groups, and more about the relationship itself. These relationships were shaped by complex ideas about what tasks women were capable of doing, but also what tasks women should be doing in relation to pre-existing social and gender expectations.

For most women entering the Land Army the work was new and few had any practical knowledge of the daily operations of a farm. Many of the women who joined the Land Army were nervous about public perceptions, work expectations, and the nature of their training. The demand for food and the need for more men to be released for military service that were a part of daily life in wartime Britain compounded the pressure these women felt and increased the pressure for the organisation to succeed. From the moment of entry into service the need for proper training and the exhibition of newly acquired skills was impressed upon the women of the Land Army. It was ultimately up to the Land Girls to eradicate prejudices against them and the operability of the Land Army scheme depended on the women's workability. Trainers and organisers were often confronted by two types of recruits: the self-confident young woman who thought that no task was beyond her abilities, and the uncertain woman who was eager to learn, but nervous about the conditions that lay ahead.[13] These divisions created an atmosphere of competition among Land Girls, which helped in the training process, but led to divisions within the Land Army. Those girls who excelled at their work were singled out to compete in agricultural competitions, thereby promoting the organisation and the successful work of the training centres. Others with the right combination of confidence, humility, and skill were sent on recruiting drives, placed on public display in parades, or participated in special envoys to meet Queen Mary and other prominent women. Land Girls were cognizant of the fact that organisers, Welfare Officers, farmers, the public, and each other were continually evaluating them. Land Girl Vera Raymond found the work challenging, but not impossible and excelled at a variety of jobs including milking, rabbit trapping, and even threshing. She was self-assured, assertive, and confident in her belief that women were not only useful on farms, but some were as capable as the men.[14] Raymond was a regular at ploughing competitions and prided herself on being a more efficient milker than most of the men and other Land Girls.

Land Girl Eva Marsh, however, struggled to work with farm machinery and/or animals and quickly found herself overwhelmed by her new experiences. Marsh was uncomfortable wearing the Land Army uniform and felt like she was on display when the men came around the training centres to watch the women work. Persistent teasing by male audiences and bet-taking by soldiers on whether or not she would fail in her duties did not entice Marsh to 'show-off' her skills; rather, it dissuaded her from joining public demonstrations or even wearing her Land Army uniform in public. Marsh preferred to go to town only when wearing 'natural' clothes and when accompanied by married women. Although Marsh described the Land Army as 'my lovely Land Army', she was distressed by the spectacle surrounding the organisation. On the one occasion when Marsh was asked to march in a procession for the Land Army, she was unable to keep step with the other girls and while she described her efforts as 'amusing', she was embarrassed by her inability to carry out the task assigned to her.[15] Marsh enjoyed being on the land with the other women, but the stress of training and *performing* was difficult for her to bear. When a family member was injured at home, Marsh took the opportunity to leave land service. The performative aspect of the Land Army was only one component of the Land Girls experience and not all women were asked to participate in parades and agricultural demonstrations. The point, however, is that not all women approached their war work in the same way. Some women who entered agricultural work considered it a viable employment option beyond the war, while others were perpetually uneasy about the choice they made to join the WLA, even when they chose to stay. Self-doubt and, for some, regret were part of the Land Girl experience and it cannot be assumed that that these feelings were unknown to organisers and potential employers.

It was not only the Land Girls who experienced a mix of responses to the conditions of war and the suitability of agricultural work for women. While many farmers appreciated the work performed by the Land Girls, the employment of women in agriculture was not simple. Some farmers accepted female agricultural workers because there was no available alternative, while others did so in an attempt to appear sympathetic at the military tribunals and to the public. Others still benefited from the use of women on the land. Women had been assisting farmers, particularly those who owned smaller farms, on the land long before the outbreak of the war. Prior to 1914, 80,000 women worked on the land in the United Kingdom and many farmers' wives and daughters often took part in farm activities, particularly around harvest time. During the war farmers could replace male labourers with female labourers for almost half the cost, and once the women were trained, production values could be maintained (of course this was not always the case). Conversely, some farmers resented the presence of women on their farms, knowing that their sons and male workforce would subsequently be conscripted. This was especially difficult for owner-occupiers. Due to gradual changes in land ownership in the late decades of the nineteenth century, owner-occupiers prospered in the early years of the twentieth century. Their farms were smaller, generally under 250 acres, employed a small, specialised labour force, with a surplus of horses and no shortage of rural workers for peak periods, which kept labour and operational costs low. The nature of farming that protected owner-occupiers in the pre-war years led to difficulties during the war as prices rose, and labour and horses became scarce.[16]

Wilfred Denning owned a 250-acre farm in western Devon that had been passed down from his father and his father before him. Denning complained,

> I worked hard my whole life. My sons and I have worked this land for 20 years and my men have been with me for 10 years or more. People think that the farms are making so much money, and some do, but many don't, especially small farms. People don't realise that this is our livelihood, we have spent our lives on the land and it is no shame to protect it.[17]

The pressures for farmers to increase domestic food production were great and some farmers simply could not conceive of succeeding in the absence of traditional labour networks. In some cases the worry was so acute that farmers abandoned the land altogether, or let their land lay fallow.[18]

For others, their prejudice came down to the belief that women were inadequate as labourers, a view that was most likely held by members of the gentry.[19] Working-class husbands were not unconcerned about the ladylike behaviour of their wives, but observing appropriate codes and conventions was most notable among the gentry, or those aspiring toward gentility. The prevalence of philanthropic work among middle-class women attests to their concern with the appropriateness of female conduct outside of the home. In the pre-war years various commissions sought to limit the employment of women in agriculture, citing the loss of moral character in women who engaged in specific activities. Reformers especially criticised married women who worked in agriculture because they were responsible for instilling a moral code of behaviour in their children.[20] Such beliefs were reinforced by high unemployment among women prior to 1914. For those women who did continue to work in agriculture, they were often marginalised due to the presence of heavier farm equipment (on large farms) and the surplus of male workers. The gender segregation of farm work reinforced the idea that 'women were inherently deficient as workers'.[21] Some farmers were thus motivated by gender presumptions and the dictates of tradition rather than by arguments based on rational efficiency.

Understanding the experiences of farmers during the war helps us to contextualise the obstacles facing the WLA, as well as to understand why the individual relationships between Land Girls and farmers were central to the success of the scheme. Just as there was no single motivating factor for women to pursue agricultural work, there was no single response of farmers to their employment. The formation of the Women's Land Army and the employment of women in agriculture generally, were not simply about the feasibility of employing women in a customarily male industry. For many farmers the issue of replacement labour became conflated with long-standing disputes between land-owners and government and the farmers' response to these disputes helped to inform the experiences of the Land Girls.

Overcoming the farmers' prejudices was only one obstacle facing the WLA; Land Girls faced many challenges that were not necessarily conquered once they were hired and placed on a farm. At the initial point of placement Land Girls were accompanied by a Group Leader (after March 1917) in order to make the transition as smooth as possible. During their first encounter with their employers many Land Girls were anxious, intimidated, and excited, but there was little time for the women to sort out these emotions. Most Land Girls arrived at their posts early in the morning, shown their sleeping quarters, and taken on a quick tour of the property before their work began. With a combination of curiosity and scepticism, some employers questioned the girls privately about their decision to enter land service. For some Land Girls these questions felt more like an interrogation when curiosity was replaced with hostility and condemnation.[22] Other Land Girls were laughed at and mocked for their presumption that any farmer would find their efforts useful.[23] Helen Bentwich worked a farm in Barkway where a farmer believed that 'his horse was more refined and better bred than any of the village-women'.[24] When in 1917 Olive Hockin inquired about farm work the farmer and his wife retorted: 'Why, think of a girl lifting that great heavy harness! ... And then there's the weather – all this snow, and the rain and cold – being out in all weathers. No woman could possibly stand it, I am quite sure of that!' Even though the farmer was reluctant to employ women, farmers were in need of labour. Even so, Land Girls had to be careful not to put too much pressure on reluctant farmers. Hockin thought it best to let one Land Girl work the land for some time before suggesting to the farmer that he hire another woman.[25]

The workability of employment contracts for women in many ways depended on how the Land Girls approached their war work. Those who understood the connection between the labour shortage and the farmers' hesitations to employ women seemed to have an easier time adjusting to their new circumstances. W. M. Bennett recalled how difficult it was to convince farmers to take on women workers. She noted that the farmers were willing to take boys, soldiers, and even conscientious objectors before they would consider women. While Lees may have been right that the women of the Land Army were either unaware of their circumstances or were indifferent to the challenges organisers, farmers, and trainers faced during the war, Bennett's account points to a reciprocal pattern of prejudice by both Land Girls and farmers. She states that the farmers were 'dated' in their attitudes. There was clearly work to be done but the farmers were too stubborn to accept women. While capable women sat around the village all day waiting for an opportunity, the farmers struggled daily to manage the workloads. Bennett believed that the farmers were risking their farms, and potentially hurting the war effort through underproduction, but the war required adjustments to be made by everyone.[26] Yet, Bennett also understood that the farmers' actions are not simply guided by prejudice. Rather, their hesitations were tied to government actions.[27] The farmers' refusal to accept women had as much, sometimes more, to do with the viability of female labour as it did a desire to disobey government directives. Cottages were full and the government refused to fund the construction of new buildings for the duration of the war. New machinery was introduced, but it continually broke down and could not be quickly repaired. Farmers hired unskilled men and boys, further diluting their skilled workforce, but complained that they worked half as well and for more money. Bennett knew that the women had to be patient and well behaved; the establishment of a positive relationship between the Land Girls and farmers could not be forced. She believed that the farmers needed women, and that they were aware of this need, but that their actions were induced by other mitigating factors.[28]

The gender division that characterised agricultural work in the pre-war years was not suspended during the war, but it did take on new meanings. Perceptions of the female worker limited her role as a member of the agricultural workforce. Changes in farming practices that were necessitated by the war, the segregation of the workforce according to skill level, and rising wages for men and women permitted a greater gender distribution in farm work and, to some degree, the relaxation of pre-existing cultural and occupational traditions. This is not to imply that work was no longer understood in gendered terms, or that women were equal to men in agriculture. Rather, women were not, and could not be, isolated from men on the land and Land Girls had to understand and evaluate their work and war experiences in relation to men who were an essential and identifiable part of the workforce.[29] Olive Hockin explains that 'with the "superior" farmers, when we saw them sneering among themselves...we would become acutely self-conscious of our breeches and lack of feminine drapery', but the labourers and working men never made them feel uncomfortable.[30] Some farmers resented their presence on the land, but for the men who were left to carry the burden, Marjorie Stone believed that they appreciated the extra hands.[31]

Hockin's experience on the land was not universal and Mary Lees and Edith Airey came to dislike the men she worked with. As a Land Girl she was trained and ready to work, yet she was also expected to carry food and drink to the workers. She was forbidden from being around the horses and machinery and spent a lot of time by herself.[32] While it appears that Mary Bale was isolated from the other workers, she recounts that despite the misjudgments of the men about the appropriateness of female farm workers, they worked together every day. Bale explained the daily operation of the farm required the participation of all workers, and although she did not find freedom on the land, she found the experience rewarding because it granted her status as a worker.[33] Airey loved the isolation of the dairy farm she worked in Suffolk, but as more men left the days were long and boring. Like Bale, Airey disliked the foreman, who she says did not like having women on the farm. Although she eventually got used to his gruff disposition, the women were always regarded as outsiders.[34] The employment opportunities opened to women in agriculture affected their sense of independence and self-potential; yet, the fact that their acceptance and successes was always dependent on the willingness of men to accept them kept the women of the Land Army in a dependent and supportive role. Bale's assertion that she found status as a worker, but not freedom helps to clarify her experience. Although women were present on the land and employed in a range of new jobs that were not traditionally done by women, the gender division that characterised the agricultural industry did not fall victim to the war. In many ways these women remained segregated either in the work they performed or spatially, and their presence on the land was rarely ever desired. The war did not grant women many new personal liberties and it did not give them financial independence, but it did allow them to make choices that directly affected their lives. Bale could have left the Land Army, but she chose to stay. Contrary to the propaganda image of the Land Army that presented it as a permanent trained labour force comprised of female recruits, the Land Girls' presence on the land was understood to be 'casual', 'seasonal', temporary.

Gail Braybon has argued women's admittance into male industries was constructed on the attitudes and needs of male workers.[35] This was certainly true in agriculture, but for women of the Land Army the female members of the farm family, notably the farmer's wife, also determined their acceptance on the land. The role of daughters and wives on small and medium-sized farms is significant because there tended to be no hired labour – male or female. Most farmers' wives were responsible for bookkeeping and accounts and daughters were typically responsible for tending to small animals, some gardening, and light fieldwork. In addition, women were required to care for the family home and family members, including mending clothing, cleaning, cooking, and managing the family economy. By the twentieth century the farm family – a family living and working on the land – faced increasing competition from commercial farms and small-holdings accounted for a decreasing share of aggregate output and income. By the outbreak of war in 1914, British farms reflected a pattern of disengagement – smallholders persisted and even prospered, but the trend was toward the land being owned by one person and farmed by another. The farm family was changing at the turn of the century and this complicated the relationship between farm families and outside organisations like the Land Army during the war years.

As the nature of landownership changed, so did the role of women. Domestic service was increasingly unpopular and it was increasingly difficult to find women willing to work as in-and-out maids in England. As a result, the work of farmers' wives was confined more and more to the family home. If the nature of their work changed, the subordinate role they played in the farm family did not. Most women entered farming through marriage, not as a chosen occupation. Even daughters who pursued agricultural work were not considered to be 'farmers'. As such, women were often cast in the role of assistant to the farmer and their work was classified as 'engaged in home duties'. They had no income, no occupational status, and no security other than that afforded through kinship. Their contribution was relegated to non-work status, despite the fact that women contributed substantially to farm production for the market and for home consumption. The division of labour along gender lines was reinforced by culture and tradition, reflecting the invisibility of women in the farming family. Yet, women were active participants in rural life and worked to improve the quality of rural life for their families.

This is not to suggest that women had no voice in the farm family. There was a clear separation between the woman's status as wife and her status as a worker. It is difficult to determine exactly how women felt about their circumstances as members of the farm family or how they saw their work in terms of the war effort, but what is known is that they were certainly significant in terms of the decisions that affected the employment of women on the family farm. The separate and subordinate status given to wives and daughters as workers is evident in the records of the Women's Land Army. Employment records for the Board of Agriculture generated by the Land Army list farmers' wives and daughters under the category 'other' or volunteer. These categories were not confined to wives and daughters and included any woman who worked on the land through the Land Army, but was not a registered Land Girl. In most cases the women in these categories were relatives of farmers, but not always. Village women who worked casually were listed under the heading 'other', but would not likely have been listed as volunteers, since few worked without pay.

The rural labour hierarchy placed Land Girls in a difficult position. As paid workers, Land Girls shared a similar status as men on the farm, even though they were paid half that of a male worker with a comparable skill set. Yet they were women, and not members of the farm family. In this way, they also shared a similar status as an in-and-out worker or a domestic servant. As female farm workers, Land Girls occupied an uncertain and unfamiliar position on the family farm. The uncertainty of this position complicated relations between Land Girls and farmers, but also between Land Girls and the farmers' families. W. M. Bennett was disappointed that more famers did not employ Land Girls on their farms, but recognised that much work could be done and was being done by the farmer's wife and female relatives. Bennett described the delicate balance of farm work and indicated that while labour supplies were short, the relationships on family farms complicated the employment of Land Girls in particular. Land Girls were instructed by Group Leaders to be careful not to interfere with the work dynamics on the farm, and in particular, not to interfere with the women already working on the land or in the home. It would take time for the farmer's wife to adjust to the presence of female non-relatives. Although support for female workers was growing in agricultural circles, many wives remained unconvinced. Bennett recalled reporting daily to a farmer who generally accepted Land Girls, but when the farmer was away, his wife shooed the women, refusing to give them a day's work.[36]

For other Land Girls the relationship with the farmer's wife was more personal and more unpleasant. Upon receiving news that a loved one had been injured in battle, Helen Bentwich asked to use the telephone to call her mother. Her request was denied because Land Girls were not permitted to use the phone. When a parlourmaid took pity on her and let her use the phone, Bentwich was carefully guarded to make sure that

she did not abscond with anything.[37] Land Girl Mary Bale explained
that the farmer's wife did not like her from the moment she arrived
and never gave her much of a chance to demonstrate her value. Bale
felt like a dependent child – always underfoot and not much help to the
female head of household. For Bale the source of tension was that Land
Girls did not know their place in relation to the farmer's wife. In her
case, the wife did not want help and resented Bale who she felt was an
added burden, one more person to be cared for.[38] Other wives adopted
the opposite approach when it came to Land Girls. Mary Lees' first work
placement with the Land Army brought her to a farm where the farmer's
wife always set aside additional work for her to complete, beyond what
was required of her on the farm.[39] For Bentwich, Bale and Lees the relationship with the farmer's wife complicated their employment.

The relationship between Land Girls and the farmer's wife was not
always so tense. Some Land Girls described an amicable relationship
between themselves and the farmer's wife and daughters. Although Rosa
Freedman had very little interaction with the farmer's family, during the
few interactions she had, she never felt mistreated. Freedman respected
the women on the farm who not only had their own jobs to do, but
were also responsible to bring the Land Girls their lunch and tea during
breaks. The women who served her were always pleasant, although few
words were exchanged between them.[40] Both Land Girls explained the
work of the farmer's wife and daughters was confined to the home and
in these cases the gender division of labour was more pronounced than
it was for Bale and Lees where the female family members interacted
daily with the hired labour force. When the division of labour was more
clearly defined the relationship between wives and Land Girls tended to
be more amicable, but when gender relations were more fluid, tensions
arose and in some cases these tensions escalated to the point of ending
the Land Girl's labour contract.

The nature of the relationship between wives and daughters and the
Land Girls was not wholly dependent on the former's treatment of
and attitude toward the latter. When Minnie Harrold arrived at Wicks
Farm for training in 1917, she expected to be trained by a skilled *male*
labourer. Harrold was surprised when the farmer's daughter greeted her
and the other Land Girls. Harrold noted that she and the other women
were disappointed. Farmers embodied self-sufficiency and were a central
part of the nation's lifeline; the Land Girls were there to learn specific
skills and they expected to be trained by a man. This prejudice on the
part of Land Girls is not surprising. Land Girls were taught not only to
respect the vital role farmers played in the war effort, but also to aspire

to help fulfil that role. Furthermore, the value of training farms was that skilled men trained the Land Girls. This type of training was preferable to Land Girls who were interested in acquiring skills beyond the basics of milking and gardening, and many women who trained on training farms went on to develop a number of different skill sets.

Harrold was disappointed that her trainer was female rather than male and quickly came to feel inadequate – not as a worker, but as a woman. The farmer's daughter was not only adroit at dairying and ploughing, but was a competent cook as well. Harrold realised that she, like many of the girls she worked with on the land, did not know how to take care of herself. A woman from the village came to the dormitory where the Land Girls were housed to cook and clean for them. When the village woman was unavailable, the girls had to rely on the assistance of the farmer's daughter.[41] Harrold, who believed she was on the cutting edge of gender and labour changes, quickly realised that within the family farm structure these changes were not in fact changes, but had long been a part of the farm system. The farmer's daughter was capable of performing the work Harrold was being trained and paid to do, in addition to her own 'women's work', and she was not paid for any of it.

Olive Hockin's account of the war provides a more balanced account of the relationship between Land Girls and the farmer's family. Hockin's early impression of the farmer's wife was that she refused to accept female workers on the farm, yet did not contribute in a meaningful way to farm production. Hockin saw that the farmer struggled everyday to meet labour demands – his wife did not work on the land and would not allow the farmer to hire women. Even after the reluctant farmer and his wife hired Hockin, the wife refused to hire more women, stating 'I'll have quite enough to do to look after you with one woman about, let alone two.'[42] Unlike a man who could fend for himself, employing Land Girls meant more work for her and moderately less work for her husband. The balance of family labour is evident from the wife's comment – she could see that Land Girls would relieve some of the farmer's burden, but only to increase her own. Eventually the farmer hired another Land Girl, Jimmy, but the wife refused to house the women on the farm, forcing both girls to move to a cottage five minutes away. The distance was short and hardly notable, but for the wife the move was essential. It removed the women from the farm thereby eliminating the encumbrance the girls presented. Living on their own in the cottage softened Hockin's attitude toward the farmer's wife and changed her opinion regarding the unequal distribution of farm work. Hockin's sympathy for the farmer and condemnation of his wife was quickly thrown into flux. She recognised that the problem with the Land Girls was that they worked long hours and by the end of the day were so exhausted that they could not take care of domestic tasks. This burden had fallen on the farmer's wife. On their own, the women were unable to keep up with the challenge of work on the land and domestic responsibilities and, like Harrold, hired a cottage wife to help care for them. Hockin noted:

> There is a theory current among some that a man needs higher wages because he 'supports' his wife ... In our troubled experiences it was made abundantly clear to us how impossible it is for a working man to live without a wife to support him. And it was also brought home to us what a thoroughly sound thing man did for himself when he designed the marriage bond. For unless she were irretrievably bound to him by law and convention, what woman would ever do the work of a working man's wife? Let no more be said about the vexed question of 'equal pay for equal work.' If either sex needs higher wages it is obviously the woman; for without the marriage convention that binds a man an unpaid servant for life, no labourer could ever have lived in a house on his own on the pre-war wage of fifteen shillings a week.[43]

Hockin's comments about the unequal distribution of 'worth' within the farm family helps contextualise the nature of gender relations in farm families that was both reaffirmed and challenged by the presence of Land Girls. Land Girls both reaffirmed traditional gender roles through their temporary and limited role on the land and challenged the gender balance that was customary in the farm family. These experiences indicate that the attitudes of female members of the farm family were as established as those of the men. For some wives and daughters their refusal to accept female farm workers was about protecting the gender hierarchy within the farm family and the employment of Land Girls complicated these relationships and led to tensions between the women.

Welfare Officers were appointed after several complaints from farmers who suggested 'more control was required to secure greater efficiency of work and better behaviour of recruits'.[44] Since farmers determined that the presence of a 'supervisor' was essential to maintaining discipline and productivity, the Women's Branch took the occasion to more closely link the labour side of the organisation with the public image of the Land Army. As noted above, Welfare Officers had certain labour duties, such as investigating complaints from both farmers and Land Girls, but from the outset these officers were also instructed to establish 'friendly relations' with recruits in an effort to make 'the women socially more contented'. In addition, the efforts of a combined labour and welfare officer would help to improve the Land Army's image and reduce public criticisms regarding the appropriateness of women's work and the necessary expenditures associated with the Land Army scheme that were ultimately borne by tax payers.[45] The scheme allowed for the hiring of up to one hundred Welfare Officers, but only half that number had been appointed by war's end.[46] The reports from the WWACs to the Women' Branch indicate relations between the Welfare Officers and Land Girls were complicated by the dual role afforded to the officers. For many Land Girls their early impression of the Welfare Officer's duties was that they played a motherly role as caretakers and role models. The impression was not wrong because this was in part what Talbot had in mind when she created the position. Many young women were comforted by the presence of Welfare Officers and felt they had someone to confide in where they might not otherwise have had anyone to talk to. In Buckinghamshire, F. Westlake noted that the farm was more like a compound or prisoner of war camp than a country estate, and although she described the welfare officer as a warden, she seemed to value Mrs Holding's presence in what she considered to be a rather inhospitable environment.[47] The implementation of the position, however, was not uniform. Some districts had both a Chief Welfare Officer and a Deputy, while other counties did not have a Welfare Officer at all. The large agricultural county of Devon did not have a single Welfare Officer, while Somerset had two initially, and a third by the war's end.[48] The rationale was that farmers in the south-west were not amenable to the employment of female labourers on their farms and Land Girls tended not to stay long when they were offered employment. Land Girls complained about the lack of social interaction and feelings of isolation and boredom, which might have been alleviated by the presence of a Welfare Officer, but the low number of Land Girls in the county meant the WACs could not justify the expenditure. The absence of a Welfare Officer perpetuated the cycle: farmers remained sceptical of the value of Land Girls, there were too few Land Girls to demonstrate their value, and there was no Welfare Officer to help overcome the inhibitions of both groups.

Where Welfare Officers did exist problems arose when the labour aspect of the officer's work superseded the welfare aspect, or at least when Land Girls perceived this to be the case. The WWACs stressed to Land Girls that they would not be alone on the land. It was the first duty of Welfare Officers to 'befriend the L.A.A.S' and assist in strengthening the organisation. With the number of Land Girls increasing, Talbot explained to the WWACs and Welfare Officers that an 'exceptional opportunity is opening out for bringing to a large number of young women that human friendliness which would do much to lessen the sense of loneliness among Land Workers and help them to lead honest, happy lives. It is incumbent upon all of us to make the most of this opportunity.'[49] Where such relationships had been established, early reports from Welfare Officers indicated that the interactions were positive and many Land Girls confided in them. While it is impossible to qualify the work of the Welfare Officers, their presence on farms helped to improve the quality of life for Land Girls and encouraged a greater sense of belonging within the organisation.

There was, however, pressure on the Women's Branch to make the Welfare Officers less friendly and more authoritative in their interactions with Land Girls. The pressure to change the role of Welfare Officers came from farmers who wanted acts of misconduct by Land Girls to be punished and all infractions to be reported and recorded for future reference. Elevating the role of Welfare Officers to inspectors was intended to fulfil this need, while simultaneously keeping the Welfare Officers in place as 'friends' to the Land Girls. Talbot was hesitant to make such changes and instead opted for a good conduct badge to be awarded for good behaviour. Poor behaviour would result in the revocation of the badge, which would only be returned once the improper behaviour had been remedied. Talbot was hesitant to modify the primary responsibilities of the Welfare Officers, but the limited number of officers and an increasing number of complaints by farmers meant that either the Welfare Officers had to take on additional responsibilities, or organisers and members would have to face the possibility that the good name of the Land Army could be compromised.[50]

Talbot's intention was to reward good behaviour and diminish the girl's willingness to stray from acceptable standards of conduct through positive reinforcement; however, the awarding of a good conduct badge created further divisions between Land Girls and complicated the relationship between Land Girls and Welfare Officers. Friendship turned to supervision, as several farmers had wanted, and some Land Girls felt victimised by Welfare Officers who meted out punishments. In Essex the War Agricultural Committee reported that two Land Girls complained of mistreatment by Miss Tritton, the Welfare Officer for the district, stating they had confided in Miss Tritton about some of their activities only to be reprimanded for misconduct.[51] Miss Williams reported that her relationship with Land Girls in Monmouthshire had deteriorated due to the conflicting roles assigned to her. Miss Williams admitted that while she had been content to listen to the girls' complaints without judgment at the beginning of her post, she was now forced to report the girls for acts of misconduct that they willingly confessed to her. Both girls felt that her actions were disingenuous, preventing them from confiding in her further, and they requested to be transferred to another district.[52]

In Kent the work of a Deputy Welfare Officer for the county was compromised after several complaints by a farmer that one of his Land Girls was disobedient. Rather than reporting the acts of misbehaviour to the WWAC, Miss McKeone imposed a curfew that prevented the Land Girls from going into town after work and kept them from attending an upcoming dance. After the girls threatened to talk to the press regarding their 'captivity', Miss McKeone was dismissed from her post.[53] Following this incident, Lyttelton stressed patience on the part of Welfare Officers and encouraged them not to abuse their powers. The role of the Welfare Officer, Lyttelton reminded them, was to support the Land Girls and placate those farmers who raised concerns about the women's behaviour, not to seek out and punish those guilty of misconduct. Certainly repeated reports by farmers against Land Girls had to be investigated, but punishments had to be carefully weighed and administered in such a way as to not dissuade Land Girls from service.[54]

Land Girls were surprised by the new tasks carried out by Welfare Officers. WWACs reported instances of Welfare Officers approaching Land Girls with a list of concerns after conversing with the farmer beforehand. In some instances the Land Girls and Welfare Officers had no previous contact and so the relationship was strained from the outset. In Morpeth Miss Wright communicated to Lyttelton that Land Girls were uncomfortable being approached by women they did not know. A Land Girl in Builth Wells attested that during their first encounter the Officer was aggressive toward her, taking her aside and forcing her to report on her work terms and conditions.[55] Even though the girl protested that no report was necessary and everything was fine, the Officer insisted. No action was taken against the Officer, but Wright encouraged Lyttelton to issue some instruction on how Welfare Officers might better introduce themselves to Land Girls and how the role of supervisor could be successfully merged with the previous duties of the Officers.[56] Communication between Welfare Officers and Land Girls was key, but the sudden supervision of Land Girls meant that complaints about inappropriate behaviour by Officers toward Land Girls became more common.[57]

Once working, most Land Girls settled into a routine and some even came to appreciate the regimentation of farm life. Beatrice Gilbert described her time on the land in Dorset as a happy time. She enjoyed the silence and solitude and found satisfaction in the time she spent conversing with the farmer and his wife. Gilbert appreciated the small pleasures in life – a hot cup of tea at the end of a long day brought her immeasurable comfort. She had everything she needed on the land: a place to sleep, good food, and pride in her work. When the war ended, Gilbert, who was engaged, gave up her work with the Land Army and went home to her family.[58] Rosa Freedman worked in a mobile group. She was picked up every day, dropped off for work, and picked up again to return to the hostels where she and the other Land Girls were housed. She had little time to herself, but came to enjoy the simple pleasures of life: a thick slice of bread, a boy singing in the field, and fresh pot of tea. The days were long, there was little time for leisure, but she valued her time on the land.[59]

Lyttelton in particular recognised that some form of recreation was essential to relieve the tedium of rural isolation.[60] This was especially important nearing the end of the war because by mid-1918 the call up of men from agriculture had restructured the demographics of many rural communities. As women took on more roles at home, the role of women in organising rural life had changed, at least temporarily, and the cultural experiences of small communities fell victim to the war, as well. Welfare Officers were too few in number to meaningfully lessen the feelings of isolation experienced by many Land Girls. Lyttelton believed that the conventions of rural life and institutions of rural communities could be used to provide entertainment for lonely Land Girls. While clubs became a feature of war work for women in the later stages of the war, few Land Girls actually took advantage of such recreational activities. The disappointing turnout at such events was the result of two factors: the inaccessibility of the events and disinterest on the part of Land Girls. Most of the recreational activities took place in large towns and cities, with the largest number held in London.[61] To attend, Land Girls had to buy a rail ticket and likely had to ask permission from their employer. Further, long arduous workdays prevented time-consuming excursions and the wages garnered by female land workers did not encourage many to spend their hard-earned money on dances that many Land Girls did not enjoy.[62] Therefore, the recreational activities of the Land Army were more appropriately part of the propaganda campaign, than they were a central feature of the Land Girl's wartime experience.

How, then, did Land Girls deal with feeling isolated and homesick, and how did they spend their leisure time? Of the surviving accounts from Land Girls, very few spoke of home or indicated what they did when they were not working. However, the accounts offer some insight into the girls' experiences beyond the work they performed. Letter writing was common among Land Girls and for many it was a Sunday evening activity. It appears, however, that letters were quite short and generally served to maintain a connection with friends and family.[63] For the most part, the women assured their families that they were safe and healthy, while others complained about the poor wages and hard work.[64] The importance of letter writing is that it provided a short mental escape from the farm and this type of mental rest was what most Land Girls coveted. Many Land Girls attended church services, even if they were not especially religious. The draw appears to have been the short excursion into the village or town and the church music. Others preferred the solitude of their cottage or room. Inactivity was not a feature of life on the land and when some women had the opportunity to do nothing, they did just that.[65] This was most common on larger estate farms where up to ten Land Girls could have been employed at one time. Mary Lees worked on a large estate farm in Newport and was happy to sit by herself while the other girls went into town. Her decision to do so reflected her work experiences. While stationed in rural Devon and isolated from fellow Land Girls and her family, Lees attended church services and went to the market whenever she could. However, once she transferred to a much larger farm with many more workers, she craved time to herself.[66]

For others, some variation of isolation was the only option. Olive Hockin and her fellow Land Girl Jimmy spent their leisure time sitting in a field away from the farmhouse. Hockin explained that 'any ordinary civilities of life, such as reading, writing letters, seeing one's friends or exploring any of the country beyond our own fields, we found were simply out of the question' in Dartmoor. So on Sundays when they did not have to work, the girls walked into a field where they sat and laughed and 'ate our bread-and-cheese, and we drank from the bubbling, busy stream ... and refreshed ourselves, absorbing the spirit and the great bare spaces and listening to the sounds of the silence'.[67] Mary Harrold explained that the women of the Land Army worked hard, endured the physical and mental strain largely without complaint and without relief and when the occasion presented it, 'we made our own social evenings'.[68] The women who were suited to the job and the women who could accept the conditions learned to endure in whatever way they could. For better or worse, those who were most contented reconciled themselves to the work they chose.

From surviving accounts it is evident that many Land Girls accepted that isolation and loneliness would be part of their work experience. Complete isolation was never desirable, and rarely the case for Land Girls. Although men and women did not perform the same tasks, nor did they necessarily occupy the same space, they did work together on the land and Land Girls, despite the hesitations of female relatives, became part of the workforce. Land Girls, who brought with them new ideas about women's work and dress, helped reduce rural isolation. Stories of home were shared both ways and the difficulties of work provided the occasion for bonding. These friendships of opportunity may not have endured, but the women of the Land Army often spoke of the bonds they formed. The efforts made by organisers to relieve the boredom and suffering of Land Girls raises questions about the nature of the relationship between organisers and the Land Girls, and the extent to which one understood the experiences of the other. The primary role of Welfare Officers to befriend the women was a step in the right direction, but greater effort could have been made to integrate the Land Girls into the farming unit, rather than solely cultivating a connection between Land Girls and the organisation that did not have a daily presence on the land.

Nevertheless, the decisions made by organisers and the Land Girl's choice to stay on the land in spite of the challenges she faced, contributed to the development of a Land Girl culture. While the experiences of women on the land varied considerably, there were patterns of behaviour among Land Girls that aided in the development of a group culture. During critical times social support was withheld and withdrawn in farming communities, forcing farm families to become increasingly insular and self-sufficient in an effort to protect the farm and family. Land Girls developed a similar strategy for dealing with the lack of public support for the Land Army and the isolation of female land workers. The Land Army organisation presented a 'them' and 'us' mentality among Land Girls – it was the responsibility of every Land Girl to demonstrate her value to the nation, a value the organisation already appreciated and understood, but the public did not. This was also a value Land Girls did not necessarily share with the female relatives of the farmers, whose war work lacked public recognition and was largely undervalued in relation to their Land Girl counterparts. The physical and mental assertion of worth publicly metastasized differently in each girl, but a common theme in the accounts offered by former Land Girls is an assertion of national worth.[69] The Land Girls and the organisation valued hard-work, self-sufficiency, respect for authority, personal value and collective worth, whereby individual wants and needs were recognised and present, but were subordinate to the needs of the farm 'family' or the farming enterprise.

Through the hard work and perseverance of the Land Girls, the Land Army displayed an organisational self-image. The role of farming was a cherished way of life, a livelihood, and a lifeline for the nation's future success. The male domain of the farm was respected, but Land Girls internalised the knowledge that everyone contributed to the success of the farm and, by extension, the war. This self-knowledge manifested itself in the Land Girls' acceptance and expectation of change that was necessary for all involved in the agricultural industry. Farmers had to accept the loss of local control as self-sufficiency clashed with national interests. The war and government intervention into agriculture meant that the farming industry was revived and elevated – no longer a personal practice or choice, farming was an essential wartime industry. The employment of women was part of this change, but in order for Land Girls to become a productive element of the farm, they too had to accept that the value assigned to the Land Girls through their training and organisational affiliation would not necessarily impress the employer or the public. Land Girls experienced a lessening of central authority as they became part of a local system and the group structure that characterised the Land Army organisation was supplanted by the individuality of farm work. This also meant that government support for the organisation was supplanted by local farming structures that undervalued women in the productive life of the farm. Rather than being part of a national organisation supported by taxpayers, Land Girls became part of the farm hierarchy that viewed women's 'new' place on the land as both a welcome relief to the labour shortage and a threat to the existing order.

Land Girls had to be both group-orientated and self-sufficient. Personal needs were always present and significant to the women's employment success, but the war filled the background, forcing individual and public attention on the larger issues of the home and war fronts. In a way, Pearl James' assertion that during the war individual identity became secondary to patriotic responsibilities is correct and the Land Army sought to take advantage of this reality.[70] The Land Army culture was built, in part, out of the propaganda image promulgated by the organisation and supported in the press. Under the shield of patriotic duty, the uniformed Land Girl's individuality was concealed. They were a unified group working toward a patriotic goal, and every woman's choice was connected to and weighed against the needs of the nation.[71]

Being group-orientated was only part of the Land Army culture, as exemplified by the individual accounts of Land Girls. Land Girls' accounts of their experiences verified the importance of the group and the nation, but they also sought to achieve self-validation for their work.[72] The code of conduct, good service badges, and length of service awards placed value and responsibility on the individual within the context of the group, but none of these things helped the women complete their tasks. Each Land Girl's worth had to be re-evaluated within a primarily local and individual context, which complicated the group-orientation of the organisation. The success of the Land Girl's interactions with farmers and their wives, or even with Welfare Officers, was determined on an individual basis. Even with regard to the more mundane matter of leisure activities for Land Girls, the individuality of the women and what they needed during their personal time was more central to their success than the organisation's attempts to provide a group solution to the nuances of personal experiences.

In spite of the group image that helped situate Land Girls on the land and orientate them to their new work and lives, the women of the Land Army were not a homogenous group of like-minded women. The disparity of their social and economic backgrounds was a factor in determining how they fared on the land, but the varying conditions faced by Land Girls was also important, perhaps more so, in explaining why some blossomed as Land Girls, while others struggled, and many retired from service. It is too simplistic to suggest that the patriotic pulse of the nation pulled Land Girls into active service and enabled them to carry out the challenges of work that most had never performed and a way of life that most had never experienced. Conflict and collaboration, individualism and collectivity, characterised the daily experiences of Land Girls. In many ways, the Land Girls shaped their own context, and were agents in conceptualising their own work experiences and their identity as women workers. The central feature of the Land Army that allows for generalisations to be made about the experiences of Land Girls is in the adaptability of the organisation. Just like Land Girls themselves, the organisation had to be amenable to change in order to meet local and regional needs.

5
'Respectable Women': The Land Army in Scotland

The number of women employed in Scottish agriculture between 1914 and 1919 remained constant at 22,000, but the introduction of the Women's Land Army in January 1917 sought to reassert and reconstitute women's value and role in the industry. Although women had traditionally made up a greater portion of the Scottish labour force than was the case in England or Wales, between 1861 and 1911 female wage earners in Scotland had been reduced by half due to the nature of pay and harsh working conditions that increasingly prevented women from seeking employment in agriculture. The introduction of the Scottish Women's Land Army (SWLA) had to compete less with the perception that women were not suited to farm work, and more with the undesirability of the work. In order to attract women to the land, organisers elected to create a new category of female worker – the respectable farmwoman. Certainly, the English model wished to recruit women of 'good character', but the organisation never rejected agricultural workers as a group. The SWLA boldly stated its preference for respectable educated women, alienating potential recruits and creating more pronounced divisions within the Scottish agricultural labour force.

In Scottish agriculture, the long-time pattern of employing single men had to be temporarily abandoned during the war in favour of continued productivity, but this did not mean that the requirements for farm labourers were relaxed. Training colleges struggled to attract recruits and the establishment of training farms was unworkable due to the nature of Scottish agricultural practices. Scottish farmers had less patience than their English counterparts for women who had little or no knowledge of farm operations and the limited need for replacement labour meant that Scottish farmers could be far choosier when selecting labourers. The alienation of potential recruits and the position of Scottish farmers meant that the SWLA struggled to make the organisation operational. Limited in size and scope compared to the English model, the SWLA received less state funding, lacked support at the local level, and was largely detached from the organisation in England. Whereas in England the creation of the WLA brought competing groups into the fold, largely operating under the umbrella of the Land Army, in Scotland early groups persisted and continued to exert power and influence over the female agricultural labour force. It was only toward the end of the war that greater cooperation with the English organisation encouraged organisers to make necessary and long overdue adjustments to the scheme. These adjustments helped to elevate the organisation and bring Scottish women under one central organisation. Unfortunately, organisational changes came too late in the war to be truly effective.

The agricultural make-up of Scotland differed significantly from conditions in England. As such, the war's impact on Scottish agriculture diverged from the English experience.[1] Consisting of just 19 million acres of land, there were only 5 million acres under crops and grass in Scotland.[2] While English trends were increasingly away from the larger estate farms and toward a growing number of owner-occupiers, there were relatively few owner-occupiers in Scotland, with most of the land belonging to a few landowners.[3] In the eastern and southern counties farms tended to be between 300 and 350 acres, and machinery was maintained at a substantial cost to the landowner. While owners were responsible for providing capital for major farming expenses, costs were spared when it came to the cottages. Living conditions were especially poor in the cottages, which tended to be small, cramped, and poorly insulated. Most of the larger agricultural lands in Scotland were in close proximity to factory towns and so wages for agricultural workers tended to be higher for Scottish labourers than their English or Welsh counterparts.[4]

Scottish agriculture differed significantly from agricultural practices in England. Of special note here is that while English farmers felt pressure to convert grazing lands into arable land, the trend away from arable land was much less complete in Scotland. Whereas in England arable land had decreased by 25 per cent between 1890 and 1914, arable lands in Scotland had only declined by 10 per cent over the same period. In addition, because less wheat and barley were grown in Scotland than in England, rotation times tended to be longer in Scotland. The rotation pattern determined how many men and horses were needed and the amount of manure required. Generally speaking, English farms expended more manpower and horsepower (one horse could plough between 16 and 25 acres depending on soil conditions) than Scottish farms, which would have important implications for wartime labour supplies.[5]

The change to crops as mandated by the Board of Agriculture during the war did not affect Scotland to the same extent that it disrupted farming practices in England.[6] Given that a considerable amount of land in Scotland was not useful for crop production, there was less pressure on Scottish farmers to abandon livestock. Livestock was especially profitable for farmers and was thus the most important branch of the agricultural industry. Most Scottish cattle farms supplied English markets – even under wartime conditions, Scottish beef was in demand and remained lucrative due to its quality. This also meant that temporary pastures were essential for continued productivity. It is here that we get a fuller understanding of the differing impact of the war on Scotland – not only did the war require Scottish farmers to make fewer changes in terms of farming practices, but livestock required fewer labourers than did crops. Whereas on the one hand the smaller number of required labourers was an asset to Scottish farmers, on the other hand the need for those labourers to remain on farms was much more pressing in Scotland than in England.[7]

Since 1890 the number of men employed on Scottish farms had fallen steadily, the result of rural depopulation and the growth of industrial towns.[8] Farmers had little access to new land holdings and farm workers were poorly paid compared to other industries and lacked modern living amenities. The Royal Commission on Labour reported in 1893 that work in agriculture was a 'rough, dirty, badly paid job with long hours and few holidays',[9] and not much had changed in the early years of the twentieth century. One of the most important challenges of Scottish rural life was the almost complete absence of community and social life. The absence of smaller farmers meant cottages tended to coalesce around a central estate, leaving rural villages largely disconnected from one another. As industry shifted to the towns and cities, villages decayed and rural society became stratified horizontally. While cottages tended to be grouped, the groups were too small to permit an active social life and the long hours left little time for socialising anyway. Women were perhaps more isolated than their husbands. Opportunities for mingling were few, and for the women who did work, the work was irregular. The extent of rural depopulation can be attributed, in part, to women who sought a better life elsewhere.[10]

In the Scottish Highlands, calls for reform forced government to take action. In 1911 the Small Landholders Act (Scotland) was introduced and created more than 430 new land holdings, mainly in the Highlands.[11] While the process was incomplete by the outbreak of the war, the new legislation had the intended effect of settling the agrarian population and setting the farmers back on track for improved agricultural production and profitability.[12] In the same year the Board of Agriculture replaced the District Boards, in operation since 1897, to promote interests in agriculture and assist in agricultural training.[13] An Agricultural Fund was placed at the Board's disposal and could be allocated for the purpose of facilitating the constitution of new land-holdings, the enlargement of holdings, or the improvement of dwellings, but the damage had already been done. By the turn of the century out-migration from the Lowlands occurred at a faster rate than population growth and there was a steady reduction in the number of skilled ploughmen and shepherds. Losses were greatest among women labourers, especially women who worked on dairy farms and the large acreage farms. The number of women employed in Scottish agriculture fell from 40,653 in 1861 to 15,037 in 1911.[14] In an attempt to stem the exodus from the land, farmers, with assistance from the Board of Agriculture, continued to increase wages, but to no avail. Wages in the countryside were lower than wages in the towns and cities and little improvement was made to housing.[15]

While housing conditions were definitely poor, T. M. Devine argues there is no direct correlation between rural depopulation and housing conditions.[16] Rather, the issue seems to have been tied to the attitudes and behaviours of the rural labour force. Scottish labourers had always been more mobile than their English counterparts and because Scottish law determined that there were only a few opportunities for workers to move in a given year, labourers often did so in search of better pay, work, and living conditions.[17] Due to the limited number of small holdings in Scotland and the difficulty of securing full-time employment, many labourers chose to leave the land altogether. The labour force was also becoming more specialised and training programmes were often a pre-condition for employment. With compulsory education came the expectation for increased productivity. The average farm labourer worked between 10 and 12 hours a day with only Sundays, hiring days, and a few holidays off a year. The burden on the family was immense and much of the work fell to women.

Although the Scottish system employed women much more extensively than did the English system,[18] women were paid half the wages of male labourers and the Royal Commission on Employment of Women in Agriculture (1870) noted that it 'is no doubt owing to the comparatively lower wages at which female labour can be obtained that Scotch farming [from] an economical point of view owes a considerable portion of its success'.[19] Of the more than 40,000 women employed in agriculture in 1871, slightly less than half were outworkers, meaning regular, full-time workers on a yearly schedule. The rest were categorised as in-and-out girls: they worked both indoors and outdoors and performed many of the same tasks as the farmer's wife. The stolid work and less than pleasurable conditions of life on the land meant that domestic service, and a growing number of positions open to women in the early twentieth century, was more desirable.

The troubles facing Scottish agriculture were not over by the outbreak of war in 1914 and would be revisited in 1919 with the introduction of the Land Settlement Act for Scotland.[20] Many historical accounts of rural Scotland in the twentieth century tend to circumvent the First World War and focus on the land riots and disturbances that characterised both the pre- and post-war years.[21] The agricultural policies adopted in Britain were, however, applied to Scotland as well. The war necessitated an increase in the domestic food supply and for Scotland this meant not only an increase in dairy and meat production, but also in the amount of land under crops, particularly oats and barley. By 1917 the government mandated an increase of three million acres of arable land for the United Kingdom, but this was not a policy that Scotland could easily adjust to.[22] Considering that root crops had been grown extensively for animal consumption, the high concentration of sheep in Scotland would make the reduction of pasturelands difficult and unprofitable, and would deprive the English markets of essential products that traditionally came from Scotland. Also of significance for Scotland was the reduction in the number of horses due to commandeering by the army and the difficulty of obtaining farm machinery from overseas markets due to the German U-boat campaign.

The war also had an impact on the labour force. The nature of the Scottish agricultural industry meant that even though inflation forced prices up, many farmers profited from the wartime markets, and agricultural wages rose as well.[23] The average wage of a ploughman doubled over the course of the war, as did the wage for shepherds. To help control employment costs, farmers chose to employ single men due to the shorter term of their contracts. This meant that contracts could be renegotiated and farmers were locked in for less time so they could take advantage of shifts in the market, and costly repairs on cottages could wait until after the war.[24] Despite such improvements, however, the agricultural labour force in Scotland declined by more than 35 per cent over the course of the war, with the greatest disruption occurring after 1916. Although a lower percentage of the labour force enlisted in Scotland than in England during the war, 28.2 per cent of farm labourers had enlisted by July 1917. The Board of Trade's Z8 reports indicate that 13.7 per cent of Scotland's permanent male agricultural labour force enlisted for military service between 1915 and 1918. Early enlistments, however, did not produce a labour crisis in Scotland. In 1916 the War Office Farm Labour Census indicated there was a labour surplus of 6 per cent on Scottish farms, suggesting there was little disruption due to the war.[25] In July 1914 the number of men employed in agriculture was 107,000 dropping to 89,000 in October 1918 and rising again to 100,000 in November 1919. The disruption was not in terms of the number of men employed, but rather the substitution of one workforce for another, and in the type of work performed. Approximately half of the above enlistees were replaced with boys over the age of 13 and other inexperienced workers.[26]

In addition, during the war arable land in Scotland increased by 5 per cent and while this was slight compared to south-east England, breaking up grasslands and speeding up crop rotations exhausted Scotland's already overworked labour force.[27] This meant more work for labourers. In order to overcome the shortages, the government made the suggestion that experienced labourers be encouraged to work another hour each day, extending the work day from 10 to 11 hours. Labourers refused and the Food Production Committees and Farmers' Unions supported them.[28]

The substitute labour provided was not sufficient to meet wartime labour needs. In December 1916 District Agricultural Committees were established to stabilise wages before the Hiring Fairs in the spring of 1917. The purpose of the committees was to prevent shifts in the labour force that inevitably came at the end of work terms and to encourage the development of a more harmonious relationship between owners and workers for the purpose of increasing productivity, but also to alleviate some of the stress of agricultural life. Over the course of the war, wages for men and women in agriculture were gradually fixed by an agreement between representatives of the farmers and workers.[29] The introduction of the Corn Production Act further solidified this agreement and District Committees were established in 1917 to fix agricultural wages for the summer of 1918.[30] Wage rates were fixed and migratory patterns that had characterised the rural labour force were abandoned, at least temporarily.

Short of stemming the tide of enlistments, more women would be needed to take on the extra work. Here, Scotland's tradition of employing women in agriculture meant that finding replacement labour was theoretically more easily accomplished. Yet, the initial efforts of organisers to bring Scottish women to the land were unsuccessful. After 1910 a decreasing number of women remained in the agricultural workforce, and the decline was particularly notable among the wives of skilled men.[31] In 1915 the Ministry of Labour, with the assistance of Employment Exchanges, encouraged the enrolment of women for employment in agriculture through newspaper advertisements. The initial scheme, which looked to women volunteers who had previous experience in agriculture, asked women to register with the local Employment Exchanges, but did not actively seek to recruit women for agricultural work.

While the Employment Exchanges recorded the names of women and men in search of work in districts where they operated, the Women's National Service Scheme (WNSS) was the organisation primarily responsible for recruiting women for work in agriculture. The organisation functioned to collect the names of workers, both men and women, and match them with farmers' needs. Unlike the future Women's Land Army, the WNSS did not require a specific service term. Reports of vacancies were collected and supplied by the War Agricultural Committee in each county and passed on to the National Service Commissioner or Sub-Commissioner in the districts, who was then responsible to match supply with demand. On the labour end, workers submitted an application form and once an interview was conducted and their skill level determined, skilled workers were placed with farmers immediately. Unskilled female workers were trained at various training farms for up to four weeks.[32] The women received 'general farm training', meaning they learned how to milk cows, hoe turnips, clear fields, and feed livestock, among other tasks considered to be acceptable women's work. Pay for training was 15s per week, with a maximum grant from the Board of Agriculture of £5 per week to cover training costs. With the cooperation of the local Employment Exchanges, if there was one, the District Selection Committee aimed to place women as quickly as possible. In instances where women were unable to find employment in their district, their names were submitted to the County Committee or the WNSS for placement in another district. The WNSS did not require women to move to undertake employment, but the possibility was there for women who were willing to relocate.

By the end of 1916 the National Service Department claimed to have enrolled more than 20,000 women for work in agriculture, which would have been a significant increase in the female agricultural labour force; however, 20,000 enrolments refers to the number of applications returned and inquiries made regarding work, not the actual number of women who had been interviewed and placed. Unfortunately, it is difficult to determine how many women the WNSS successfully recruited and placed on farms. Between 1914 and 1917 the Ministry of Labour indicated that 4,000 women had been brought to the land in Scotland, but there is no breakdown to specify what this number means.[33] There were fluctuations in the number of women working in agriculture over the course of the war and it is likely that the WNSS in Scotland placed approximately 3,000–4,000 women over this period. In June 1917 the number of women *enrolled* in the WNSS was 2,855, but only a quarter of this number were indicated as 'effective'.[34] By mid-1918 only 1,500 women were successfully employed in agriculture in Scotland, even though there were 2,600 vacancies to be filled. In July 1917 the number of women in agriculture dropped to 19,000, but rebounded to 22,200 by the following July.[35]

The central challenge facing organisers of the WNSS was farmers' preference for male labourers and the desire for in-and-out workers. Farmers' prejudices against women workers were not as pronounced in Scotland as they were in England, but many of the applications for labourers specified a desire for skilled men. The WNSS had to determine what was fair and in an effort to appease farmers tried at least partially to meet their preferred manpower requests. While early volunteer groups did advocate the use of female labour on the land, the policy adopted by the WNSS was to use female workers to compliment skilled men, often placing several men and one woman when filling openings. This way, women could attest to their value, one or two women at a time.[36] Also of concern was that while many women enjoyed farm work and eagerly filled positions, vacancies for in-and-out workers tended to remain unfilled. In-and-out workers assisted farmers with livestock and helped with fieldwork, but the day was very long, often 5 a.m. to 7 p.m., and the pay was insufficient.[37] In instances where vacancies could not be filled, the District Committees recommended that less arduous tasks such as fruit picking or turnip hoeing would be a more fruitful use of the organisers' time and efforts, rather than trying to fill vacancies for in-and-out positions. The goal was to maintain good will on both sides: to encourage farmers' acceptance, but also avoid dissuading women from farm work on the basis of in-and-out work.[38]

In January 1917 an arrangement was made between the Board of Agriculture and the Minister of National Service for the creation of the Women's Land Army for Scotland. Although the Women's Land Army was a national organisation, its management was divided between two offices, one in England and the other in Scotland. The implementation of a single Land Army scheme for Britain was unrealistic due to regional differences; therefore, the SWLA differed in its orientation, operations, and outlook from the English scheme. The SWLA was intended to serve as an umbrella organisation that would be responsible for the management of women's labour in agriculture, as it did in England, but the Women's National Service Scheme was responsible for organising women's employment in agriculture and it continued to serve in this capacity even after the Women's Land Army was formed in Scotland. In England, integrating the efforts of early volunteer organisations had begun in 1915 and while there were certainly a few disruptions along the way, the Women's Branch eventually assumed responsibility for coordinating women's labour for agriculture. Unfortunately, in Scotland the scheme's introduction interfered with the WNSS's local recruiting efforts and there was some confusion about what role each organisation would play.[39] This had happened in England as well, but there was a longer transition period between the inception of a single administrative body and its birth. Until mid-1918 the SWLA worked in conjunction with the Women's National Service Scheme but did not supersede its authority. It was not until July 1918 that the WNSS was dissolved and replaced by a single scheme under the SWLA.[40]

The SWLA also faced governmental challenges in terms of organisation and oversight. Under the Scottish scheme an Interdepartmental Committee was formed between the Ministry of National Service, the Scottish Divisional Office of the Employment Department of the Ministry of Labour, and the Board of Agriculture (Scotland) to coordinate efforts in an attempt to maximise output, reduce the reliance on skilled men, and further integrate women into the agricultural industry.[41] A separate Women's Branch was not established under the Board of Agriculture for Scotland; rather, a Joint Advisory Committee consisting of representatives of the Ministry of National Service, the Scottish Divisional Office of the Land Army, the Board of Agriculture and the Employment Department of the Ministry of Labour were responsible for all work carried out under this scheme. The Joint Advisory Committee operated under the Interdepartmental Committee and was responsible for coordinating all departments dealing with the employment of women in agriculture. In addition, organisers for the SWLA worked in cooperation with the Women's Branch for England and Wales. The two groups corresponded through letters and conferences in an effort to make the Land Army scheme run as efficiently as possible. Organisational and training responsibilities for the SWLA were the responsibility of the Board of Agriculture (Scotland), with the exception of training allowances and travel funds that were paid by the Ministry of Labour, and the cost of uniforms that was paid for by the Ministry of National Service.[42] In Scotland the National Service Sub-Commissioners carried out the functions of the National Service Department, which included recruitment to and the promotion of the Scottish Women's Land Army. Seven Agricultural Co-operating Officers were appointed by the Ministry of Labour to assist in the formation of the Women's Agricultural County Committees in 1917. Together these two groups helped to amalgamate the efforts of the SWLA and the WNSS. The Cooperating Officers were also responsible for training programmes, as well as for the placement of women in their areas. This was to be done in an overseer's role and was not intended to be a daily function for Cooperating Officers. In addition, the Cooperating Officers worked under the immediate supervision of the Agricultural Organiser of the Employment Department for Scotland.[43]

As of April 1917, 47 Women's Agricultural County Committees had been formed, but not all of them were fully operational. The WACCs worked closely with the District Agricultural Executive Committees and were responsible to ascertain farmers' needs and assist them in meeting labour requirements by supplying women. They were also responsible for reporting vacancies to the Employment Exchanges. The WACCs could make recommendations for women to be brought in from other districts in instances where labour needs exceeded the number of women workers in the district, but this was done at the discretion of the District Agricultural Executive Committees. The Board of Agriculture's initial expectation was that women would be able to assist men in agriculture generally, but this would be in terms of supplementing reduced farm staffs, and employment opportunities would initially be domestic.[44] Although the District Committees sought to steer employment away from in-and-out work, the demand for in-and-out workers persisted. The assumption among farmers was that if the Executive Committees and the Board of Agriculture promoted the use of women in traditionally female roles, they should have been able to find women who would continue to perform these tasks. The District Committees and WACCs expected it to take some time for farmers to agree to use women as substitution labour – meaning skilled work that would not ordinarily have been done by women – on their farms. So the expectation was that women would increasingly replace skilled men, and not just serve as general farm labourers. Here the issue for farmers was not the employment of women in agriculture, but the substitution of skilled men, whose responsibilities were vast compared to skilled men in England, with women.

The procedure for enrolment with the SWLA generally followed the English model with a few notable exceptions. Women seeking employment with the SWLA were required to fill out an application form that could be obtained from the District Representatives, Local Registrars, or Employment Exchanges. From here a preliminary interview with the applicant was conducted, but unlike the English model where a travel warrant was included, the SWLA tried not to incur expenses for the interview process.[45] The interview process was also streamlined in Scotland. Rather than several stages of interviews and reporting on the interviews, the Interviewing Officer filled out a single form and made her recommendation to the Selection Committee. An Interviewing Officer conducted a second interview once the recommendations made to the Selection Committee were compiled; rather than a continuous process of interviews, selections, and a second interview followed by a wait time to gather references and medical reports, the Scottish Committee decided on a two-stage process. When contacted for the preliminary interview candidates were instructed to present their references, which were done by form rather than personal letters. Medical Certificates, also done by form in Scotland, had to be presented before an interview was conducted. The SWLA kept a list of available doctors, but in instances where the applicant was unable to see one of the doctors vetted by the Land Army, the list of doctors could be supplemented in particular circumstances. This process required doctors to register with the Land Army in order to sign the appropriate forms. Under this scheme, the doctors were responsible to the organisation, not their patients. The hope was that doctors would provide honest assessments of the women's physical heath and not report on the women's character or presumed suitability for the work based on a personal/familial relationship between doctor and patient. Ultimately, doctors were responsible to carry out the examinations, complete the appropriate forms, and return them to the Employment Exchange or Agricultural Co-operating Officers. Letters were not brought in by applicants thereby negating the need for the organisation to contact the doctor in order to verify the information in the letter, which was the method adopted by the English scheme.[46]

The method of selection and enrolment was also more concise in Scotland than in England. The Selection Committee interviewed candidates and made a decision in person. Written confirmation of acceptance or rejection would also be provided, but the policy of immediate acceptance or rejection was designed to speed the process along so that girls were registered, and their training and placement could take place straightaway. An identity card was issued to a candidate on the day of acceptance and provided all of the particulars of her enrolment, although the section of the card that detailed her work placement would be left blank until a placement had been made. By reducing the lag time between interview and acceptance it was hoped that women would then enter the Land Army and losses to other industries would be reduced.[47]

Once enrolled, training procedures had to be initiated. In Scotland, three options were available: training with a farmer whereby the farmer would undertake tuition for unskilled workers for up to three weeks and offer an employment term of three weeks following the training; farmers would provide training for up to three weeks but with no offer of further employment; or the women could train at an Agricultural College Instructional Centre. In the first two options the vacancies were described as Training Centres, whereas in the third option the vacancy was described as an Instructional Centre. The distinction is important. While the training period was the same, the type of training was not. At Training Centres the farmers appointed lead hands with various skill sets to complete a range of training exercises, depending on need and the availability of skilled men/instructors. The women, however, would quickly specialise and once the training period ended after three weeks, the specialised training would continue through the employment term. Instructional Centres provided training in general farm labour. This was likely to be group instruction led by a skilled worker and was intended to help women learn their way around the farm and to perform certain tasks such as milking or hoeing. Here the ratio was kept at two to three girls per skilled instructor, so the level of instructor-student interaction was favourable.[48] Courses at the Agricultural Colleges also lasted three weeks, but the training was much less intensive and the scope was generally narrower. Again, the training courses focused on mastering a few specific tasks. Arguably, the best form of training came from the farmers at Training Centres.[49]

One of the most important differences between the Scottish Land Army and the English version is the provision that prevented women who were already employed full time in agriculture from joining the SWLA. The reasons for this policy are twofold. First, women working in agriculture were already undertaking work of national importance and it would be counterproductive to remove employed women from their work for the purpose of enrolment with the Land Army.[50] As the

SWLA worked closely with the National Women's Service Scheme and the Women's Agricultural County Committees, drawing women from pre-existing employment in agriculture would simply mean a transfer of numbers from one group to the other. It would also mean additional paper work, which would slow down the rate of enrolment and complicate the selection and interview process. Although the policy of rejecting women already employed full-time in agriculture is outlined in Section 2 subsection (b) of the charter for the establishment of the Scottish Women's Land Army, there was a provision to grant enrolments based on exceptional circumstances.[51] Unfortunately, the 'exceptional circumstances' provision was not carefully outlined in the charter, but it indicated that an Agricultural Cooperating Officer could make a recommendation to the Interdepartmental Committee who had the authority to allow enrolment if the tasks the woman would perform with the SWLA were of greater national importance than her current employment. No permission, however, would be granted if it seemed the woman would simply abandon her existing position. The Land Army sought to recruit women who would commit for the long term and did not wish to enrol those who would leave their posts for a more preferable position.

Permission for enrolment would also not be granted if no suitable local labour were available to replace the woman worker; here the issue was that the absence of labour would be detrimental to the farmer, which had the potential to negatively affect the relationship between the organisation and the farming community. Given the strenuous relationship between the Board and Scottish farmers in the pre-war years and accusations that the government pried unnecessarily in landownership rights, steps had to be taken to prevent the perception that the Board of Agriculture wished to interfere needlessly in local employment contracts.[52]

The second reason for the rejection of women already employed full time in agriculture was that the SWLA wished to produce 'a new and better class of woman worker', what they termed the 'respectable woman'.[53] Organisers believed that the 'special selection' of quality workers had raised the standard of women's work in agriculture and resulted in the improved treatment of women workers by farmers.[54] The official enrolment guidelines for the SWLA did not indicate such a restriction, nor did the organisers fully define what 'respectable woman' meant. Correspondence, however, indicates that respectability was a combination of idealised gendered behaviour and ideas about a woman's proper place. Notably, the SWLA did not indicate a preference for women who were suitably feminine, as had been a significant aspect of the propaganda model adopted by the English scheme, but as is evident in the recruiting poster '4,000 Women Wanted for Fruit Picking', femininity was idealised (Figure 5.1). Respectability, however, was always part of the ideals and values upon which the Land Army was founded and while it was intuitively valued by organisers, it was negotiated and expressed in different ways and was dependent upon varying conceptions of class, work, and family.

Respectability was not generally a quality associated with women agricultural workers in Scotland. Women employed in agriculture were frequently described as 'loose' and 'straying from the path of virtue'.[55] Agriculture was considered to be among the most dangerous occupations for women in terms of the threat it posed to their morality and respectability, and by the twentieth century women who worked full time in agriculture were considered to be 'unwomanly'.[56] The presumption that women employed in agriculture were unwomanly was not a deterrent for Scottish farmers, generally, but it did discourage women from seeking work in the industry. The determination made by Scottish organisers that the Land Army should be restricted, as much as possible, to a particular kind of woman reflected a larger discourse about the nature of farming in twentieth-century Scotland and the proscription

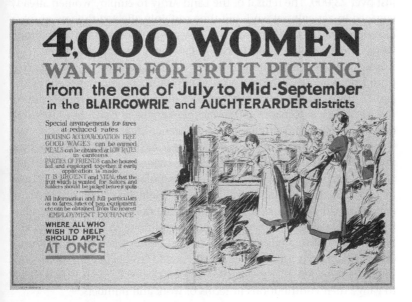

Figure 5.1 'Women Wanted for Fruit Picking'
Source: The National Archives, NATS 1/109 (2).

of specific roles, including work relations, for men and women. In this way, it is necessary to avoid the binary good/bad distinctions of respectability for women because it obscures the complexity of women's roles in agriculture. As women had been traditionally part of the employment contract between tenant farmers and landowners, the organisation of a 'land army' of semi-trained women had to overcome not just traditional ideas about masculine and feminine behaviour, but also the nature of work relations in Scottish agriculture. Between 1870 and 1914 most women employed in agriculture in Scotland were the daughters or wives of farm workers and this familial connection to working the land meant that landowners tended not to employ female labourers who were not already part of the farm system.[57] Given the familial nature of Scottish farming, the SWLA added an amendment to the enrolment forms indicating that consent *should* be obtained from the husbands of married women who applied for work with the Land Army.[58] This was an attempt by organisers to placate expectations regarding the pre-existing farm system.

Certainly, the growth in numbers during the war points to a level of success, but ultimately the number of women employed in agriculture in Scotland during the war never reached the pre-war employment figure of just over 23,000. The refusal of the Land Army to employ women already engaged in agricultural work full-time certainly affected the raw number of enlistees as recorded for the Land Army and for women agricultural workers in general – in most cases, each woman recruited into the Land Army was a new agricultural worker rather than one being transferred from one type of work (i.e., on a family farm) to another (i.e., for the Land Army). That the total number of women agricultural workers during the war never exceeded the pre-war totals suggests that the Land Army did not have a significant impact on the agricultural workforce. However, we must also be aware of the fact that these 23,000 women were not the same women from 1914 through 1918 – many women left agricultural work for munitions, transportation, and manufacturing jobs, so the Land Army was successful in maintaining a stable female presence on the land amidst considerable flux due to the requirements of other wartime industries. The Land Army aimed to recruit part-time or casual labourers and convert them into a full-time, semi-trained labour force. The Land Army drew heavily from this group of workers and thus opened up more room for casual, uncounted workers to take their places. As such, it is difficult to gauge their contributions in terms of work and numbers.[59]

While the Scottish Women's Committees struggled with early enlistments and a lack of clear direction from the CWAC on how to effectively place women on farms, the prevalence of women in agriculture prior to the war actually worked against their efforts. In the pre-war period the typical mobility of the agricultural labour force meant both men and women had the freedom to move in search of better wages and living conditions. Between January and March 1917 the Land Army tried to regulate the labour supply by contracting workers to particular farms for a one-year period and even when the work terms were six months (after March 1917), the goal was to keep the labour force stable.[60] The increase in pay for women in Scotland was also a deterrent for Scottish farmers. The attraction of employing women in agriculture centred on the fact they were a plentiful, cheap source of labour, and while their wages were a fraction of that of male labourers, farmers argued the rise in labour costs was notable and not necessarily justified. Farmers thought the rise in pay should reflect training and experience, but the Land Army could not necessarily guarantee either. Rather, the Land Army asserted the potential value of women workers, but it did not aim to establish a fully skilled labour force. The rise in wages for women was connected to the wartime labour market and from the perspective of the Land Army was a necessary incentive to lure women to agricultural work.

There was hesitation on the part of rural women to enlist with the SWLA after January 1917, most citing that there was no need to formally enrol. Labour was in demand, so why be tied to one scheme? The lack of popular support in Scotland led to the integration of the Women's County Agricultural Committees and the abandonment of training centres operated by the Women's Committees. In the Highlands farmers were unsupportive of the early organisational efforts of women's labour and the partial training provided by the newly formed training centres. The first training programmes were initiated in the spring of 1915, but they were not well coordinated and lacked a central training plan, as well as skilled instructors. The Women's Committees, which supported women's work locally and worked with the Town Councils for the promotion of women in the community, were ill-equipped to handle the organisation of training facilities, in part because they did not have the financial support to do so, and also because they lacked the appropriate networks to reach potential trainees.[61] Initially, the training programmes were not tailored to suit the particular needs of Highland farms. Training for work on dairy farms lasted between nine days and two weeks. Farmers argued that learning to milk a cow efficiently and effectively took longer to master than a few days, and many farmers refused to employ women who went through the training programmes.[62]

In early 1918, Miss Strange, the Agricultural Organiser for the Women's National Service Scheme in the northern counties, indicated that the training facility at Kilmarnock was forced to close due to poor enrolments. According to Miss Strange, the instructional centre was unsatisfactory and women were not able to get the full training needed to meet the requirements of Highland dairy farmers. The training facility was not abandoned, however, and was instead converted for the purpose of training disabled soldiers for agricultural work. The training facility was taken over by the Ministry of Labour, the building was refurbished, and the training programme was overhauled to focus on milking and stable work. In addition, the training period was extended from three weeks to six weeks: the first four weeks involved instruction at the centre and in the last two weeks the men travelled to farms for real work experience, an option that was not available to women through the centre.[63] In Inverness the training camp, which focused mainly on livestock, also closed due to a lack of interest; the camp organisers noted that at its peak ten women trained at one time, but the numbers were generally two or three trainees. Part of the problem was that the training time and routines had not been changed since the formation of the Land Army in early 1917. While the English Women's Land Army recognised that the short training period of only three weeks was insufficient and that the women had to be trained beyond the basics of farm work, the Women's Nation Service Scheme stuck to the three-week training programme and continued to partially train the women for a variety of jobs.[64]

The failure of training schemes was a major source of concern for the Board of Agriculture, the Ministry of Labour, and the SWLA. Between autumn 1917 and spring 1918 an additional 200,000 acres were put under crop. In September 1917 the Board of Agriculture hoped not only to maintain its current acreage, but to increase it the following spring. The Board noted that although 1,500 women were employed with the SWLA, a far larger number were working independent of the organisation. In terms of the 1,500 Land Girls, the Board determined that the work carried out by these women was 'negligible'.[65] The central problem facing the Land Army was that it undertook work that was traditionally done by women and unlike in England there was little willingness on the part of the Board of Agriculture to alter existing practices. The organisation of women's labour was certainly different in wartime Scotland, but the opportunities for expansion created by the war did not change the structure or output values of the Scottish agricultural labour force. The Board of Agriculture wanted the number of women enrolled in the Land Army to increase by 20 per cent over the next six months, but recommended that the gendered division of the agricultural labour force should be maintained, even once the war was over. The demand for women would not increase, the Board argued, but it would continue to be an important addition to male labour. This division of labour and the recognition of the part played by women in agriculture was intended to prevent Scottish agriculture from returning to its pre-war low, whereby both men and women had abandoned the land in favour of employment elsewhere, but was not necessarily an effort to advance the role of women in the industry.[66] To prevent further losses from agriculture, the Board of Agriculture encouraged the SWLA to offer new incentives to attract and keep women on the land. The details of the incentives offered were to be worked out by organisers and a report submitted to the Board of Agriculture detailing the plans and the progress made.[67]

The question of incentives was a difficult one. More pay was an option, but wages were fixed and already agreed upon by farmers and the Ministry of Labour. One area in need of attention was procuring appropriate housing. While organisers believed that better training facilities would help to promote agriculture and encourage women to consider a career in horticulture or related areas, any future changes to the training scheme would have to be preceded by housing reforms. The housing situation was dire and few improvements had been made to cottages since the turn of the century. Although a housing shortage persisted in England as well, and housing reforms had been put on hold in 1914, Land Girls in Scotland were forced to live in caravans or tents (in the warmer months) due to the unsuitability of housing in rural districts. While payment for the caravans came from the Ministry of National Service, there was much criticism of the scheme from the Interdepartmental Committee. The SWLA was supposed to be self-sustaining in terms of housing Land Girls, meaning the Land Army was responsible to find suitable accommodations, for which the Land Girls were expected to pay no additional costs.[68]

In October 1917, however, the Royal Commission on Scottish Housing lamented the 'incurably damp labourers' cottages on farms, [and] whole townships [that were] unfit for human occupation in the crofting counties and islands'.[69] With some pressure from the Housing Commission, in November 1917 the Board of Agriculture issued the Land Army £250 for housing. Rising costs and labour shortages meant repairs were not easily made to existing structures. Undoubtedly, the difficulty in finding suitable accommodations affected the number of potential recruits, limited the number of women in training facilities, and stalled the placement of women on farms where suitable accommodations could not be found.[70]

Linked to the housing issue was the problem of deficient training facilities. Any movement on improved wages for women would require substantial changes to the Land Army's training programme, which would cost the government more money for training facilities and instructors. Organisers were not opposed to extended training times, but the Board initially failed to see the benefit and refused to cover the costs.[71] Instead, the plan was to consolidate training efforts and, to this end, the Board of Agriculture and the Ministry of Labour requested that the West of Scotland Agricultural College offer training for women interested in agricultural work in the five northern counties. This plan followed, generally, the training initiatives recommended by the Board of Agriculture – training would last for three weeks and cover tasks traditionally done by women – but the College denied the request, seeing no benefit to the plan laid out by the Board.[72] Organisers of the SWLA also rejected the plan. Miss Strange, who was responsible for recruitment and training in northern Scotland for the Land Army, thought it was impractical to initiate a new training programme in the northern counties unless the programme itself was first improved.[73] But recruitment and training were carried out by both the WNSS and the SWLA and the efforts of one were often detrimental to the efforts of the other. Miss Strange believed consolidation should take place under the Land Army proper where the recruits and organisers would be brought under a national scheme with national leadership to properly train, market, and place the newly skilled workers. Stopping short of a complete overhaul of the existing system, she argued, would be a further hindrance to the scheme that already struggled to attract recruits.[74]

In spite of Miss Strange's argument that changes to the current system were needed, a new plan was put forward in August 1918 and epitomises the problematic relationship between housing and training. In August a new training facility in Rossie, Auchtermachty was proposed. Mrs A. MacDonald put forward a proposal for the Ministry of Labour to lease the training facility at a rate of £5 per annum and requested an additional £20 to furnish the cottage. The facility was not fully operational, but Mrs MacDonald argued it could be made operational through the training process.[75] The plan was to bring women into a training facility that could not fully accommodate them in an effort to demonstrate the facility could be functional if the recruits worked out. Initially capable of training three or four women at a time, the facility required two women trainers and two women to staff the facility and provide training to the next group of recruits. Under this scheme, the women who were responsible to train the recruits were also responsible for their placement and to oversee their work once placed. Training lasted three weeks, which meant every new group of recruits required the hiring of new instructresses. One group's expansion was dependent on the others, and with a three-week training rotation, the hope was the facility would increase its numbers quickly and shortly become fully operational. The proposal, however, did not include a housing plan. The facility was not equipped to house the trainees and no offer for billets was presented with the plan. In September 1918 the proposal for the new facility was approved by the Interdepartmental Committee, but the requested funds to furnish the facility were not approved for another three months while the Committee weighed projected costs against the intended benefits of the facility. Ultimately, the Interdepartmental Committee, which continued to doubt the feasibility of training more women under current conditions, ultimately approved the new training facility, but limited its access to funds that were required to make the programme work.[76]

A second training centre was proposed in October, this one to be opened at Beechwood Farm, Inverness. This training facility, however, would be paid for and administered by the Board of Agriculture and the SWLA, not the Ministry of National Service. Here the Land Army would have greater say over training and the operation of the facility. The Scottish Women's Land Army requested £517 to be issued by the Treasury Authority of the Board of Agriculture (Scotland) to cover the set-up costs for the facility.[77] After considerable discussion between the military authorities (who weighed in regarding leaves for soldiers and the workability of substitute labour beyond soldiers) and representatives of the Board of Agriculture, permission was granted by the Ministry of National Service to complete the transfer of responsibilities to the Board of Agriculture in October 1918 for Beechwood Farm.[78] All training facilities operated by the Board of Agriculture would be paid for by the Board's Treasury Authority, with the exception of Land Girls who trained at trial facilities or on experimental farms. Maintenance costs for Land Girls at these facilities would continue to be paid for by the Ministry of National Service through the Ministry of Labour.[79]

Part of the problem of solving the training or housing problem associated with the employment of women in agriculture was that the WNSS and the SWLA continued to pursue divergent policies into the autumn of 1918. Without a single strategy, or a single organisation, organisers for both groups had to compete for limited government funds. Further, the budgets of the National Service Department and the Board of Agriculture were separate and allocated by two different authorities, which prevented the establishment of a national scheme.

In addition to their requests for appropriate housing and better train-ing facilities, organisers recommended that the conditions for service be reviewed and that more applicants be accepted on a provisional basis to widen the pool of potential recruits.[80] In 1918 the majority of women who had been placed in work terms with the WLA (538 of 800) were registered on two- to three-month terms, with relatively few (136) com-mitted to nine months or a one-year term (126). The highest number of applications received in 1918 was in the months April through July. During these four months 1,317 women applied for enrolment with the SWLA. Of these applicants, 753 applications were either withdrawn by the applicant or rejected by the Selection Board.[81] While the records do not indicate how many women withdrew their applications or why, they do indicate that the Selection Board rejected the majority of applications in this category. As noted earlier, the Selection Board had very stringent requirements for employment and tended to reject women who were employed in agriculture at the time of their application to join the Land Army, and it had specific requirements in terms of the women's respect-ability. These two factors potentially reduced the number of 'desirable' women and provide plausible explanation for why approximately half of all initial applicants were rejected.

While the Scottish application and enrolment process was less cumbersome and time-consuming than the English schemes, the end result was fewer women enrolled, proportionally, with the Land Army in Scotland. Nevertheless, a report from the Interdepartmental Committee in June 1918 indicated that the SWLA's approach to screen-ing applicants and the problems of training resulted in wasted time and resources. The Interdepartmental Committee stressed to organisers that the role of the Land Army was not to create a new class of agricultural worker, or even to advance the potential role of women in agriculture in the long term, but rather to meet manpower demands under present conditions. It concluded that thus far the SWLA scheme's management was haphazard and immediate changes were needed. Most pressing was the need for Regional Headquarters to agree to a single scheme for Scotland, which meant significant reorganisation, and for each branch and sub-branch to respect the financial commitments of the Scottish government by streamlining women's agricultural work into a single organisation.[82] Calls to reorganise the SWLA had been voiced in early

1918 and the desire at that time was to restructure all women's volunteer organisations involved in agriculture under a Women's Division at the Board of Agriculture. Ultimately, this would place women's agricultural work under the umbrella of a single organisation, the SWLA, as was the case in England and Wales. This would reduce competition between groups, streamline application, enrolment, and training, prevent crossover, and maximise the efforts of organisers.[83]

The request for a Women's Division of the Board of Agriculture was not granted approval due to budgetary concerns, but in response to this decision and to the Interdepartmental Committee's report on the work of the SWLA, a special meeting of the representatives of the Women's National Service Scheme, the Ministry of Labour, and the Scottish Board of Agriculture was called. Meriel Talbot was also asked to attend the meeting, as well as two additional representatives from the Women's Land Army for England and Wales. While Talbot did not attend, she sent a recommendation along with Mrs Hugh Middleton, the Organiser for Northumberland. The purpose of the meeting was to consolidate efforts to improve women's employment in agriculture, to discuss training periods and conditions, and to advance public perceptions of women workers. Talbot recommended reconfiguring the WNSS and SWLA to bring it into line with the English model.[84] In October 1918 representatives of the WNSS and the SWLA met to discuss changes to the scheme. Mrs Middleton was the guest speaker and gave a talk titled 'The Women's Land Army in England'. Here, Mrs Middleton discussed the organisational structure of the WLA and how oversight by the Women's Branch helped to coordinate efforts between volunteer organisations, the Women's County Agricultural Committees, and other groups working to promote the employment of women in agriculture during the war. The Scottish representatives were especially struck by the degree of oversight in the English model and what they believed was a costly and unnecessary coordination of activities. They were also surprised by Middleton's report that the sending of women to farms to be trained by farmers (not a formal training centre) had been largely abandoned in favour of training programmes in agricultural colleges or farms that operated as an approved Training Centre for the WLA. Connected to this point was the English position that six weeks of training was considered insufficient and that the women really benefitted from a training programme of between eight and twelve weeks in duration.[85]

Middleton also explained that one way to get around the need for specialised training (i.e. fully skilled workers as opposed to semi-trained workers) and the shortage of workers with a specific skillset in certain areas, was to use travelling gangs. These gangs were compiled based on specific skills and sent to areas where those skills were needed. A travelling gang leader assisted the gang system by reporting deficiencies to the local office or back to the Women's Branch. The gang leader did not work with the gangs but rather travelled from place to place to see that work progressed satisfactorily and to report specific needs for designated areas. The WLA could then deploy gangs to undertake the work required. The SWLA organisers were aghast that the gang leader was paid £2 per week and allocated a subsistence wage during travel. Perhaps more surprising for the Scottish branch was the employment of a Welfare Officer to make sure that the women were comfortable and taken care of according to the terms of their work contract, and to make sure that the farmers/employers were satisfied with the Land Girls' work. In Scotland the Welfare Officer position did not exist; rather, Land Girls reported to the Employment Exchange or to a District Representative. Each was responsible to 'interest herself' in the welfare of the Land Girls, but they tended not to travel to locations throughout the district, as was the case with Welfare Officers under the English scheme.[86] This is not to say that the Land Girls were cared for less under the Scottish scheme; rather, independence and isolation were a necessary part of the job. One organiser expressed her opinion that 'unnecessary coddling will produce weak minded workers', and would interfere with the success of the scheme.[87]

The purpose of the meeting, however, was to improve the organisation in Scotland, and Mrs Middleton unveiled several options to improve the retention rates for the SWLA. Awarding badges for service was one option that had not been adopted by the Scottish division and Mrs Middleton seems to have been convincing in her assertion that the badges were viewed as 'badges of honour' for the women. They served as a visible symbol of the women's service and encouraged friendly competition and camaraderie within the ranks of the Land Army. The wearing of official Land Army uniforms also helped to promote solidarity and made the women feel that they were part of the national organisation. In Scotland, many Land Girls went without uniforms. In part this was due to shipping delays and supply shortages. But it was also because retention rates did not justify the expenditure incurred.[88] Nevertheless, organisers adopted the Good Service Badge and pressed for extra funds to be allocated to the Land Army for the purchase of additional uniforms, and instituted a new policy of wearing the uniform during training. To this end, the SWLA proposed offering Land Girls a second free uniform, in line with the English scheme.[89] They hoped that if the women wore a uniform from the moment they enrolled with the Land Army, it would aid in the development of a sense of belonging and potentially keep the women on the land indefinitely.[90]

Following the recommendation made by Mrs Middleton, the training period for the SWLA was extended to six weeks on a trial basis. This meant that certain programmes and training centres extended their training period, but officially the training period was not extended to six weeks until 1919, not long before the demobilisation of the Land Army.[91] The extension of the training period had been discussed earlier in the year and was open to great debate in August 1918 when it seemed that the training programmes had failed to produce favourable results, but such an extension was considered to be organisationally impracticable and financially unfeasible. Middleton insisted, however, that not only would farmers likely be more receptive to the use of substitution labour provided by the SWLA if the Land Girls received proper training, but the Land Girls would take more pride in their work and gain more satisfaction from their wartime service if they felt valued. This could only be achieved with adequate training.

The meeting was not simply a lecture by Middleton about the benefits of the English model; rather, there was an exchange of information and questions from both delegations. For example, the Scottish committee was very interested in the possibility of employing women under the age of 18. They argued that lowering the age of enrolment would not only help to increase the number of enlistees, but it would also open recruiters up to a new group of women who did not have previous employment experiences and could be freshly trained with a new skill set. These women would also not be targeted by other wartime industries due to their age and so there would be less competition for the Land Army. The English committee did not endorse the employment of women under the age of 18 due to the fact that the housing deficiency would not accommodate such an arrangement. The primary concern raised by Mrs Middleton was the question of the women's welfare. Without the women being able to stay in the farmhouse they could not be assured of their personal safety. The Scottish Women's Land Army did not employ the same regiment of women's inspectors and so there was less official oversight and more reliance on cooperation among farmers, Land Girls, and the Women's Land Army to ensure suitable living arrangements. When living arrangements were not satisfactory, there was no proximate intermediary, so the Land Girls had to report to the central office. From here arrangements had to be made and most often it simply meant the Land Girls were removed from their posts and reassigned.[92] What Middleton did not know was that the SWLA had knowingly, on occasion, employed women under the age of 18 and the point of raising the issue at the meeting was to feel out the English delegation on the matter.[93]

Nevertheless, the Joint Committee meeting provided Scottish organisers the opportunity to hear recommendations for change. Even though the Scottish organisers believed that the English Land Army suffered from over-regulation leading to excessive expenditure, the Scottish delegation did welcome recommendations for improvements in recruitment and retention. Scottish organisers used this information to recommend that a meeting take place in one year's time in Perth and to request increased funding for the day-to-day operations of the Land Army. The request for additional funding was of central importance with regard to the enrolment and retention of women workers. For example, the SWLA was only able to provide a train or bus ticket for women from their home to their place of employment. This level of funding was considerably less than what was provided under the English scheme. In some cases the method of transportation or the duration of travel required a night's stay in a bed and breakfast, but the Ministry of Labour had not approved the cost of a night's accommodations in the past. While the Ministry of Labour was responsible for training and travel allowances, funds had not been released in a timely manner, and sometimes not at all.[94]

Inadequate funding for travel and training had been a long-standing problem for the organisation. Dating back to August 1918 Alice Younger of the Divisional Office requested that not only should past allowances be paid in full, but that the terms of the contract between the SWLA and Land Girls had to be changed to include all costs associated with travel for the Land Army.[95] The Ministry of Labour also had to recognise the potential for the accruement of additional costs connected to training and travel and felt that the Divisional Office should have access to a limited amount of discretionary funds to cover the cost of travel to training centres, from training centres to the place of employment, from the place of employment to the Land Girl's home, and for any change of employment while remaining with the Land Army. While funds could be obtained from the Ministry of Labour for the travel listed above, they had to be requested and there was a considerable waiting period between the date the request was made by the Divisional Officers and when a decision was made by the Ministry of Labour, and even if funds were granted, they were not always awarded. In cases where Land Girls were forced to abandon their position of employment, which could be due to unsuitable housing, an unexpected change in labour conditions/contract, or abuse by farmers, their wives, or other employees, the cost of travel (including accommodations) was paid by the Land Girl. It was expected that the Land Girls would be compensated, but in many instances they were not. Younger pointed out in her request that similar expenses had been allowed and payment had been received by the Queen Mary's Army Auxiliary Corps, which also received training and travel funds from the Ministry of Labour. The Queen Mary's Army Auxiliary Corps had been permitted expenses for a night's lodging, breakfast, and an evening meal for the original date of departure.[96] In terms of enrolment and retention, it was most effective if travel and training costs were borne by the Ministry of Labour and not the Land Girls.

The extension of the Land Army's operational budget was dependent on the outcome of the ongoing discussions between the Board of Agriculture (Scotland), the Ministry of National Service, and the Ministry of Labour, but ultimately the request for additional funding had to be approved by the Ministry of Labour. The approval of funds was stalled, however, by the war's progress. The approval of a Joint Meeting of agricultural organisations for Scotland was dependent upon the continuation of the war because the SWLA was, at its core, an emergency organisation. Although it hoped to transition into a permanent post-war organisation, it was always possible that it would be disbanded once the war came to an end and the Ministry of Labour saw no point in holding a Joint Meeting whose findings could be irrelevant if peace terms were met. Earlier in October 1918 the three bodies engaged in lengthy discussions regarding their financial responsibilities for the Scottish scheme. Part of the reason it was difficult to resolve problems around training facilities, uniforms, and travel allowances was because of the difficult relationship between these bodies. Since the formation of the Scottish Women's Land Army, the Ministry of Labour and Ministry of National Service increasingly requested the transfer of financial obligations for the Land Army to the Board of Agriculture.[97] The Board also assumed responsibility for the payment of travel allowances, but the request for a discretionary fund for travel was rejected in November with the recommendation that payment of allowances be revisited at a later time.[98] The Board of Agriculture also agreed that travel allowances for training and work terms should follow the model for the Queen Mary's Army Auxiliary Corps, making it easier for the SWLA to place women and to meet farmers' need. Government oversight would not be diminished under the new arrangement; all requests for the transfer of travel credits had to be done in writing and justified under the terms of the new agreement.

The process for obtaining credits for travel warrants could be arduous and tedious. If a Land Girl wished to travel during an approved period of leave, she had to have her employer sign the forms for a travel warrant. Once the forms were received by the Employment Exchange, the employer would be telephoned for confirmation. Once this was done a one-way ticket could be issued. The same process was required for the return journey. Once the Employment Exchange issued the travel warrant it had to be approved by the Divisional Office, which had to get approval from the Ministry of Labour and then the Ministry of Labour had to be reimbursed by the Ministry of National Service.[99] The process was not simplified when the Board of Agriculture assumed responsibility for travel allowances, but because the Board's assumption of this responsibility took place over a month's time, there was a four-week period when the Labour Exchanges were uncertain as to where to send the paperwork. Each government body required different forms and requests and approvals varied from body to body. Forms that were filled out incorrectly, or filled out in the wrong coloured ink, were returned and the process was restarted. Further, between April 1918 and the end of the war, paperwork submitted to one branch of government may have had to be resent to another branch as the transfer of financial obligations for the SWLA changed hands.[100] The recommendation to revisit the allotment of funds for travel would also depend on the extension of the SWLA after the war and the possible restructuring of the scheme in the immediate post-war period.

At the end of October 1918 the Interdepartmental Committee concerned with the SWLA met to discuss the specifics of the report initiated by the SWLA upon the recommendations made by Mrs Middleton. In addition to the SWLA report, a separate report was sent by Miss Talbot based on Mrs Middleton's experience. Talbot's report came as a surprise to the Interdepartmental Committee. Like the SWLA, the Interdepartmental Committee was amazed at the degree of intra-organisational oversight and the costs associated with maintaining the English scheme. The Committee found that the Board of Agriculture and Food Production Department had been quite generous in their funding of the English Land Army. Training allowances for Land Girls were higher in England, 25s per week in England and Wales compared to 19s per week in Scotland, and travel warrants were granted with little fuss and were more readily distributed. The English scheme had also benefitted from considerable financial support for the furnishing of training centres, which the Board of Agriculture for Scotland argued it could not afford. The Interdepartmental Committee, however, did agree to the appointment of

Group Leaders and Welfare Officers along the English model and at the English rates of £2 and £3 per week, respectively.[101] There was also general agreement that the training period for the SWLA should be increased from four weeks to six weeks and that an increase in the stipend for training facilities was necessary. The six-week training period was accepted by the Committee in late November 1918 and the SWLA was directed to continue to register and place women until further notice.[102] Although there was backing for the extension of financial support for the improvement of training facilities, this matter, like the matter of training allowances and travel funds, could not be resolved until the end of the war due to budgetary considerations.[103] In the short term, the Land Army was granted an operational budget for the next three months, at which time a further decision would be made as to the continuation or disbandment of the Scottish Women's Land Army.

The Women's Land Army was a national organisation formed and made operational in January 1917, but the Scottish scheme demonstrates the importance of local experiences and regional variations within Britain. Regionally, the Land Army both supported and fractured the national image of the organisation. Whereas the Women's Branch and Women's Land Army took on the responsibility of organising women's work in agriculture in England and Wales, in Scotland organisers for the Land Army had to compete with the Women's National Service Scheme for recruits and government funding until very late in the war. Competition between organisations encouraged division within the agricultural labour force and prevented the establishment of a unified effort to increase the number of women employed on Scottish farms. While the number of women employed in agriculture remained steady at an average of 22,000 over the course of the war, training schemes for both the SWLA and WNSS were compromised by interorganisational competition for recruits, and housing shortages deterred women from enrolling for land service.

The predicament of low enrolments and the lack of government funding when divided between the two competing organisations led to a damaging cycle of behaviour. While the Board of Agriculture (Scotland) pressed for better results, it also demanded that the gender divisions that characterised the Scottish agricultural labour force remain in place, preventing the meaningful advancement of women in the industry. In turn, the SWLA attempted to attract women to new employment opportunities on the land, but could not promote a future for women in the industry. Instead, it offered women limited training, meagre accommodations, insufficient wages, and a lack of government support in terms of training and maintenance allowances. Although the WNSS was disbanded in August 1918 making way for the advancement of the SWLA after that time, it was not until the joint meeting of the English and Scottish branches in October that meaningful changes were made to the organisational structure of the Scottish Land Army. By the time the Interdepartmental Committee heard and debated the recommendations for changes, the war was coming to an end and budgetary approval for such changes had to be carefully weighed against the potential cessation of hostilities. Without the national emergency created by the war there was no need for an army of women land workers and the outlay of money to promote the organisation would be potentially wasted. Organisers of the Women's Land Army in Scotland worked hard to advance the role of women in agriculture, but the conditions of farming in Scotland that marginalised women in the pre-war years continued to alienate potential recruits during the war and the resistance of landowners and farmers to government intervention prevented the Board of Agriculture and Ministry of Labour from further interference in the industry. While there are no exact figures as to the number of women enrolled in the SWLA, the organisation did help to maintain the overall number of women employed on the land. Unfortunately, the organisation's late start limited its ability to effectively promote the role of women on the land and its designation as a wartime organisation meant it suffered the same fate as its English counterpart when the Women's Land Army was demobilised in 1919.

6
Back to the Land: The Land Army after 1918

Following the armistice on 11 November 1918, Britain's food situation remained uncertain. The shift from a wartime to a peacetime economy would be carried out piecemeal and the return of men from the theatres of war would take many months to complete. Even once the demobilisation process was under way, there was no guarantee that the men who left agricultural work for military service would return to their pre-war employment. The agricultural industry was in a state of uncertainty. The depletion of the labour force in the decades prior to the war and Britain's growing dependence on overseas markets was temporarily reversed between 1914 and 1918 as the domestic food economy was revitalised, but it was quite possible that these changes were temporary and the reliance on homegrown food would diminish again once pre-war markets were restored. In November 1918, neither Talbot nor the Board of Agriculture knew for certain what lay ahead for the Women's Land Army. Organisers hoped for the Land Army's lengthy continuation, but knew that the organisation faced potentially insurmountable obstacles. The difficulty was in making the wartime organisation – which had marketed itself as a temporary, albeit necessary, instrument in the nation's successful prosecution of the war – vital after 1918. The government was not unsympathetic to the Land Girls' efforts – although the WLA represented a small percentage of the agricultural labour force, the 27,000 women of the Land Army voluntarily left their homes to settle in an unfamiliar area of the country where they endured months or years of hard labour. Despite hopes for the future, in August 1919 the government revealed that the Land Army's service was coming to an end and in November of that year announced that the WLA would be demobilised. This chapter explores organisers' attempts, and ultimately their failure, to transform the Land Army into a peacetime organisation and to justify its continuation into the post-war years. The difficulty for organisers in making their case for the continuation of the Land Army lay in the paradoxical realities of the Land Army's existence. A temporary army of selfless women workers, who were inspired by national need, and who were willing to work endless hours for little pay with limited potential for future employment, simply would not entice women to seek employment in agriculture once the war was over. While Talbot saw potential in the Land Army and in the Land Girls who filled its ranks, many of the volunteers who served with the Land Army, and even the Land Girls themselves, willingly gave up their war work and returned home or left the land in search of other employment opportunities. But the demobilisation of the Land Army was not conditioned by the desires of those personally involved in its operations; the reality was that in the absence of the war, the Land Army failed to find relevance.

Church bells rang out across the country on 11 November 1918 signifying that the Great War had come to an end. Victory celebrations marked the days that followed and in the excitement of the time, few Britons gave much thought to the future of the Women's Land Army. Even before the armistice was signed, however, Meriel Talbot knew this day would come. The war would be over and the future of the Women's Land Army would be unclear. Talbot was optimistic, believing the Land Girls had proven themselves during the war and that the country and her government would recognise the WLA's contribution to Britain's victory. The war had, after all, demonstrated the dangers of allowing homegrown food production to fall to dangerous levels. In the uncertain years that lay ahead, it would be in the best interests of the nation to maintain British food independence.[1]

Talbot's optimism, however, was not echoed in the press, at least not with regard to the future of the Land Army. In the days following the war's end the press picked up on the now uncertain position of the WLA. Although the press heralded British women as the 'Best Women in the World', it did not stop some from inquiring about 'What to do with the Girls'.[2] Several newspapers suggested that the women of the Land Army should emigrate – to find greener pastures and the tranquility of farm life that they coveted and came to love. Others offered the potential for marriage, suggesting that perhaps the 'Rural Romances' of the war years would result in marriages between returning farm hands and the Land Girls.[3] Others still were much more speculative and pessimistic, or perhaps realistic, and questioned what purpose the women of the Land Army could serve now that the men were returning home.[4] Talbot was unsurprised by doubts surrounding the continued relevance of the Land Army and knew the Land Army's future would face serious opposition, not because the organisation was unappreciated or disrespected, but because its continuation was unnecessary.

For now, all that could be said with any degree of certainty was that the Land Army had not received dismissal orders from the Board of Agriculture and Britain's food situation, while not dire, had to be carefully managed by government. The questions that Talbot confronted were not limited to whether the Women's Land Army as an organisation would continue its work after the war in the same capacity as it had done during the war. She was certain that its role would have to change and that the Land Army organisation would have to make itself adaptable to post-war circumstances. Even questions regarding the appropriateness of women's work in agriculture were not a major source of concern. Talbot believed that women had demonstrated their value on the land and supposed that those who were convinced would continue to employ women and those who were not would continue to resist. Rather, the question of central importance was what role would women, Land Girls or not, play in agriculture post-1918? For Talbot, the role of women in agriculture was not tied to the continued existence of the Women's Land Army, but rather to the work the Land Army carried out. At the same time, Talbot did not wish to see the role of women in the industry revert to the pre-war period when the number of women on the land was greatly reduced and employment opportunities were limited to fruit picking and providing extra hands during harvest time. So for now, the WLA presented an opportunity for Talbot and other organisers to continue to advance the position of women in agriculture. In the long term they hoped that the Land Army could be transformed into a peacetime organisation aimed at bringing more women into the agricultural industry, both as labourers and farm managers. Educational opportunities for women would have to be expanded and more funding for women interested in agricultural training would have to be made available.

In addition, a sense of camaraderie was important. Talbot understood that farming would not be an easy industry for women to break into, and those women who tried would need a strong support network. The WLA would provide that support network, while at the same time promoting agricultural training and education for women. Government, however, would determine what role the Women's Land Army could play in this venture.

On 12 November 1918 an interdepartmental meeting of the Women's Branch, Board of Agriculture, Ministry of Labour, National Service Department, and representatives of the Women's War Agricultural Committees met to discuss the food question. How to organise agriculture for peacetime was the main issue on the agenda, but there was little agreement on what should be done. The Board of Agriculture had proposed a plan to bring all agricultural matters under the auspices of two county committees. This would relieve the County Councils of the burden of overseeing agriculture, but would also mandate a new organisational structure for dealing with issues pertaining to the agricultural industry, thus reducing the authority of the County Councils. It would also mean that the women's committees would no longer be responsible for organising women's labour.[5] What this meant for the WLA was never sorted out because the County Councils objected to the plan and there was disagreement as to which government division would be responsible for overseeing the county committees. With no decision reached, the de facto plan was to allow the County Councils to continue to oversee agricultural production with the assistance of the women's committees. In the meantime, demobilisation orders for soldiers and sailors meant that the Ministry of Labour would begin to release pivotal men in agriculture in advance of general demobilisation. Ploughmen in particular were needed to assist with the harvest and it was expected that 6,000 ploughmen would be released from service and returned to agricultural work without delay. In addition, training facilities allotted space specifically for disabled soldiers. By October 1919, 495 disabled men were either placed on farms or were training at one of eight facilities that offered modified training programmes in milking and gardening.[6] The 3,904 War Agricultural Volunteers, however, were released from their service, and all subsistence allowances associated with the coordination of women's volunteer efforts ceased immediately. The National Service Department, which had been responsible for their initial recruitment, informed the volunteers of this decision.[7]

The WLA would remain in place in England, Wales, and Scotland and continue to function as it had during the war. The Board of Agriculture funded the Land Army, while the National Service Department oversaw recruitment, and the Ministry of Labour managed employment contracts. This arrangement was temporary and likely only to remain in place for one year in order to assist with the reintegration of military servicemen back into the domestic work force.[8] For now, the Women's Branch was requested to maintain very high standards with regard to recruitment for the Land Army. Fresh applicants would be expected to perform physically demanding tasks and there would be little choice for Land Girls with regard to their place of employment. With the advance demobilisation mentioned above, the need for female labour on farms was at present equal to the supply. Recruiters and organisers could, therefore, afford to be much more fastidious in the selection process and were expected to do so.

At a meeting of representatives for agricultural districts in Scotland, Alice Younger, Divisional Officer for Edinburgh, tabled the formal adoption of the Women's Land Army Scheme for Scotland for the post-war period. By way of an inter-committee report, Mrs Hugh Middleton, Organising Secretary for Northumberland, had explained to the organisers in Scotland how the scheme was to operate in England and how funds were to be allocated for various committees and officers. Based on the English model, the new scheme in Scotland, renamed the Scottish Women's Land Army Scheme, called for the disbandment of all other volunteer organisations for agriculture in December 1918 to reduce competition and streamline recruitment, training, and placement. The end of the war and changes to labour needs meant the Scottish Scheme, as in England and Wales, was expected to produce workers of superior quality. Convincing farmers to keep women on, even as the men returned, meant the women had to be skilled or had to have considerable work experience.

Housing also presented challenges for the organisation. In Scotland, housing had generally been part of the employment contract for agricultural labourers, and with men returning from the war, housing would have to be made available to them. This meant that the number of women housed would have to be reduced. Recognising that the housing shortage in Scotland was no small obstacle and that circumstances were unlikely to be remedied quickly, organisers decided to carry over 1,860 women who had not been employed in agriculture before the war and who were enrolled with the SWLA between 1917 and November 1918 into the new scheme. The remaining Land Girls, approximately 1,000 women, were released from service. Of the 1,860 women enrolled, approximately 300 indicated a desire to continue with agricultural work, even if the Land Army was disbanded. While the reduction in the Land Army's numbers may seem peculiar, organisers in Scotland knew that the women's experiences on the land and their relations with farmers was paramount to the scheme's success. Therefore, organisers decided to reduce the number of Land Girls, keeping only those most suited to the work, in an effort to improve the viability of the organisation. With the end of the war and the return of the men, organisers expected that enrolments for land service would decrease; however, organisers reasoned that the notable pay increases for women in agriculture and improvements to accommodations, which organisers hoped would be possible in the post-war period, would convince more women to pursue agricultural employment in the long term. The reduction in the number of Land Girls would be temporary and in the post-war period the absence of a national emergency would allow Scottish organisers to carefully select and train future Land Girls. Learning from mistakes made earlier in the war when the SWLA competed with other organisations, notably the WNSS, Scottish organisers were confident that the new organisation would increase its enrolments quickly, thereby justifying the extension of the organisation – not just its survival – in the years to come.[9]

The new demands on the Land Army provided an opportunity for organisers to transform the image of the Land Army to bring it more in line with the initial vision of January 1917: a permanent, well-trained, disciplined, and effective labour force of educated women who were capable of hard work, and who possessed the proper skills and background to manage the challenges of life on the land. Numbering just 14,754 at the end of November 1918, influenza attacks and the uncertainty of the organisation's future had greatly reduced the Land Army's numbers.[10] Nonetheless, Talbot instructed the Women's Agricultural Committees and Labour Exchanges to be careful when selecting women for agricultural work in order to meet the standards indicated by the Board of Agriculture and Ministry of Labour, but also to encourage public support for the continuation of the Land Army scheme. This was the organisation's opportunity to reinvent the Land Army as a viable employment opportunity for women, meaning their employment would be seen as work, not service. As Talbot expected, demobilisation would be slow and there was no guarantee the men who left the land in 1914 would be willing to return in 1919. It was possible their experiences in the Great War conditioned them to avoid the solitude and drudgery of rural life and their mandated return in the fall of 1918 gave little indication of their plans. Unfortunately, the fact that more than 14,000 Land Girls remained on the land immediately following the armistice, down from 27,000 during the war, gave little indication of their plans either.

Talbot's resolve to promote and encourage the role of women in agriculture post-armistice had to be communicated to the Land Girls who awaited news about their employment prospects. The timing was critical. The Land Girls had to receive reassurance before they abandoned their posts, but Talbot wanted to wait until she was more confident that she had something positive to report. A letter was sent to every Land Girl informing her that although the future of the Land Army remained uncertain, the food situation remained precarious. Europe had been devastated by war and agricultural production in Britain would need to be maintained, not only to feed the domestic population, but to help supply Europe's markets. Although she could make no guarantees, she assured Land Girls that 'Your country still needs you' and that their work was not yet finished.[11]

In addition to her letter, in January 1919 Talbot instructed the Labour Exchanges and Women's Agricultural Committees to divide the Land Girls into two classes. Those women in class (a), who had expressed a desire to find alternative labour, would be released from WLA service and their employment information made available to future employers through the Labour Exchanges. Those women in class (b), who desired to remain with the Land Army or who preferred to pursue agricultural employment should the Land Army be disbanded, would have their employment information retained by the Women's Agricultural Committees for future use. To maintain numbers and skilled workers, Talbot recommended a comprehensive survey of agricultural needs in England, Wales, and Scotland and she encouraged organisers to place Land Girls wherever a position became available. The wartime policy was to have women move wherever in the country their services were required, but post-war the hope was to expand the scheme to attain greater coverage in all counties, especially in the West Country, so that Land Girls would be located closer to home. For Talbot, Younger, and the Women's Agricultural Committees, the challenge was not simply convincing government of the need to keep the Land Army in place, but also convincing Land Girls that their work was valued and that their services were still required.[12]

Furthermore, some of the women organisers who were responsible for the daily operations of the Land Army in the counties had to be convinced their work was similarly valued. In Shropshire, Mrs Fielden failed to see why organisers should continue in their work when it was just a matter of time before the WLA was disbanded. Even if it continued for a year, she argued, much of the local staff had already left their posts and the number of Land Girls was reduced monthly. Further promotion of the Land Army would only meet with short-lived success and the staffs and rank-and-file would have to be resupplied without any guarantee that their work would be meaningful. Mrs Fielden and Mrs Alexander, both from the Shropshire Committee, were not alone in submitting their resignations to the Director of the Women's Branch in late 1918.[13] In Berkshire the Women's Organising Office, which dealt with women's work on the land, lost several of its full-time staff members and reported to Talbot that it would take some time for replacements to be interviewed and recommendations for hire to be made to the Women's Branch.[14] In Perthshire and Roxburghshire staffs were reduced and in Perth the office closed for a few days following the armistice due to a staff shortage.[15] Letters arrived daily to the Women's Branch regarding declining staffs and insufficient numbers to satisfy demands, especially in smaller regions. Organising committees expressed their concerns that the situation would only be exacerbated once demobilisation was fully underway. Women, both organisers and Land Girls, would want to return home to their husbands and families and the Land Army would be unable to meet whatever labour demands remained.

The matter of the continued demand for Land Girls was difficult to assess. The German army's push westward in March 1918 meant that the food situation could remain ominous for some time to come. At that time, there had been much discussion about the continuation of the Land Army's services and the Women's Branch was encouraged to increase the number of recruits monthly and to amplify the propaganda campaign for the scheme. Talbot carefully monitored the publicity campaign, having the Publicity Section of the National Service Department inform her daily of newspaper stories and advertisements related to the Land Army.[16] In Scotland, the propaganda campaign was similarly enlarged and a greater proportion of the operating budget was allocated to the distribution of fliers and posters. Younger also approved several parades and fairs in the spring of 1918 to encourage enrolments and also to showcase the women's skills to local farmers.

While Talbot had been eager to increase enrolment, she, like her Scottish counterparts, did not want to do so without proper consideration of the potential long-term implications for the organisation. Filling the Land Army's rank with women who were unsuited to the task of farm work had always been a source of anxiety for Talbot. But with the Spring Offensive underway, the possibility that the food situation could deteriorate if more men were needed for military service persuaded Talbot to be less prudent with regard to the Land Army's promotional campaign.[17] In the autumn of 1918 the allied counter-offensive renewed hopes that the war would soon be over, but cast doubt once more on the future of the Land Army.[18] The publicity campaign was scaled back, and the call for Land Girls was removed from the 'wants' columns of newspapers.[19] While it could not be known that the German government would call for an armistice in November, there were only a few months between the elevation of the Land Army's position on the home front and the organisation's potential disbandment. There was much confusion at the Women's Branch in the closing months of the war and the cessation of hostilities in November did not provide clarification. Much could change in a year, so organisers had to operate with the understanding that although the Land Army had survived, there was no way to know for how long.

In January 1919 all organisations that dealt with agriculture were asked to carry out assessments of the farmers' needs in their districts. This was the first stage in assessing labour requirements. With the end of the war many farmers indicated their preference for a return of their male workers and communicated to Group Leaders and Welfare Officers that labour arrangements worked out in the immediate post-war period would be temporary.[20] Although the Women's Committees continued to advocate for the employment of women, some farmers revived familiar arguments against their employment – training was insufficient, the work was not suitable for women, and without the pretext of a national crisis, few women would willingly stick with farm work. With the number of Land Girls already in decline, there was little organisers could say to change the farmers' minds. The farmers' renewed reluctance to hire women was not so much about the quality of their work or their suitability for the job, but rather reflected a desire among farmers to return to perceived normalcy. Farmers, generally, did not deny, or did not intend to deny, that the Land Army had offered assistance during the war years, although it surely felt that way to organisers in early 1919. Most farmers kept the women they already had in their employ, but the request for more women workers dissipated with each passing month after the armistice was signed.[21]

For Talbot and the Women's Committees the situation was disorientating as an early reprieve from government met with resistance from farmers. Talbot decided that some reorganisation was needed. If the institution was to outlive its wartime roots, it had to demonstrate its continued importance. Tackling the farmers' opposition meant that Talbot had to return to the major issues that plagued the Land Army from the outset: training, billeting, and ambiguous public support. In late January the Women's Committees were encouraged to make recommendations for extended training periods beyond the allowable six weeks. This would also require the government to continue to pay for four weeks of training, as it had during the war, plus an additional two weeks. Under this plan the government would pay for six weeks of the eight-week training programme (the other two weeks were to be paid by the employer). The case made by the Women's Committees was that the transformation of the land under peacetime conditions would require new farming knowledge. Many women came into the Land

Army in late 1917 or 1918 when the plough campaign was already well underway. Training had focused on the needs of farmers at the time and not a general education in farming practices and techniques. The new training programme would offer a general education in farming, including land management, horticulture, agricultural science, and livestock management and aimed to teach women the basics of agricultural production and marketing.[22] What is notable about the programme is that it was not intended to meet an immediate need; rather, it offered a stepping-stone for those interested in pursuing long-term employment in the industry. In addition to extended training and educational programmes, billeting would have to be supplied by employers, or the government would have to bear the costs of caravans. This was a risky move. With the Land Army facing disbandment, Talbot opted to press for scarce government funds to extend training programmes without any assurance from the farmers that the women's services were still needed or desired.

With the new training scheme quickly rejected by the Board of Agriculture a conference was held in February to begin the laborious task of re-facing the Land Army. Many challenges lay ahead, but the most pressing were discussions about finances, wages, transportation troubles, and billeting. This conference was, however, unique in that representatives of the farmers' union were present and gave voice to concerns similar to those put forward by the WLA. Without the war, farmers feared that the government's attentiveness to the industry's needs would diminish. Related to this point were the farmers' concerns that farming conditions were not likely to improve in the near future. Machinery and suitable housing remained in short supply and, despite the efforts of the Land Army to revitalise rural living, farm work and life remained isolating.[23] The farmers' desire to make room for the returning men was a hopeful gesture toward encouraging their homecoming on the land. Both farmers and the Land Army were concerned that government assistance would not last long, and that many farmers would struggle to keep their farms once the wartime markets and government price guarantees evaporated. The fact was that the calibre of agriculture labourers had declined in the latter years of the war. Certainly recruitment took its toll – even once the need to restrict the call up of men from essential industries, and agriculture in particular, was understood – but the increased reliance on boys, women, and POWs meant that the quality of the labour force declined. Unskilled workers now performed tasks that had previously been done by skilled men and the quality of food production was negatively affected in the process.

In the immediate post-war period there was a feeling of pessimism among farmers. While government protections during the war came as a result of the work carried out by the Selborne Committee, a sub-committee of the Ministry of Reconstruction, one farmer described the government's pre-war approach to agriculture as 'criminal neglect'.[24] Some of the farmers' uncertainty diminished when the Royal Commission on Agriculture (1919) offered farmers price protection for four years, but in exchange the Ministry of Agriculture subjected farmers to 'good husbandry' inspections, which monitored aggregate output and ensured that farmers paid the minimum wage for farm workers that had been introduced in 1917.[25] This arrangement was solidified with the introduction of the Agriculture Act in June 1920 and eased relations between the farmers and government.[26]

Rents, however, were offered no protections and the threat of rising rents and concerns about the productive value of agriculture encouraged many farmers to sell their land. The assertion that up to one-quarter of the land in England was under new ownership by 1922 has been recently revised; nevertheless, the years 1919 and 1920 were notable in terms of land sales in England.[27] The farmers who found themselves vulnerable at the end of the war were the small estate farms, those with land but no capital. Dairy farmers also suffered during the war. While the number of cattle remained steady, the cattle were smaller as a result of the reduction in feedstuff. The smaller estate farms and dairy farmers had been the prime supporters of the Land Army because they were most in need of their labour. This was especially true in Scotland where a high percentage of women employed with the SWLA worked on dairy farms. Women became skilled milkers during the war and Land Girls with this skill set remained in demand.

Likewise, the smaller estate farms had relied on a smaller labour force and so were in more need of the semi-skilled Land Girls than were the larger estate farms. The decline of these groups, and even the transfer of land itself, meant that the Land Army had to convince a whole new group of landowners of its value, at the same time that the men were returning home. In many ways, the fate of the Land Army was tied to the willingness of the farmers to accept female labour, but more importantly, the fate of both groups was tied to long-term trends in agriculture.

Government and public support were needed to keep the Land Army operational, but once again organisers faced overwhelming challenges. On 16 November 1918 the National Service Department, which had been responsible for the recruitment and promotion of the Land Army, announced that it would no longer provide these services. Talbot was informed that the termination of the war necessitated the end of the relationship between the Women's Branch and the National Service Department, and that all responsibility for recruitment would be transferred to the Board of Agriculture. Talbot protested, but the National Service Department offered no support, considering the matter to be closed.[28] With the war over the National Service Department was to be disbanded at the earliest opportunity. Therefore, it was not possible for the Department to continue in its former role with regard to recruitment. The promotional campaign for the WLA was once again forced to reinvent itself. Rather than full-page pictures of women on the land, calls for recruits were reduced to small advertisements and were generally not accompanied by pictures. Throughout 1919 the *Times* printed a few articles that drew attention to the women's abilities, especially in dairy work, and the *Globe* printed several articles about the 'new class' of Land Girls and reiterated what the Land Army had accomplished during the war. In most cases, recruitment efforts focused on the WLA's role in the war and the continued need for home food production.[29]

Emphasising that the new skills acquired by Land Girls did not replace their domestic capabilities was also a central theme in promotional advertisements. An article in *Royal Magazine* entitled 'The Woman of To-Morrow' assured the public that just because women learned to hoe potatoes did not mean they had forgotten how to prepare them for dinner. The accompanying pictures showed a woman being dragged by a discontented cow, while another woman was seen holding a teacup while her husband sipped from it. The story assures men that the wife of tomorrow would be better equipped for the challenges ahead than the wife of yesterday. She would not offend him with incessant questions about his work or the details of each day. She would still sew, prepare meals, tidy the house, and tend to all domestic matters. While the story seems to suggest that women were made more capable by their wartime experiences – stating that many women now had the 'strength of three servants' – the articles were satirical. The woman that the public desired simply did not exist in reality, but the article speaks to a public desire to return to 'normal', thereby stressing the need for women to embrace domesticity and avoid blurring the boundaries between public and private life.[30] Just as men were changed by the war, women were also changed by their experiences; change, however, did not mean women were less capable of caring for a family. The article implied that in many ways the pre-war status quo persisted, in that gender roles had not been contravened the way that many feared.[31]

The public's discomfort about the conflated role of men and women in the post-war period can be understood by looking at news articles about the WLA and women's war work in general. In the limited number of articles that appeared in the first half of 1919, several made reference to replacement trends, with specific mention of agricultural work.[32] In the absence of public opinion surveys it is difficult to determine the articles' effect on public attitudes, but Talbot must have had her concerns because she initiated a new promotional campaign that focused on what the Land Girls could do in terms of work, avoiding the language of 'replacement'.[33] Talbot feared the language of 'replacement' would create a negative link between the Land Girls and wartime casualties. In an effort to construct a positive association between the Land Army and the nation's success in the war, stories about the Queen's visit to Land Girl training facilities featured prominently, as did the good work of the Land Girls in their continued *support* of Britain's farmers.[34] The campaign to prolong the Land Army's operations as a peacetime organisation did not appear overtly in the press. Talbot preferred to make her case for women's work in agriculture by reassuring the public and Land Girls that the WLA, and organisations like it, continued to have relevance post-1918 due to women's abilities as workers.[35]

In the summer of 1919 the promotional campaign for the Women's Land Army was stalled. The government's decision to reorganise the War Agricultural Committees, including the Women's War Agricultural Committees, had dire consequences for the WLA. In July the Board of Agriculture decided that the Executive Committees should assume control over the WWACs. The former WWACs were invited to form sub-committees in most counties, and executive sub-committees in the counties where the number of women employed in agriculture warranted such representation. The sub-committees were to have no more than ten elected members and would meet annually to elect members, as well as to participate in a day conference on the role of women in agriculture. The sub-committees were responsible for supervising the work of women in agriculture and making assessments about the effects of agricultural work on women and its impact on rural life. The Village Registrars were to assist the sub-committees by keeping in contact with the women employed in agriculture in each village and to keep track of the farmers' labour needs.[36] The Executive Committees were also reorganised as a result of the disassembly of the Food Production Department in March 1919. The Executive Committees, which previously fell under the authority of the FPD, were brought under the control of the Board of Agriculture in order to assist with the plough campaign for 1919 and in order to help stave off the predicted shortage of cereals that was expected over the next two years. The duty of the Executive Committee was to supervise all agricultural work in the counties, including cultivation and planting orders, but it was left up to the individual counties to determine how much latitude the women's sub-committees would have within this organisational framework.

The main concern for the WLA was that both the Executive Committees and the women's sub-committees had significantly less power as a result of the reorganisation. In addition, the introduction of the Corn Production (Amendment) Act of 1918 reduced the Executive Committees to an advisory role by 1920. In the immediacy of the 1919 restructuring plans for agriculture, the Executive Committees were now responsible to submit monthly reports to the sub-committees, rather than attending monthly meetings, thereby fashioning a more passive relationship between the groups than had existed during the war.[37]

In Scotland, the Women's Committees were also reorganised. The War Agricultural Committees absorbed the 47 Women's War Agricultural Committees and formed a joint advisory board that included representatives of the former WWACs. A subsidiary branch was also formed to work in an advisory capacity to the colleges for agricultural education. This subsidiary branch was also responsible for the handling of juvenile labour, which was expected to persist as a viable alternative to women workers in the post-war years. This subsidiary branch and its authority over the employment of juvenile workers (in conjunction with the Educational Authorities) elucidated that farmers, and women, wished to return to pre-war trends where women were increasingly absent from the land. In these initial stages of reorganisation, a plan for the reintegration of men into the agricultural workforce had not yet been established. The indication was that the reorganisation was temporary to provide additional time for the Board of Agriculture in Scotland to work out a long-term plan for agriculture in the counties. Gradually, the number of boys and women would be reduced, as skilled and semi-skilled labourers were reintroduced into the agricultural labour force.[38]

Talbot expected changes to the Land Army as well. The news came quickly. In August, Prothero informed Talbot and Lyttelton that the Women's Land Army would be demobilised on 28 November 1919. In Scotland, the Board of Agriculture sent a similar letter to Alice Younger announcing that the SWLA would be demobilised on the same day and that the Board would assume full responsibility for the placement of women in agriculture.[39] Demobilisation, the positive end of service, was meant to coincide with the government's plans for the general demobilisation of Britain's military forces. Demobilisation was not an easy task, and plans for demobilisation of the armed forces had begun in the summer of 1916. The Ministry of Reconstruction's sub-committee, responsible for the demobilisation of the army, was concerned to avoid mass unemployment. Under Edwin Montague the sub-committee devised a plan to release men based on industry's ability to absorb men back into the workforce. This was a unique, and somewhat bizarre, demobilisation scheme because it called for the release of individual men, not units, and took no account of the men's service records, age, or injuries.[40] By creating classes of soldiers, the government determined that some men were more valuable to the domestic economy than others, a notion that defied the very basis of the national war effort. The assumption that all service was valued equally and that Britain would be a land 'fit for heroes' was jeopardised by the approved demobilisation scheme.

The WLA fit into this scheme in that its continued operations after November 1918 demonstrated its value as a wartime service, but also that the continued importance of agricultural production at the time of the armistice meant that serious disruptions to food production had to be avoided. Take, for example, that female munitions workers began to experience lay-offs in 1917. With Russia's withdrawal from the war its armament orders no longer had to be filled. Further lay-offs came in the spring of 1918 and finally mass lay-offs occurred after the signing of the armistice.[41] This is not to suggest the WLA was valued above other women's organisations; rather, its continuation was based on government priorities with regard to men's work in essential industries and the care taken to minimise the danger of unemployment. Just as industries had to be prioritised during the war, they also had to be prioritised with the resumption of peace.

The Land Army, like the armed forces, was *demobilised*, not *disbanded*. In many ways this emphasised the women's *service* to their country.[42] The Land Girl's employment, and the Land Army itself, was temporary, not permanent, and with the end of the war, the Land Army could 'stand down' from active service. Unlike the military, however, the desire for relaxation and distance from the strain of wartime service did not apply to the Land Army, or other domestic groups.[43] Those who remained with the Land Army after the signing of the armistice most likely enjoyed their work, or they liked the pay, and wished to remain employed for the time being. The positive connotation of demobilisation – released from service, not fired or dismissed – was not received in the intended positive fashion by Land Girls. The end of the war meant the Land Girls would be forced from their place of employment, with many returning to domestic service.[44]

Talbot was not unprepared for the news and had undertaken work toward the formation of a new organisation to support the role of women in agriculture. Plans were underway for the creation of the National Association of Landswomen (NAL) and while Talbot cared for the demobilisation of the Land Army she worked on gaining government support for the NAL. With regard to the demobilisation of the Land Army, no immediate action was taken. Talbot did not inform Land Girls of the change until October 1919 and although the Women's Committees were abreast of the situation, they were instructed to proceed as usual for the time being.[45] Talbot's actions to obscure the Land Army's future were exemplified by the events surrounding the Great Rally in Northampton. The Great Rally was intended to be a celebration of the excellent work done by the Land Army and its continued role in post-war reconstruction. The announcements of the Land Army's demobilisation came with a reduction in its operating costs, so the funds for the Great Rally were no longer available.[46] Instead, the Women's Committees would have to raise the money to pay for the rally and restrict participation to just fifteen Land Girls from each county. Canvassing for donors and the promotion of the Great Rally was somewhat muted without the assistance of the National Service Department and, as a result, the counties failed to raise the money they needed. Urged to practise further economy by the Board of Agriculture, the Northampton Committee, with much regret, was forced to cancel the Great Rally on 6 September 1919.[47] The Organising Secretaries, following Talbot's instructions, informed Land Girls that the cancellation of the Great Rally was due to post-war austerity measures and that the Land Army's future was still unknown.

As part of the 'business as usual' approach, Land Girls continued to be registered[48] and the Women's Committees were also encouraged to maintain a good relationship with present employers, especially those farmers who participated in training schemes. For those women who wanted long-term prospects on the land, training scholarships and, later, the possibility of emigration was suggested for those who were exceptionally skilled and able to make a living at farming. The possibility of a future training scheme for military servicemen was introduced with the Gifts for Land Settlement Act (1916) that granted the Board of Agriculture and the County Councils the ability to accept land gifts for the settlement or employment of servicemen in agriculture in England and Wales.[49] The land was intended to provide training opportunities for men wishing to pursue farm management or ownership and was accompanied by grants for the purchase of land overseas and scholarships to attend approved training universities or colleges in England, Wales, and Scotland.[50]

In 1919 the opportunities for land ownership overseas and training scholarships were extended to members of the Women's Land Army under the Free Passage Scheme (1919–22).[51] Under the Scheme, ex-servicemen and women were granted free passage to the colonies or dominions where land grants from the Board of Agriculture could be used for the purchase of farmland.[52] Although emigration and land ownership were offered as a reward for men and women who had served in the war, the scheme offered a potential solution to the problem of the female surplus. While the scheme was opened to men and women, it was gendered. Men who served during the war were able to partake in the scheme, regardless of their time of service, but women had to have a service record of six months or more. Further, the scheme allowed for the relocation of a 'superior quality of woman' to the colonies or dominions.[53] Such distinction, while servicing the connection between state and empire, was in itself state recognition of the value of the work performed by the WLA. Once the demobilisation of the Land Army was announced, emigration became more than just a remote possibility.

The furtherance of alternative opportunities for Land Girls was necessitated by a memorandum received by Talbot from the Board of Agriculture in September 1919 requesting a further reduction in staff at the Women's Branch, but also in the counties. The women's sub-committees in England, Wales, and Scotland were ordered to reduce their staffs to one clerk and eight elected members (six in Scotland). The reductions would be based on service records and duties. Lists of all members and support staff were to be compiled, with duties and service periods indicated, along with recommendations for dismissals. The lists were to be turned over to the Board of Agriculture no later than 30 September 1919. Each committee was given the opportunity to decide where the cuts should be made, but personal circumstances were to be given no weight in the decision-making process. The lists turned over to the Board of Agriculture were to ensure that dismissals were based on duties and service histories, not personal or political relationships. In addition, checks were placed on travel allowances and travel accommodations. While the Board of Agriculture accepted that travel was necessary for agricultural promotion and productivity, it requested that travel be used sparingly and that accommodations should be meagre.

There was also to be no disruption to services provided to agricultural workers in spite of the funding cuts.[54]

With the reorganisation of the Board of Agriculture in October 1919, Talbot was forced to address the demobilisation of the Land Army. Plans had to be made for the final months of the Land Army's operations and a ceremony for the presentation of distinguished service awards had to be organised for those women who had stayed with the Land Army in its closing days. The loss of momentum from the war years had taken its toll on organisers and Land Girls. In August 1919 the number of registered enlistments remained healthy at 22,000, but only 13,000 women were trained and fewer than 8,000 were working.[55] Talbot recognised that the time had come to inform the remaining Land Girls of the government's decision to demobilise. In a letter to the Organising Secretaries dated 14 October 1919, Talbot explained that now that the men had returned from the war it would 'no longer be right to spend public money on the equipping and transport of the Land Army, which, in time of war was a necessity'. She assured the women of the Land Army that just because this meant the 'withdrawal of the war time Organisation; it will not mean, I hope, the withdrawal of anyone of you who has proved herself to be a good farm hand and of service, therefore, to her employer and to her country'.[56] Talbot's wording is important: the demobilisation of the Land Army was not a reflection of the Land Army's work, or a criticism of women's employment in the industry, but rather a consequence of post-war austerity measures. Talbot informed the Women's Committees that after 30 November Land Girls would be regular employees, and would no longer be associated with the Board of Agriculture, nor would they be permitted to wear the Land Army uniform. She offered assurance that there was still much agricultural work to be done across the country, and urged women to consider joining the National Association of Landswomen after the Land Army officially completed its service. Talbot offered encouragement by reminding the women of the Land Army that they had not only served their country, but they had improved their health and gained a better understanding of and appreciation for rural life. Their work was not only in service to their country, but in service to themselves and all women who experienced enjoyment and personal improvement as a result of their work. In her closing remarks, Talbot wrote:

> And so the time has come when I must, as Director of the Women's Land Army, say 'Good-bye' to you. But it is'nt [*sic*] really 'Good-bye', for in the days to come, through the Association and in other ways,

I shall hope to come across women farm workers who, during the Great War, belonged to the Women's Land Army. I am proud, and always shall be of all of you. The Land Army has won a good name for itself throughout Great Britain, and indeed, in other countries of the World.[57]

The letter issued by Talbot to the Organising Secretaries was to be communicated to the Land Girls, but a letter was also sent to every active Land Girl explaining the details of the organisation's termination. Talbot and Younger arranged for those women who remained with the Land Army after 1 October 1919 to receive a special service certificate, apart from the distinguished service awards, and to assist them in finding employment once the Land Army's contracts were concluded.[58] It was important that every woman employed with the Land Army who wanted to continue to work after the war submit her name to the Women's Branch before the end of November, as several other women's organisations, as well as a number of government employees, were to be released from their employment by Christmas. The Women's Branch offered to assist those women from London (or women who wished to settle in London) in finding a job and accommodations. In addition, transportation costs by train to London were to be covered by the Women's Branch, but such assistance was only possible until the end of December 1919 when the operations of the Women's Branch would come to an end.[59] In order to coordinate the arrival of Land Girls in London and arrange job placements, Talbot organised a final Land Army rally in December 1919. All women arriving in London were expected to be in full uniform, including organisers who desired to show their support of and appreciation for the good work carried out by the Land Girls. Talbot planned to use the occasion as a final showing for the WLA, but also as a promotional event for the National Association of Landswomen, which was still in the planning stages.

If the wearing of the Land Army uniform at the assembly in London was intended to be a final, and perhaps appropriate, showing of the Land Girls since the cancellation of the Great Rally a few months before, Talbot, who frequently wore the Land Army uniform for public appearance, was saddened by the retirement of the LAAS uniform. In her memorandums to the women's sub-committees, she stressed the need to collect the uniforms as quickly as possible and to ensure that the Land Army coat and hat did not find their way into the hands of village workers. In her final instructions the tone of Talbot's letters had changed. She was less direct in her commands, frequently beginning with 'I have to inform you', 'It is necessary to inform you', or 'I regret to inform you', hesitations that were uncharacteristic of her previous correspondence. She also acknowledged, subtly, the difficulties of shutting down the organisation and the disorienting effects of the month's events.[60] In a public statement Talbot expressed her belief that the Women's Land Army had opened a new door for women, for it was just a short time ago that the wearing of trousers and breeches had been the subject of public unease and now the Land Army uniform was a symbol of women's service in the Great War. She hoped the door did not soon close and that women continued to have a central role in the rural life of the nation. Talbot trusted that the revitalisation of the land would be more complete and more successful if women played an active role, but the onus was now on the former Land Girls to continue to pursue employment in agriculture on their own.[61]

It is with the formation of the National Association of Landswomen that we see Talbot's true intentions with regard to the WLA. In August 1919 Lord Lee replaced Rowland Prothero as President of the Board of Agriculture. Lee was sympathetic to the Land Army's situation and attached importance to the continuation of women's agricultural organisations. When Talbot approached Lee about the possibility of forming a National Association of Landswomen she found much support and was instructed to use what time was left for the Land Army to take the initial steps in bringing the organisation to life. The organisation of the NAL was the responsibility of the Women's Branch and was supported by the women's sub-committees in the counties. While Lee expressed his support, he was also clear that the NAL would have no official association with the Board of Agriculture. The NAL was formed on a self-governing basis, meaning the organisation was to be managed by its subscribing members. The time between the conceptualisation of the NAL and official support from the Board of Agriculture happened quickly and there was consequently little time to canvass the Land Army organisation for support before plans were set in motion.[62]

It was only after the initial planning stages that the Women's Land Army organisation was informed of the development. Once official approval was given, a provisional committee representing the interests of women in agriculture was formed and the general framework of the scheme discussed. At this stage it was determined that a close working relationship with the Women's Farm and Garden Union and the National Federation of Women's Institutes was desirable and that this cooperation should be solidified from the outset. Every county committee was contacted, by way of a circular letter, explaining the scheme and requesting assistance and support. The idea was that the NAL would operate in much the same way as the WLA, in that close cooperation with the county committees would be an asset to the organisation. General meetings of Organising Secretaries would encourage discussion and allow for the election of representatives to a central organising committee, serving much the same function as the Women's Branch. There was much disagreement, however, about the need for a central office. The Women's Committees believed that a central office was only required for the distribution of uniforms and the issuing of contracts, while the Organising Secretaries argued that a central office was essential for efficient work and the integration of the NAL. General agreement tended toward the establishment of a central committee, so the provisional organising committee added a provision for a central office in its recommendation to be put before the first Council meeting in the new year.[63] Once a formal council and central office were formed, the provisional committee would cease to exist. After the Board of Agriculture gave its approval for the new scheme, the Provisional Committee set to work preparing an operational plan to put before members. It also established committees to oversee marketing and enrolments, and arranged for the first council meeting of delegates from the counties. At the time of the Land Army's demobilisation there was still much work to be done, as only eight counties had signed on to support the NAL.[64]

The NAL was intended as an extension of the WLA. Talbot believed it would encourage a similar sense of camaraderie and purpose, and would provide further opportunity for the Organising Secretaries, Welfare Officers, and Group Leaders of the Land Army to continue to do all in their power to show that even though 'this subsidized form of labour can no longer be justified; at the same time by the good work they have done, women have proved their worth, and that the country has still need of the best service they can give'.[65] Talbot hoped the majority of women employed with the Land Army would continue as permanent workers on the land and that they would continue to support one another through the National Association of Landswomen.

Upon the demobilisation of the Land Army, the Land Girls who remained to the end were given a certificate of discharge. The certificate contained remarks about the women's work and their personal character during the period of service, and, in cases where it was possible, a statement from the woman's employer was included. The certificates were to be accurate, but generous. Any woman who was discharged after 1 October 1919 for poor conduct or unsuitability for the job was not presented with a certificate.[66] In addition, the remaining Land Girls were given a free uniform from the Board of Agriculture and the uniform was retired to commemorate the Land Girl's service.[67]

The Demobilisation Outfit, as it was termed, was also intended to signify to the counties that the Land Army was no longer an official organisation.[68] It was also a way to denote to the Organising Secretaries that their service had come to an end. When the demobilisation date for the Land Army was announced, the Women's Branch and Organising Secretaries in the counties were allotted an extra month of operational time to bring Land Army matters to a close. While the Organising Secretaries busied themselves with certificates and uniform presentations, by the end of December the process to close down the county offices was only partially complete. In late December 1919, Talbot issued a memorandum instructing the county organisers that 'your duties with regard to placing women and filling demands of employers must in no case be carried on'.[69] Talbot also informed the Organising Secretaries that the meeting of the National Association of Landswomen held on 18 December inaugurated the organisation as an independent body; therefore, the Organising Secretaries were not permitted to spend official time working to advance the interests of the organisation. To avoid disadvantaging the NAL, Talbot reminded those involved with the WLA and NAL that the two organisations were 'sisters', but independent of one another. The fact that the WLA could not be transformed into a peacetime organisation prevented closer association between the organisations. Talbot wanted to start anew, building on the work done by the Land Army, but with the benefit of a fresh start for a brand new organisation.[70] Talbot, therefore, requested that the Organising Secretaries in the counties accept that their time with the Land Army had come to an end, that the Women's Land Army no longer existed, and that all work associated with the organisation would cease immediately.[71]

In the Christmas 1919 edition of the *Landswoman*, Lord Ernle, President of the Board of Agriculture, and Meriel Talbot thanked the Land Girls for their service. Both acknowledged that conditions had not been easy and while public support was not always forthcoming, the nation would not 'soon forget that, when every pound of sod and every pair of capable hands were urgently needed, the women of the Land Army worked early and late, for meager wages, at tasks which were often monotonous and physically exhausting'. The Land Girls' dedication had been tested and although not every woman who entered the Land Army succeeded, the women of the Land Army 'have shown what women can do and be in the most important of our national industries'.[72]

Lord Ernle's statement captures the sentiments of many organisers of the Land Army and 'showing what women could do' was precisely what Talbot had set out to accomplish when she accepted the position of director of the Women's Branch. She believed that women played a central role in the welfare of the nation and that the WLA had helped to propel women into fields of work and associations that they might not otherwise have undertaken. Her efforts were about more than just the promotion of women's work in agriculture; rather, she sought to make a connection between women's work and the future strength of the nation, which would be vital to recovery efforts in Britain and Europe during the years of reconstruction. To this end, Talbot and her fellow organisers did not wish simply to continue the propaganda version of the Land Army post-armistice. Rather, she, Alice Younger, and others like them hoped to reinvent the Land Army – to create a group of women workers who took pride in their work and who found support and inspiration in one another, locally and nationally. This helps us to understand why Talbot waited so long to announce the WLA's demobilisation orders and why Younger readily dismissed hundreds of women from service with the SWLA. Talbot and Lyttelton hoped to use the remnants of the old organisation to create a new association of women land workers, and while both women had hoped to retain government support for their work financially and politically, they knew how to operate on their own. The creation of the National Association of Landswomen speaks to the success of the Land Army scheme. Although the Women's Land Army was demobilised in 1919, land women were a permanent factor in the agricultural life of the country and the Land Army concept found new life in the post-war period.

Conclusion

Although the Women's Land Army no longer existed after 1919, for a time it continued to occupy a space in the public imagination. Berta Ruck's *A Land Girl's Love Story* (1919) rehearsed a familiar narrative of women workers inspired by a sense of duty and patriotism, but with the addition of a love story that came to define the women's wartime experiences. *A Land Girl's Love Story* tells the tale of Joan, who left her work in a London office after being scorned by her lover, Harry, to find a more meaningful way to support the war effort. After being distracted by a bold sign bearing the words 'England must be fed', she decided to join the Women's Land Army and despite her initial hesitations, stuck with it through to the end of the war.[1] Ruck reiterates time and again that the women of the Land Army were doing work of national importance, focusing on the parallel between the Land Girls' service and the soldiers in the trenches. As part of this connection, Ruck focused on the soldiers the girls met, fell in love with, and eventually married.[2] This romanticised version of the Land Army and its future-looking narrative was perhaps appropriate in the immediacy of the return to peace. In Ruck's story, the heroine and her soldier-suitor represented a newly constructed wartime identity for women – where patriotism, marriage, and motherhood were conflated but not necessarily in conflict – that could carry into the post-war period. This story, and others like it,[3] also helped to contest accounts from the war such as Olive Hockin's *Two Girls on the Land: War-Time on a Dartmoor Farm* (1918), which many contemporaries interpreted as a feminist statement on the threat the Land Army posed to conventional gender roles and the male dominion over the land.[4] The view of the patriotic Land Girl serving her country was imposed on society by the press, government, and organisers who sought to avoid any notion that acceptable gender behaviour was being transgressed. The need for this reassurance did not end with the conclusion of the war, and re-establishing gendered standards was seen as vital to the nation's recovery. If the Land Girls' contribution was seen as service to the nation, despite the intensity of the work, then the distinction between how men and women exercised their patriotism was not clouded and war service within this framework did not represent unwanted social change.

During the war the images of Land Girls were used to inspire patriotism, but also to make a connection between the war and home fronts. The absence of men on the land necessitated the formation of a national organisation like the WLA, with the intention of cultivating nationalism and inspiring resolve among the British populace. Unfortunately, the role of women in agriculture was complicated by assumptions about gender and class. It was expected that female land workers would experience prejudice and discrimination in spite of the appropriation of the Land Girl in the national war campaign, but the expectation was that Britons would come to understand the importance of her work. The knowledge that the absence of men from the land was temporary was supposed to soothe public anxiety surrounding the employment of women in a traditionally male industry; yet, the presence of women on farms challenged the preservation of rural paternalism and complicated the dynamics of the farm family. The presence of women land workers posed a threat to male labourers who were left vulnerable to conscription, including the farmers' sons.[5] Prejudice against Land Girls was not simply a matter of gender presumptions about the suitability of women working the land, but also a matter of survival for those farmers whose livelihood depended on the work of a relatively small male labour force. Further complicating matters was the fact that the Land Girls not only posed a threat to the sustainability of small holdings, but also to the domestic sphere of the farm house. The work of wives and daughters was essential to the household economy, but the separate spheres assigned to them made their work less visible and more undervalued. The arrival of Land Girls threw national attention on this new labour force, but continued to consign female relatives to the realm of volunteerism, further devaluing their work both in terms of the farm economy and the war effort.

The viability of the WLA was dependent on organisers finding the 'right' women to help overcome prejudices. The belief was that if the right women could be recruited, trained, and placed, then farmers would see the potential value in this labour force and the public would be more tolerant of the women's new role. Finding the right women, however, proved to be a futile undertaking. While the WLA aimed to recruit only educated women from the middle classes, poor pay and the nature of farm work failed to secure the numbers required to make the scheme successful. The opening of the Land Army's ranks and the large number of domestic servants who enlisted resulted in a mixing of the classes that threatened the middle-class orientation of the Land Army. Although the type of women enlisting for land service after mid-1917 were not the desirable recruits Talbot had hoped for, organisers had to make do. Berta Ruck's *A Land Girl's Love Story* offers commentary on the appropriateness of women's work on the land, both in terms of class and gender. Although there was no difference in the training or status of women land workers based on class, the ideal Land Girl was independent, modest, and posed no threat to the social order. While Joan at first found the mixing of the classes 'queer', Mr Price (the farmer) offers assurances that although 'some were one thing and some another' they were 'good little workers, all'.[6] The classlessness of the organisation was not detrimental to its operations and Ruck argues Land Girls and farmers alike benefitted from the 'wealth of new ideas' that everyone 'gained from the inter-mingling of class with class'.[7] Ruck's optimism aside, the classlessness of the Land Army was never a reality. Organisers yearned for the early days of the organisation when the well-intentioned and well-educated middle-class Land Girls were placed without incident, only to be replaced by the unruly women (referring to domestic servants and rural working-class women) who came to dominate the organisation's ranks in the final year of the war. Although organisers were always concerned to manage the women's conduct, complaints about inappropriate behaviour intensified as the war progressed, linked in part to the continued isolation of workers and the difficulty of the work, but also to the assumption that the new class of recruits did not have the social skills necessary to endure the privations that came with land service.

While the Land Army's operations during the Great War elucidate these presumptions, the formation of the WLA also revealed that women had much to say about the war and their role in it. The efforts of early volunteer groups to promote women in the agricultural industry found relevance and vitality in the war years. The early efforts of groups like the Women's Farm and Garden Union to advance the role of women, economically, in the agricultural industry were transformed by wartime food shortages where women's work in the industry was not a matter of personal choice, but vital to the nation's future. The government's utilitarian approach to women land workers as tools in the successful prosecution of the war degraded the success of the organisation, the obstacles organisers faced and overcame, and the importance of the Land Army's work. Through a collective effort, the organisers of the Land Army and affiliated groups successfully recruited, training, and placed an agricultural labour force that helped the British government manage losses to imports through the revitalisation of domestic farming. The Board of Agriculture acknowledged these efforts through a series of comparisons made between the efforts of Land Girls domestically and soldiers in the trenches through a national propaganda campaign, and thanked the women for their service as the organisation faced disbandment, but the public acknowledgement of their effort came from the Women's Branch by way of a rally in 1919 that honoured the Land Girls and celebrated their war work.

Yet, the chosen battleground for women's economic advancement, the agricultural industry, was not only difficult for women to gain a foothold in, but even for those who were able to do so, the war stifled their ambitions. As Cecilia Gowdy-Waygant has argued, the 'very political choice of agriculture as a wartime service by women served a political purpose of gaining recognition and respect in labour and society. The devastation of the war, however, complicated societal expectations for women, and changing political roles removed agriculture as that springboard of political equality.'[8] The role of the WLA in the war was retrospectively assigned to the sphere of war service, rather than as a catalyst for a brighter political and economic future. In many ways the Land Girls themselves helped foster this perception. They worked long hours for little pay, made do without the comforts of home, and managed the isolation of rural life. While physical betterment was trumpeted by propagandists as the advantage of such work, the real value was in the service to the state. Certainly not all Land Girls understood their war work in this way, and their personal motivations for joining the WLA were diverse, but the women were, in large part, attentive to the nation's needs and eager to answer the call to service.

The unassuming portrait of the Land Girl served a national need, and helped to inspire women who might otherwise have been less than enthusiastic about pursuing farm work, but of equal importance is that the call to service was made by other women who were committed to the task of enlisting women for land service. The efforts and motivations of individual organisers were too diverse for the purpose of this study to explore further, but whatever their reasons, they were invested in the women's work, the viability of the Land Army scheme, and their collective and individual contributions to the war effort. The formation of a national organisation did not, however, diminish the need to promote agriculture as a viable economic opportunity for women in Britain. As was evident in Talbot's desire to continue the organisation's activities after November 1918, the Land Army was a positive symbol of women's success in the industry. The promotion of women on the land did not begin with the First World War and the propaganda used by the organisation harkened back to the traditional role of women in farm work. The Land Army's birth and development were exercises in character building for both men and women, locally and nationally. The presence of women at markets was not altered by the war in any significant way, but their presence in relation to the absence of men intensified public unease. Likewise, the predominantly male county authorities were now interspersed with women's committees dedicated to the promotion of women in a traditionally male industry. The sharing of authority and the perceived loss of local control contravened the traditionally insular and male farming community. The modification of women's (and, to a lesser extent, men's) behaviour during the war meant it was important for organisers to earn the farmers' and the government's trust. First, organisers had to demonstrate that an organisation of women workers that was administered by a women's branch was operable and second, organisers had to provide proof that the intended goal of the scheme, to increase home food production, could meaningfully and effectively be carried out. The efforts of organisers went into verifying the functionality of the organisation and toward meeting its prescribed goals.

It was not until the post-war period that we see the resumption of earlier efforts to advance the role of women in the industry. In many ways, the war years represented a break between the early efforts of volunteer groups to expand work and educational opportunities for women and the renewal of those efforts after the war's conclusion. The central challenge facing organisers was how to reface efforts that had already been refaced to accommodate wartime needs.[9] The perception was that the Women's Land Army was the first public attempt by women to make inroads into the agricultural industry, but that such attempts would expire once the men returned home. The promotion of the Land Army and the image of the well-intentioned, patriotic Land Girl informed the public that neither the work nor the money were motivating factors in her employment. The challenge for organisers, and Talbot in particular, was not simply that they could not overcome this perception, but that the circumstances that made the organisation a matter of public interest ceased to exist after 11 November 1918. The demobilisation of the Land Army in 1919 had little to do with the perceived quality of the women's work, nor was it a political statement about the WLA's overall rate of success, neither of which were easily quantifiable; rather, the demobilisation of the Land Army came as a consequence of the return to pre-war conditions. Just as *A Land Girl's Love Story* represented a revolution against undesired change and the reaffirmation of pre-war norms, the demobilisation of the Land Army was seen as a necessary consequence of the return to *normal* conditions. With the demobilisation of the Women's Land Army the personal experiences of Land Girls and organisers and the account of women fighting for a place in the labour force, was replaced by the well-known story of women's war service.

Notes

Introduction

1. A. Offer, *The First World War: An Agrarian Interpretation* (Oxford: Clarendon Press, 1989), 93; C. S. Orwin and E. H. Whetham, *History of British Agriculture, 1846–1914* (Newton Abbot: David & Charles, 1971), 341–2; P. Dewey, *British Agriculture in the First World War* (London: Routledge, 1989), 15–17; P. Dewey, *War and Progress: Britain, 1914–1945* (London: Longman, 1997), 19.
2. A. Gregory, *The Last Great War: British Society and the First World War* (Cambridge: Cambridge University Press, 2008), 1–8. See C. Pennell, *A Kingdom United: Popular Responses to the Outbreak of the First World War in Britain and Ireland* (Oxford: Oxford University Press, 2012).
3. C. Gowdy-Wygant, *Cultivating Victory: The Women's Land Army and the Victory Garden Movement* (Pittsburgh: University of Pittsburgh Press, 2013), 10–11.
4. P. Horn, *Rural Life in England in the First World War* (New York: St Martin's Press, 1984), 81–2, 72–86, 136.
5. Dewey, *British Agriculture in the First World*, 240–1, 242.
6. A. Marwick, *The Deluge: British Society and the First World War* (London: Norton, 1970), 92. Marwick expanded his emancipation thesis in his *Women at War* (London: Fontana, 1977), which was a further spur to feminist revisionism. See G. Braybon, *Women Workers in the First World War* (London: Routledge, 1981), 105–9, 148–9; S. Boston, *Women Workers and the Trade Union Movement* (London: Davis-Poynter, 1981), 96–130, 132–4; J. Lewis, *Women in England* (London: Wheatsheaf, 1984), 145–58; G. Braybon and P. Summerfield, *Out of the Cage: Women's Experiences in Two World Wars* (London: Routledge, 1987), 1–7, 77–8, 111–13, 129; A. Woollacott, *On Her their Lives Depend: Munitions Workers in the Great War* (Berkeley, CA: University of California Press, 1994), 1–14, 188–92, 214–16; D. Thom, *Nice Girls and Rude Girls: Women Workers in World War I* (London: I. B. Tauris, 1998), 53–74, 203–6; C. Culleton, *Working Class Culture, Women, and Britain, 1914–1921* (London: St Martin's Press, 1999), 4–5, 51–75.
7. D. Cannadine, *The Decline and Fall of the British Aristocracy* (New Haven, CT: Yale University Press, 1990), 9, 99, 126.
8. Woollacott, *On Her their Lives Depend*, 14–15, 215–16. For a different interpretation of the role of women in the First World War see S. Pyecroft, 'British Working Woman and the First World War', *Historian* 56.4 (1994): 699.
9. See N. Mansfield, *English Farmworkers and Local Patriotism, 1900–1930* (Farnham: Ashgate, 2001), 127.

1 Answering the Call: The Formation of the Women's Land Army

1. C. S. Orwin and E. H. Whetham, *History of British Agriculture, 1846–1914* (Newton Abbot: David & Charles, 1971), 341–2; P. Dewey, *British Agriculture*

in the First World War (London: Routledge, 1989), 15–17; P. Dewey, *War and Progress: Britain, 1914–1945* (London: Longman, 1997), 19; A. Offer, *The First World War: An Agrarian Interpretation* (Oxford: Clarendon Press, 1989), 93; J. Sheail, 'Land Improvement and Reclamation: The Experiences of the First World War in England and Wales', *Agricultural History Review* 24: 2 (1976): 111; P. Dewey, 'Nutrition and Living Standards in Wartime Britain', in *The Upheaval of War: Family, Work and Welfare in Europe, 1914–1918*, ed. R. Wall and J. Winter (Cambridge: Cambridge University Press, 1988), 201.

2. T. H. Middleton, *Food Production in War* (London: Oxford Clarendon Press, 1923), 86–97.

3. Orwin and Whetham, *History of British Agriculture*, 341–2; Dewey, *British Agriculture in the First World War*, 15–17; Dewey, *War and Progress*, 19. The only executive action of note in the first 18 months of the war was the establishment of a Sugar Commission (August 1914). Dewey, 'Nutrition and Living Standards in Wartime Britain', 201.

4. M. Barnett, *British Food Policy during the First World War* (Boston: George Allen & Unwin, 1985), xviii–xix, 63–5.

5. Dewey, *War and Progress*, 27.

6. T. Wilson, *The Myriad Faces of War: Britain and the Great War, 1914–1918* (Cambridge: Polity Press, 1986), 536.

7. R. Houh, *The Great War at Sea, 1914–1918* (Oxford: Oxford University Press, 1984), 307–8.

8. D. Cannadine, *The Decline and Fall of the British Aristocracy* (New Haven, CT: Yale University Press, 1990), 72–3.

9. B. Hibbard, *Effects of the Great War Upon Agriculture in the United States and Great Britain* (New York: Oxford University Press, 1919), 183; Middleton, *Food Production in War*, 176–80; Lord Ernle, *English Farming: Past and Present* (London: Frank Cass & Co., 1961), 403–8; A. F. Cooper, *British Agricultural Policy, 1912–1936: A Study in Conservative Politics* (Manchester: Manchester University Press, 1989), 1, 22–30; M. Olson, *The Economics of the Wartime Shortage: A History of British Food Supplies in the Napoleonic War and in World Wars I and II* (Durham, NC: Duke University Press, 1963), 73–7, 93–9, 115. The Board of Agriculture was created in 1889 and during the war it was responsible for all agricultural matters, including food safety. The Ministry of Food on the other hand was created in December 1916 to regulate the supply and consumption of food in the counties, as well as to encourage food production. Orwin and Whetham, *History of British Agriculture, 1846–1914*, 182; Middleton, *Food Production in War*, 103.

10. 'Land Improvements for Britain', *Daily News*, 15 October 1914.

11. Cooper, *British Agricultural Policy*, 22–3; Dewey, *British Agriculture in the First World War*, 23–24; Wilson, *The Myriad Faces of War*, 163, 216.

12. Report of the Devon Farmers' Union, 22 December 1914, Devon Record Office (DRO), Fortescue of Castle Hill, 1262M/114.

13. Offer, *The First World War: An Agrarian Interpretation*, 91.

14. Report of Farm Holdings for the County of Devon, 21 August 1914, DRO, Fortescue of Castle Hill, 1262M/L/OD/138; 'Women on the Land: Wages – Are They High Enough? Many Difficulties', *The Sheffield Daily Telegraph*, 1 June 1916.

15. J. Brown, 'Agricultural Policy and the National Farmers' Union, 1908–1939', in *Agriculture and Politics in England, 1815–1939*, ed. R. J. Wordie (New York: St Martin's Press, 2000), 182.
16. Dewey, *British Agriculture in the First World War*, 24–7. Milner Committee Report on Home Production of Food, 28 December 1915, The National Archives (TNA), MAF 42/9/3.
17. Dewey, *British Agriculture in the First World War*, 26–8.
18. Devon War Agricultural Committee, 29 December 1915, DRO, Fortescue of Castle Hill, 1262M/L138.
19. Milner Committee Report on Home Production of Food, 28 December 1915, TNA, MAF 42/9/3.
20. Dewey, *British Agriculture in the First World War*, 29–30.
21. J. Kendle, *Ireland and the Federal Solution: The Debate over the United Kingdom Constitution, 1870–1921* (Kingston: McGill-Queen's Press, 1989), 180–2; I. Chambers, *The Chamberlains, the Churchills and Ireland, 1874–1922* (London: Cambria Press, 2006), 283–4.
22. Lord Selborne to H. H. Asquith, 12 July 1915, TNA, LAB 2/172/LE1823/81/1915. See B. White, 'Feeding the War Effort: Agricultural Experiences in First World War Devon', *Agricultural History Review* 58 (2010): 95–112.
23. Lord Selborne to Mr Campbell, 14 September 1915, TNA, MAF 39/23.
24. 'War Agricultural Committees: County Committees', TNA, 15 September 1915, Board of Trade, MAF 39/23. See also J. Grigg, *Lloyd George: War Leader 1916–1918* (London: Penguin, 2005), 129.
25. 'Food Prospects in 1917', TNA, 30 October 1917, CAB 24/2; 'Food Prospects in 1917', TNA, November 1916, CAB 24/2.
26. 'War Agricultural Committees: County Committees', 15 September 1915, TNA, MAF 39/23.
27. Selborne to T. H. Middleton, 13 November 1915, TNA, MAF 39/23.
28. See B. White, 'Volunteerism and Early Recruitment Strategies in Devonshire, August 1914–December 1915', *Historical Journal* 53 (2009): 651–2.
29. 'Report of progress of forming county committees for agricultural labour and on the work of these committees', 21 March 1915, TNA, LAB 2/172/LE1823/81/1915.
30. 'Report of progress of forming county committees for agricultural labour and on the work of these committees', 1 April 1915, TNA, LAB 2/172/LE1823/81/1915.
31. 'Labour on Farms Conference between Walter Runciman and Earl of Selborne, and the County Councils Association', TNA, Board of Trade, 16 June 1915, LAB 2/172/LE1823/81/1915.
32. 'Farmers' Woes', 6 July 1915, *Western Morning News*; 'Farmers' Labour: Swansea', *North Devon Herald*, 17 May 1917.
33. Mansfield, *English Farmworkers and Local Patriotism*, 124, 176–7.
34. County Executive Committee, 26 December 1916, DRO, Lord Fortescue Papers, 1262M/L151 Bundle 27.
35. Devon War Agricultural Committee, 23 March 1917, TNA, MAF 80/4998; A Farmer, 'The Farmer's Position', *Western Times*, 9 March 1917.
36. Conference between Runciman, Selborne, and County Council Associations regarding Labour on Farms, 16 June 1915, TNA, LAB 2/172/LE1823/81/1915.
37. 'Circular to the Secretaries of the County War Agricultural Committees', 29 November 1915, TNA, MAF 59/1.

38. Corn Production Act, 1917, Agricultural Wages Board (England and Wales), 1919, The Women's Library, 7DMB10; A. C. Franklin to Miss Barton, 24 December 1918, Food Production Department, The Women's Library, 7DMB10.
39. 'Circular to the Secretaries of the County War Agricultural Committees', 29 November 1915, TNA, MAF 59/1.
40. 'Circular to the Secretaries of the County War Agricultural Committees', 29 November 1915, TNA, MAF 59/1.
41. Michel Augé-Laribé and Pierre Pinot, *Agriculture and Food Policy in France during the War* (New Haven, CT: Yale University Press, 1927), 40. In French propaganda the female peasant working in the field became a symbol of French heroism and strength. See Margaret H. Darrow, *French Women and the First World War: War Stories of the Home Front* (New York: Berg, 2000), 178–9; 'Women on the Land in France: State Helps Patriotic Effort', *The Evening Standard,* 10 January 1917. M. P. A. Hankey, Secretary to the War Cabinet, was also impressed by the role of women in French agriculture and reported on their work in July 1915. See C. Twinch, *Women on the Land: Their Story during Two World Wars* (Cambridge: Lutterworth Press, 1991), 1.
42. Surrey Committee for Women and Farm Labour, 26 February 1916, The Women's Library, 2/LS/WF205; M. Gosse to Noeline Baker, 24 February 1916, The Women's Library, 2/LS/WF205.
43. 'Work of Women's War Agriculture Committees, Week Ending August 1916', August 1916, TNA, MAF 59/1.
44. P. Horn, *Rural Life in England in the First World War* (New York: St Martin's Press, 1984), 118.
45. Madeleine Greenwood, 'The Women's War Service Legion: Horticulture Section', *The Common Cause,* 17 May 1918, 52.
46. 'The Women's Farm and Garden Union', *The Ladies' Field,* 16 November 1915; 'Women and their Work: Short Training', 16 September 1916, *The Daily Express*; 'Improving Prospect for the Poultry Farmer; Short Training', Farm and Garden Union, *The Daily Express,* 16 October 1915.
47. 'Women and Farming: Need for Adequate Training', *Hereford Times,* 10 July 1915.
48. 'Circular to the Secretaries of the County War Agricultural Committees', 29 November 1915, TNA, MAF 59/1.
49. Report of Women's Employment Organisations, 4 October 1916, TNA, MAF 59/1.
50. Philip Cambray, 'War Work at Home: Employment of Women on Farms, Growing Demand', *The Standard,* 12 June 1915.
51. Margaret Farquharson, 'Women and the Land', *Sunday Times,* 31 December 1916. Women of 'gentle birth' refers to women of high social status, implying that they have acquired the proper manners and behaviours of the upper class. This definition was meant to exclude working-class women.
52. Bernard Wale, 'Women Workers on the Land', *Western Independent,* 31 December 1916.
53. Training Women in Farm Work Report, Board of Agriculture, TNA, MAF 59/1, 30 September 1916.
54. Hereford War Agricultural Committee, Successful Scheme of Women Working on the Land in Gangs or Parties, 8 October 1916, TNA, MAF 59/1.
55. Mrs Thorno to Women's Agricultural Committee, 23 June 1916, TNA, MAF 59/1.

56. 'No Men for Farms: Why Suitable Women are Scarce. Compulsion for all Workers?', *The Daily Express*, 16 June 1916; 'Success Achieved', 2 June 1916, *The Surrey Express*; 'Women at Men's Tasks: Some Difficulties of Employment', *The Times*, 2 June 1916; 'Why Women Won't Go to the Land', *The Glasgow Weekly*, 25 October 1916; '20,000 Women Needed', *The People*, 11 June 1916; 'Women on the Land: Farmers' Difficulties in Glamorgan', *The Western Mail*, 20 October 1916; 'The Flapper Farmer: Devon Girl as a Champion Land-Worker', *The Daily Sketch*, 1 June 1916.
57. Circular to the Secretaries of the County War Agricultural Committees, 29 November 1915, TNA, MAF 59/1.
58. Organisation of the Women's County Committees, 19 October 1916, TNA, MAF 59/1.
59. Report on the Women's County Committees, 4 October 1916, TNA, MAF 59/1.
60. Dewey, *British Agriculture in the First World War*, 50–5.
61. While Dewey notes that the highest number of women registered was in Durham with 4,938, the report indicates higher numbers in Cornwall. Dewey, *British Agriculture in the First World War*, 53; 'Summary of the World of the Women's War Agricultural Committees for the Year Ending 1916', 4 October 1916, TNA, MAF 59/1.
62. Dewey, *British Agriculture in the First World War*, 56.
63. Meriel Talbot to WWACs, 4 June 1916, TNA, MAF 59/1.
64. Meriel Talbot to Lord Selborne, 5 May 1916, TNA, MAF 59/1.
65. Register report for Women in Agriculture, Board of Agriculture, 4 October 1916, TNA, MAF 59/1; Board of Trade Employment of Women in Agriculture Report, 15 September 1916, TNA, MAF 59/1.
66. Mr Sommerville to J. Whilputte, 21 September 1916, TNA, MAF 59/1.
67. Board of Trade Employment of Women in Agriculture Report, 15 September 1916, TNA, MAF 59/1. The question of substitute labour fits in to a larger debate about workers' rights and the value of state intervention into industry. See Gerry Rubin, *War, Law and Labour* (Oxford: Clarendon Press, 1987), 95–6, 138–9; J. N. Horne, *Labour at War: France and Britain, 1914–1918* (Oxford: Oxford University Press, 1991), 78–83, 295–301. Also see B. Waites, *A Class Society at War: England 1914–1918* (New York: St Martin's Press, 1987), 200–1; K. Grieves, *The Politics of Manpower, 1914–18* (Manchester: Manchester University Press, 1988), 4, 70–1, 181–99.
68. Report from Board of Trade on the Women's Agricultural Committees, 14 February 1916, TNA, MAF 59/1.
69. Memorandum in Regard to Women's Work in Agriculture, Board of Trade, 4 August 1916, TNA, MAF 59/1.
70. M. Kirby, 'Industry, Agriculture and Trade Unions', in *The First World War in British History*, ed. Stephen Constantine et al. (New York: St Martin's Press, 1995), 63, 64.
71. Jocelyn Dunlop to Noeline Baker, 2 March 1916, The Women's Library, 2/LS/WF205.

2   Female Preparedness, Male Authority: Organisers and the Board of Agriculture

1. R. E. Prothero, *Whippingham to Westminster* (London: Murray, 1938), 318.
2. Christabel S. Orwin and Edith H. Whetham, *History of British Agriculture, 1846–1914* (Newton Abbot: David & Charles, 1971), 182; T. H. Middleton, *Food Production in War* (London: Oxford Clarendon Press, 1923), 103.

3. Lord Ernle, *English Farming: Past and Present* (London: Frank Cass & Co., 1961), 403–8.
4. Minute Books 1917, Glamorgan War Executive Committee, Glamorgan Archives, GC WG/1-3.
5. Although the Women's Branch was placed under the authority of the FPD, both departments were still under the authority of the Board of Agriculture.
6. J. Bush, *Edwardian Ladies and Imperial Power* (London: Leicester University Press, 2000), 92. The Victoria League was an apolitical, predominantly female, imperial propaganda society that promoted colonial loyalty to the mother country, but accepted self-governance in the dominions. The League encouraged the participation of women in colonial politics and endorsed women's capabilities outside of the home, but worked within traditional gender norms and the societal limitations of the Edwardian period. See Eliza Riedl, 'Women, Gender and the Promotion of Empire: The Victoria League, 1901–1914', *The Historical Journal* 45 (September 2002): 569–99. Talbot never envisioned a complete separation of the sexes in League membership and believed that the League would benefit from male expertise and support, a view that she carried into her war work. Nevertheless, Talbot was a life-long suffragette. Meriel Talbot, diary, 22 October 1910, Kent Archives, Talbot family papers, U1612 F222; Meriel Talbot to Lord Gladstone, 8 March 1912, Gladstone Papers, British Library, MSS Add. 46072 fo. 201. Supporters and new branches of the Victoria League publically celebrated Talbot's leadership and expansion of the League between 1901 and 1914. See 'Victoria League: Reception to Miss Talbot', *The Mercury*, 13 January 1910.
7. Edith Lyttelton, diary, 10 September 1900, Churchill College Archives Centre, Chandos Papers, Chan. 6/3.
8. Lyttelton was a determined nationalist who believed that British authority was dependent on its strength and health at home. Lyttelton saw separation between Britain and its colonial holdings, which she believed was essential to the health of the mother country, but advocated a mutually beneficial industrial and economic relationship. Edith Lyttelton to Viscount Milner, 9 July 1903, Bodleian Library, Milner Papers, MSS 216/102.
9. Labour Division Report, Food Production, Employment Agriculture, 10 October 1917, TNA, CAB 24/28; Labour Report Food Production Department, Women's Branch, 22 August 1917, TNA, CAB 24/24.
10. Agricultural Executive and District Committees, no date, TNA, MAF 42/2.
11. A. F. Cooper, *British Agricultural Policy, 1912–1936: A Study in Conservative Politics* (Manchester: Manchester University Press, 1989), 1, 22–30.
12. M. Olson, *The Economics of the Wartime Shortage: A History of British Food Supplies in the Napoleonic War and in World Wars I and II* (Durham, NC: Duke University Press, 1963), 73–7.
13. Labour on Farms Conference Between Walter Runciman, Earl of Selborne and Count Council Associations, 16 June 1915, Board of Agriculture, TNA, LAB 2/172/LE1823/1915.
14. Village women who worked with group leaders were employed through the National Service Department and not the Land Army proper.
15. Group Leaders are also known as Gang Leaders. Instructions to Employment Exchange Managers and Agricultural Co-operating Officers, Board of Agriculture, 21 March 1917, TNA, LAB 2/172/LE 1823/81/1915.

16. Responsibilities of Women's County Committees, 20 October 1916, Board of Agriculture and Fisheries, TNA, MAF 59/1; Women's County Committees and Associated Committees, 20 October 1917, Board of Agriculture and Fisheries, TNA, MAF 59/1.
17. Organisation of the Women's County Committees, 19 October 1916, Board of Agriculture and Fisheries, MAF 59/1.
18. Report on the Work of Women's War Agricultural Committees for the Year Ending August 1916, 4 October 1916, Board of Agriculture and Fisheries, TNA, MAF 59/1.
19. Organisation of the Women's County Committees, 19 October 1916, Board of Agriculture and Fisheries, TNA, MAF 59/1; Meriel Talbot to Organising Secretaries, 12 March 1918, TNA, MAF 42/8.
20. Lyttelton to Lady Mackworth, 2 August 1917, TNA, NATS 1/1279; Talbot to Miss Crowdy, 31 January 1918, TNA, MAF 42/8.
21. Ministry of Labour, Employment Department, Employment Exchanges, no date, TNA, LAB 2/172/LE1823/81/1915.
22. For example, Dorset did not have a WWAC and instead dealt with agricultural matters through various sub-committees. Dorset declined to establish a WWAC because the Farmer's Association for the county found that working with the Labour Exchanges and Village Registrars was cumbersome and largely unsuccessful. Meeting of Representatives of Dorset County Council and Farmer's Union Association, 30 November 1916, TNA, LAB 2/172/LE1823/1915.
23. Report on Organisational Problems Land Army and Women's War Agricultural Committees, Board of Agriculture and Fisheries, 20 February 1917, TNA, MAF 59/1.
24. Miss MacDonald to Meriel Talbot, 21 May 1917, TNA, MAF 59/1; Miss Hepburn to Meriel Talbot, 6 June 1917, TNA, MAF 59/1.
25. Miss Pullar to Edith Lyttelton, 20 July 1917, TNA, MAF 59/1.
26. H. Bentwich, *If I Forget Thee: Some Chapters of Autobiography, 1912–1920* (London: Paul Elek Books, 1973), 115.
27. Training Test Instructions for Land Workers, Women's Branch, 18 November 1917, TNA, MAF 42/8; Percentage of Applicants Surviving the Test, Women's Branch, no date, TNA, MAF 42/8.
28. Miss Biddle to Meriel Talbot, 23 May 1917, TNA, MAF 59/1.
29. Miss Baker to Meriel Talbot, 1 June 1917, TNA, MAF 59/1.
30. Meriel Talbot to Organising Secretaries, 8 May 1917, TNA, MAF 42/2.
31. Report of Women's Employment, Board of Agriculture and Fisheries, 29 September 1916, TNA, MAF 59/1.
32. Mrs Jones to Meriel Talbot, 13 July 1917, TNA, MAF 59/1.
33. The National Service Department was responsible for the advertising campaign for the Women's Land Army, with the assistance of the Publicity Department of the Women's Branch (see Chapter 3).
34. Report of the Organising Secretaries to Meriel Talbot, 18 July 1917, TNA, MAF 59/1.
35. Training of Women in Farm Work, 4 October 1916, TNA, MAF 59/1; Report on Women's Employment, 4 October 1916, TNA, MAF 59/1; Report on Training Centres and Women's Education, 7 September 1917, TNA, MAF 59/1.
36. Farm Training in Report Food Production Department, 17 June 1919, TNA, CAB 24/82.

37. Women's Branch Training Centres in the Counties, England and Wales Only, 1 March 1917, TNA, CAB 24/7; Report Board of Agriculture for Scotland, Women's Land Army, 23 May 1917, TNA, CAB 24/24. For farms located in remote areas farmers were responsible to secure appropriate accommodations for Land Girls, preferably in the farmhouse or in a cottage.
38. Report on the Women's Land Army issued to the Food Production Department by Neville Chamberlain, Director-General of National Service, 10 May 1917, TNA, CAB 24/13.
39. Durham to Rey, November 1917, Ministry of Labour, TNA, NATS 1/1298; Memorandum to the District Commissioners and Sub-Commissioners, Women's Branch, 30 March 1917, TNA, MAF 42/3.
40. M. Winter, *Rural Politics: Policies for Agriculture, Forestry, and the Environment* (New York: Routledge, 1996), 85; Lord Ernle, 'The Food Campaign of 1916–18', *Journal of the Royal Agricultural Society* 82 (1921): 1–48. For more on Prothero's attitudes toward agricultural reform and government intervention in the industry see R. E. Prothero, *The Pioneers and Progress of English Farming* (New York: Longmans, 1888).
41. Corbridge and District Farmers' Club and President of the Board of Agriculture and Fisheries, 6 July 1917, TNA, MAF 42/3.
42. WWAC Withdrawals and Rejections for Land Service, 24 November 1917, TNA, NATS 1/1296; Talbot to Dunham, 26 December 1917, TNA, NATS 1/1298; Number of Women offering themselves for service in the Women's Land Army, Report Food Production Department, 21 June 1917, Women's Branch, TNA, CAB 24/17.
43. Edith Lyttelton to Sir George Riddell, 19 November 1917, TNA, NATS 1/1298.
44. Women's War Agriculture Committee and Food Production Department. Land Army Scheme, 24 May 1917, TNA, MAF 42/3. This work was generally done by gang leaders who were responsible to recruit, organize, and place unskilled and untrained village women on local farms. Gang leaders did this work with the assistance of the Village Registrar – normally a woman of gentle birth.
45. Minutes of Meeting Held at the Food Production Department, Women's Branch, 5 November 1917, TNA, MAF 42/8; Meriel Talbot to M. Dunham, 19 November 1917, Women's Branch, TNA, MAF 42/8; M. Dunham to Meriel Talbot, 22 November 1917, Food Production Department, TNA, MAF 42/8.
46. Lucy Whitman to Sir Auckland Geddes, 16 November 1917, TNA, NATS 1/1298.
47. Report on meeting of Representatives of WWACs and WACs to Meriel Talbot, 5 June 1918, TNA, MAF 59/1.
48. Meriel Talbot to Organising Secretaries, 26 May 1918, TNA, MAF 42/3.
49. Meriel Talbot to Travelling Inspectors, 10 June 1918, TNA, MAF 42/4.
50. Meriel Talbot to County War Agricultural Executive Committees, 30 March 1917, TNA, MAF 42/7.
51. Meriel Talbot to Chairs of WWACs, Special Probationary Training Centres, 6 July 1918, TNA, MAF 42/4.
52. Meriel Talbot to Organising Secretaries, Billeting of Land Girls. Girls' Friendly Society, 22 June 1917, TNA, MAF 42/3. For more on the Girls' Friendly Society see A. L. Money, *History of the Girls' Friendly Society* (London: Wells Gardner & Company, 1911), 1–11.

53. The Women's Land Army operated on a budget determined by the Board of Agriculture. Specific numbers as to the operating budget of the Women's Branch or the Women's Land Army do not exist; however, the Board of Agriculture was responsible to cover expenses associated with the scheme, including training, housing, offices expenses, travel, and publicity. The members of the WWACs were volunteers, as were the Organising Secretaries, but all manual labour positions within the Land Army were paid. Report on Rates and Pay and Terms of Service Food Production Department, 2 April 1917, TNA, MAF 42/1.
54. T. L. Heath to Roland Prothero, 21 June 1918, Treasury Chambers, TNA, MAF 42/8.
55. Meriel Talbot to Rowland Prothero, no date, Women's Branch, TNA, MAF 42/8.
56. K. H. Armitstead to Meriel Talbot, 30 September 1918, Food Production Department, TNA, MAF 42/8.
57. Food Production Department Report on Agriculture, Women's Branch, Women's Institutes, 11 September 1918, TNA, CAB 24/63.
58. Back to the Land movement refers to a period in the nineteenth century when the land and the people who relied on it were out of balance, meaning that people who owned land were not producing food for daily consumption for themselves and others around them. Politically, reformers like Joseph Chamberlain attempted to restore the imbalance through Acts of Parliament that protected land tenure and kept land in the hands of the privileged. See G. Parker, *Citizenship, Contingency and the Countryside: Rights, Culture, Land and the Environment* (London: Routledge, 2002), 98–9.
59. Women's Institutes and Promotion of Women on the Land, Report Food Production Department, 22 April 1919, Women's Branch, TNA, CAB 24/78.
60. First Annual Meeting of the National Federation of Women's Institutes to December 31, 1917, NFWI, The Women's Library 14/59/31.
61. M. Morgan, 'The Women's Institutes Movement: The Acceptable Face of Feminism', in *This Working-Day World: Women's Lives and Culture(s) in Britain*, ed. Sybil Oldfield (Bristol: Taylor & Francis, 1994), 30–1.
62. Rules for the National Federation of Women's Institutes of England and Wales Passed by the General Annual Meeting of October 1918, no date, NFWI, The Women's Library 15/40/09; First Annual Report of the National Federation of Women's Institutes to December 1917, no date, NFWI, The Women's Library 14/53/41.
63. Women's Institutes and the Land Army, Meeting of Secretaries of the Women's Institutes, 9 November 1918, NFWI, TNA, MAF 42/3; Women's Institutes, Report Food Production Department, 7 October 1919, Women's Branch, TNA, CAB 24/89.
64. Welfare Officers and Land Army, Minute Sheets of Food Production Department, 23 October 1918, TNA, MAF 42/8.
65. Duties of a Land Army Welfare Officer, Women's War Agriculture Committee, no date, TNA, MAF 42/8.
66. Meriel Talbot to WWACs, Appointment of Land Army Officers, 20 June 1918, TNA, MAF 42/8; Meriel Talbot to WWACs, Land Army Officers and Welfare Scheme, 9 July 1918, TNA, MAF 42/8.
67. Duties of a Land Army Welfare Officer, Women's War Agriculture Committee, no date, TNA, MAF 42/8.

68. The Land Army and Need for More Effective Control, Food Production Department, 18 June 1918, TNA, MAF 42/8.
69. Food Production Department and Ministry of Labour report on Control of Labour under the Women's Branch, 10 May 1917, TNA, CAB 24/13.
70. Memorandum of 1917 Issued to the Women's Branch and Ministry of Labour, Women's Land Service Corps. Land Army, June 1918, TNA, MAF 42/4; Memorandum with Regard to the Organisation of Women's Work in Agriculture, 3 August 1917, TNA, MAF 59/1.
71. Minutes of Merioneth Agricultural Executive Committee, 15 September 1919, TNA, MAF 80/4951.
72. Report on Wages Given to Women of the Land Army, 7 October 1919, Women's Branch, TNA, CAB 24/13. Past precedent made some farmers reluctant to pay women a fair wage. See Wages and Hours of Labour 1906, no date, Board of Trade, TNA, LAB 41/1578. For more on women's work and wages before the war see G. Braybon, *Women Workers in the First World War* (London: Croom Helm London, 1981), 15–40.
73. H. Kenworthy to Meriel Talbot, 16 June 1918, Women's Branch, TNA, MAF 42/8.
74. M. Story and P. Childs, *British Cultural Identities* (London: Routledge, 2002), 120. See N. Verdon, *Rural Women Workers in Nineteenth-Century England: Gender, Work, Wages* (New York: Boydell Press, 2002), 92, 161.
75. Some farmers were blacklisted for their treatment of female workers. See Bentwich, *If I Forget Thee*, 111.
76. For more on labour productivity in the pre-war years see E. H. Hunt, 'Labour Productivity in English Agriculture, 1850–1914', *The Economic History Review* 20 (August 1967): 280–92. For more on labour relations in the late nineteenth and early twentieth centuries see Ernle, *English Farming: Past and Present*, 405–7. Duties of a Land Army Welfare Officer, Women's War Agriculture Committee, no date, TNA, MAF 42/8; Meriel Talbot to Mrs Armitstead, 24 August 1918, Women's Branch, TNA, MAF 42/8; H. Kenworthy to Meriel Talbot, 16 June 1918, Women's Branch, TNA, MAF 42/8.
77. J. Sheail, 'The Role of the War Agricultural and Executive Committees in the Food Production Campaign of 1915–1918 in England and Wales', *Agricultural Administration* 1 (1974): 142–3.
78. Horn, *Rural Life in England*, 81–2, 72–86, 136.
79. Changes to Agriculture in Wartime, Wiltshire Agricultural Executive Committee, January–March 1918, Wiltshire and Swindon Archives, F1/100/23/4-5.
80. Relationship between Women's War Agricultural Committees and the Agricultural Executive Committees, 9 August 1918, Food Production Department, TNA, MAF 42/8.
81. Reports of Essex Women's War Agricultural Committee, November–December 1917, Essex Record Office, D/Z 45/15/4-6; Reports of Berkshire War Agricultural Committee, Women's Sub-Committee, 28 May 1918, Berkshire Record Office, WA/5/2/7; Reports Oxfordshire War Agricultural Committee, Women's Labour, Oxfordshire Record Office, CC1/17/2; Reports Bedfordshire War Agricultural Committee, Women's Sub-Committee, May–June 1917, Bedfordshire and Luton Archives, PK8/1/8/3.
82. Minute Books Worcestershire Agricultural Executive Committee, 1917–1918, Worcestershire Archive and Archeology Service, BA 179/6-9.

83. The Land Army Organisation and Control, 18 September 1918, Food Production Department, TNA, MAF 42/8.
84. Report Operational Costs of Land Army Scheme, Treasury Chambers, 21 June 1918, TNA, MAF 42/8; Meriel Talbot to Superintendent of Passenger Traffic, May 1918, TNA, MAF 42/3.

3   Gender, Service, Patriotism: Promoting the Land Army in Wartime Britain

1. G. Clarke, *The Women's Land Army: A Portrait* (Bristol: Sansome & Company, 2008), 12.
2. Report of the War Cabinet on Women in Industry, 1919, TNA, Cmd. 135. While the total number of women employed in munitions work is uncertain, it is possible that the number reached one million by the spring of 1918. In comparison, a small number of women pursued employment with the WLA, the Voluntary Aid Detachment, or the First Aid Nursing Yeomanry. This number is likely a reflection of the expansion of the industry during the war and the pressing need for workers. A. Woollacott, *On Her their Lives Depend: Munitions Workers in the Great War* (Berkeley, CA: University of California Press, 1994), 19; Iris A. Cummins, 'The Woman Engineer', *The Englishwoman* 46 (April 1920): 38.
3. National Service, 'Women! Enrol for Service on the Land', 1915, NATS 1/1308.
4. J. Harris, *Private Lives, Public Spirit: A Social History of Britain, 1870–1914* (Oxford: Oxford University Press, 1993), 67–8.
5. S. Grayzel, 'Nostalgia, Gender and the Countryside: Placing the "Land Girl" in First World War Britain', *Rural History* 10: 2 (1999): 156–7, 159. See B. White, 'Sowing the Seeds of Patriotism: The Women's Land Army in First World War Devon', *The Local Historian* 41 (2011): 13–27.
6. See Arthur Marwick, *The Deluge: British Society and the First World War* (London: Norton, 1970), 300.
Some of the major works that deal with the social and cultural impact of the war as a whole since Marwick are: J. M. Winter, *The Great War and the British People* (London: Macmillan, 1985), 249–79, 261–7; T. Wilson, *The Myriad Faces of War: Britain and the Great War, 1914–1918* (Cambridge: Polity Press, 1986), 751–9; J. M. Bourne, *Britain and the Great War, 1914–1918* (London: Edward Arnold, 1989), 199–240; J. Winter, *Sites of Memory, Sites of Mourning* (Cambridge: Cambridge University Press, 1995), 29–77; G. DeGroot, *Blighty: British Society in the Era of the Great War* (London: Longman, 1996), 257–70; P. Fussell, *The Great War and Modern Memory* (Oxford: Oxford University Press, 1976), 3–35; S. Hynes, *A War Imagined: The First World War and English Culture* (London: Bodley Head, 1990), 57–98.
7. 'Women's Work in War-Time: Girl Gardeners as Substitutes for Men', *The Graphic*, 27 May 1915; 'Women Gardeners: Temporary Posts to Fill Absent Men's Places', *The Evening Standard and Chronicle*, 8 January 1916; 'Super Cowgirls: Work on the Land for Period of the War', *The Daily Chronicle*, 6 January 1916.
8. *All the Year Round. A Weekly Journal Conducted by Charles Dickens, with which is incorporated Household Words* (London, 1866), 588.

9. Braybon, *Women Workers in the First World War*, 108. 'Feminisation' generally applied to office and shop work where women were seen in increasing numbers in the early twentieth century. The process was gradual and aroused no social concern.
10. Board of Agriculture Report: 'How to Enrol [*sic*] Country Women for War Service in their Spare Time', 22 March 1916, DRO, Fortescue of Castle Hill, 1262L/L14.
11. 'Girls Who Play at War Work', *Sunday Pictorial*, 24 March 1918; 'Women's Labour', *Mark Lane Express*, 17 September 1917; 'A Holiday on the Land', *Birmingham Mercury*, 30 April 1915.
12. See War Cabinet Reports for the Women's Branch held at TNA, March 1917 – November 1918, TNA, CAB 23 and Reports on the Food Supply of the United Kingdom, January 1916–November 1918, TNA, CAB 24.
13. Circular letter to the Women's County Farm Labour Committee, 5 December 1916, DRO, 1262M/L141; Organisation of the Women's County Committees, 19 October 1916, TNA, MAF 59/1.
14. 'Women on the Land: The Value of Training', *The Daily News and Leader*, 6 October 1915; Meriel Talbot to WWAC, 'Special Training Centres', 6 July 1916, The Museum of English Rural Life (MERL), SR WFGA/9/5; 'Training of National Service Volunteers', Food Production Department, 21 August 1917, MERL, SR WFGA/9/5.
15. Report on Conference between Representatives of County Committees and The Right Hon. The Earl of Selborne: 'Women's Labour on the Land', 31 December 1915, DRO, Fortescue of Castle Hill, 1262M/L141.
16. Braybon, *Women Workers in the First World War*, 168.
17. 'The Happy Ploughmaid', no date, WWI: Home Front and Land Girls Farming, The Women's Library, 10/51; 'Society Women as Dairymaids and Hoppers', no date, WWI: Home Front. Land Girls (Farming MISC), The Women's Library, 10/51; 'A Judge's Daughter Works on a Sussex Farm', MERL, D DX892/2.
18. Interim Report, Board of Trade, 28 October 1915, TNA, MAF 42/8.
19. Memorandum on the Training of Women for Employment in Practical Farm Work during the War, Cornwall County Council's Scheme, August 1915, TNA, MAF 59/1.
20. Instruction to Employment Exchange Managers for the Women's War Agricultural Committees, Scotland, 6 January 1916, TNA, LAB 2/171/ED29202/1916.
21. 'Suggestions for the Recruiting Campaign in Wales for Work on the Land', Conference of the National Service Committee, 12 September 1915, TNA, NATS 1/1279.
22. 'Women in War Work: Agriculture and Labour Needs', Report for Board of Agriculture, 26 November 1915, TNA, MAF 42/9.
23. Training facilities for women tended not to reach capacity. 'War Work at Home: Training Women for the Land: Many Vacancies', *The Standard*, 10 July 1916.
24. Report on Labour Supplies for Devon, Dorset, Somerset, and Cornwall, June 1917, DRO, 1262M/141.
25. Circular to the Secretaries of the County War Agricultural Committees, 29 November 1916, TNA, MAF 59/1.

26. Report of a Conference between Representatives of County Committees and the Right Hon. The Earl of Selborne, 'Women's Labour on the Land', 31 December 1916, 5.
27. S. Ouditt, *Fighting Forces, Writing Women: Identity and Ideology in the First World War* (Chapel Hill, NC: University of North Carolina Press, 1999), 53. The 'women in war work' propaganda campaign initiated by the Board of Trade encouraged women to undertake work of national importance, not just work in agriculture. P. Horn, *Rural Life in England in the First World War* (New York: St Martin's Press, 1984), 113–14.
28. 'Is Womanliness in Danger? Confessions of a Girl on the Land', *Sunday Pictorial*, 24 December 1916.
29. 'Join the Land Army: A Call to the Women of Britain', pamphlet, TNA, NATS 1/1308, 1–3.
30. Women's War Service Committee for Devon, reports for May and June 1917, DRO, 1262M/141.
31. 'To the Women of the Nation', May 1917, MERL, U54 1371 SR WFGA/F/1–2.
32. *The Times*, 7 April 1917. See also National Service Department recruiting poster, '10,000 Women Wanted for Farm Work', TNA, NATS 1/1308.
33. Alice Mildmay, 'Employment of Women on the Land', *The Salcombe Gazette*, 27 April 1917.
34. National Service Department, '10,000 Women Wanted for Farm Work'.
35. National Service Department, '10,000 Women Wanted for Farm Work'.
36. W. E. Shewell-Cooper, *Land Girl: A Handbook for the Women's Land Army* (London: English University Press, 1942), 8–9.
37. Clarke, *The Women's Land Army: A Portrait*, 20.
38. Letter to Prothero, meeting of Food Production Department, Women's Branch, 4 May 1917, TNA, NATS 1/1303; Meriel Talbot to Organising Secretaries, 31 December 1917, MERL, SR WFGA/9/5.
39. Devon War Agricultural Committee, 29 January 1917, TNA, MAF 80/4998.
40. S. Grayzel, *Women and the First World War* (London: Longman, 2002), 42–3.
41. Demonstrations – Cornwall, Women's County War Committee, Report June 1917, MAF 59/1; 'Girl Students in Farm Work Test', no date, WWI: Home Front. Land Girls (Farming MISC), The Women's Library, 10/51.
42. 'Women Land Workers Welcomed by the Lord Mayor at the Mansion House', Women's Land Army at Work, Women's War Work Collection, Imperial War Museums (IWM), SUPP. 40/62.
43. Herefordshire War Agricultural Committee, Agricultural Demonstration for Women's Land Army, May 1917, TNA, MAF 59/1.
44. 'Women Land Workers Welcomed by the Lord Mayor at the Mansion House', Women's Land Army at Work, Women's War Work Collection, IWM, SUPP. 40/62.
45. 'Women Work on the Land: Series of Competitions at Exeter', *The Morning Post*, 29 May 1917.
46. 'Women's Work on the Land: Series of Competitions at Exeter', *The Morning Post*, 29 May 1917; Report on Agricultural Competitions, Alice Mildmay, WWAC, May 1917, DRO, 1262M/141.
47. Joint Conference of the Board of Agriculture, Women's Committees, and Women's Branch on Enrolment and Agricultural Demonstrations for the Women's Land Army, June 1917, TNA, MAF 42/8.

48. 'Girls on the Land: Chaperones and Umbrellas Holders Not Provided', *Daily News and Leader*, 27 May 1916.
49. Kathleen Macleod, 'Women and Farm Work', *The Daily News*, 12 February 1915; 'The Shortage of Farm Labour', *The Morning Post*, 24 May 1916; 'Women in Agriculture', *Eastern Daily*, 2 February 1916; 'Arboath Advisory Committee', *Dundee Courier*, 19 May 1916; 'How to Enrol [sic] Country Women for War Service in their Spare Time', 22 March 1916, DRO, 1262L/ L14; Report on women's labour in war time, Devon Agricultural Committee, WLA, DRO, 1262M/L122.
50. A. Goodwin, 'Early Years of the Trade Unions', in *Women in the Labour Movement: The British Experience*, ed. L. Middleton (London: Croom Helm, 1977), 96–7. See A. Howkins, *Poor Labouring Men: Rural Radicalism in Norfolk* (London: Routledge, 1985); P. Hollis, *Ladies Elect: Women in English Local Government, 1865–1914* (Oxford: Clarendon Press, 1987).
51. Women's Land Army, Agricultural Section, Terms and Conditions of Service, no date, TNA, MAF 42/8; 'Join the Land Army: A Call to the Women of Great Britain', pamphlet, TNA, NATS1/1308.
52. 'Women for Farm Work: Candid Criticism at Totnes Farmers' Meeting', *The Western Guardian*, 3 February 1916.
53. 'Women for Farm Work: Candid Criticism at Totnes Farmers' Meeting', *The Western Guardian*, 3 February 1916; 'Women and Farm Work', *The Weekly News*, 1 January 1916; 'Women's Land Army: Launceston', *The Weekly News*, 27 July 1916.
54. *The Dartmouth & South Hans Chronicle*, 17 March 1916. The use of school children could be troublesome and although they were used on the land throughout the war there were strict regulations in place regarding their employment. *The Western Morning News*, 6 July 1915; *The North Devon Herald*, 17 May 1917. See also 'Duchess of Atholl and Women for the Land: Persuading the Farmers', *The Dundee Advertiser*, 13 April 1917; 'Trained Farm Girls: Obstinate Farmers' Refusal to Employ Them', *The Daily Mail*, 12 May 1917; 'Women Waiting for Work', *Northern Echo*, 12 July 1917; 'Our Stubborn Farmers: Will Not Employ Women or Pay the Minimum Wage', *Sunday Herald*, 13 May 1917; 'An Appeal to Durham Farmers: The Training and Employment of Women Volunteers', *Auckland Chronicle*, 24 May 1917; 'Women and the Land: Substitution Not Sufficiently Quick. Farmers' Prejudice', *Pall Mall Gazette*, 16 December 1916.
55. 'The Reluctant Farmer in Norfolk', 24 May 1917, Women's War Work Collection, IWM, SUPP. 40/62.
56. In Devon the competitions were held in Exeter and the women who participated were from the Seale Haynes Agricultural College. While some demonstrated exceptional skill in milking, during the competitions several women had trouble ploughing in different soil conditions and experienced difficulty running a team of horses that they were unfamiliar with. 'Women at Men's Tasks: Some Difficulties of Employment', *The Times*, 2 June 1916; 'Why Suitable Women Are Scarce', *The Western Daily News*, 14 June 1916; 'Devon Women Who Are Willing to Do Work on Farms: Official Statement', *The Western Times*, 5 May 1916; 'Women's Work on the Land: Series of Competitions at Exeter', *The Morning Post*, 29 May 1917; Report on Agricultural Competitions, Alice Mildmay, WWAC, May 1917, DRO, 1262M/141.

57. 'Patriotism or Profits? Mr. Prothero's Appeal to Farmers', *The Daily Express*, 4 June 1917; 'Sweater's of Women's Labour', *The Western Daily Mercury*, 14 February 1917; 'How to Help on the Land: Poor Farmers!', *The Daily Mirror*, 27 February 1917; 'Farmers' Profits', *Express and Echo*, 8 October 1917; 'Women on the Land', *Totnes Times*, 28 October 1916.

58. 'The Women's Land Army', *The Landswoman*, January 1918 (Vol. 1, No. 1), 2; 'Sticking It!' *The Sheffield Telegraph and Dispatch*, 26 February 1917.

59. 'The Prime Minister's Appeal to Women', January 1917, MERL, SR WFGA/9/5.

60. Report of a Conference between Representatives of County Committees and the Right Hon. The Earl of Selborne, 'Women's Labour on the Land', 31 December 1915, 5–6.

61. Report of a Conference between Representatives of County Committees and the Right Hon. The Earl of Selborne, 'Women's Labour on the Land', 31 December 1915, 5–6.

62. 'The Women's Land Army', *The Landswoman*, January 1918 (Vol. 1, No. 1), 2. Prothero is quoting Walt Whitmans' 'Song of the Open Road'.

63. *The Book of Husbandry* is attributed to Sir Anthony Fitzherbert and is considered to be the first book on agriculture published in the English language.

64. 'Land Lass in Wonderland', *The Landswoman*, July 1918 (Vol. 1, No. 7), 1.

65. See Fussell, *The Great War and Modern Memory*, 231–40.

66. For more on the countryside at war see C. Dakers, *The Countryside at War, 1914–1918* (London: Constable and Company Limited, 1987), 14–15.

67. 'The New Land Lady: Miss Talbot, Revivalist', *The Daily Chronicle*, 15 December 1917.

68. 'To the Women's Land Army', *Casswell's Saturday Journal*, 17 August 1918; 'The New Land Lady: Miss Talbot, Revivalist', *The Daily Chronicle*, 15 December 1917.

69. 'Lure of the Land: Appeal to Liverpool Women. A Month's Recruiting Campaign', no date, WWI: Home Front (Land Girls: MISC), The Women's Library, 10/51; 'Women's Land Army: Recruiting and Badging', March 1918, MERL, D DX892/2.

70. C. Twinch, *Women on the Land: Their Story during Two World Wars* (Cambridge: Lutterworth Press, 1990), 33.

71. 'The Women's Land Army', *The Landswoman*, January 1918 (Vol. 1, No. 1), 28.

72. 'The Women's Land Army: A Jolly Sisterhood', *The Daily News*, 27 May 1918.

73. 'Happiness and Success: Possibilities of Outdoor life for Women', *Bristol Evening Times*, 19 May 1915; 'Outdoor Life for Women: How They Can Live it Happily and Successfully', *The Birmingham Dispatch*, 6 May 1915.

74. Meeting Food Production Department, Women's Branch, 23 May 1918, TNA, MAF 42/8; National Service Committee Report from Arthur Collier, 20 April 1917, TNA, NATS 1/1308.

75. Care of Women in the Counties, Women's Land Army, Leaflet W. 62, TNA, NATS 1/1308.

76. National Service Department (Women's Section), Holiday Resorts Campaign, 6 July 1917, TNA, NATS 1/1308; Holiday Resorts Campaign, Poster W. 52 & W. 60, no date, National Service Department, TNA, NATS 1/1308; Leisure and Recreation, Women's Land Army, Women's Branch, 26 June 1918, TNA, NATS 1/1308.

77. 'The Wartime Bo-Peep', *The Daily Sketch*, 31 May 1916; 'Fair Roses of England as Wartime Farmers', MERL, SR WFGA/9/5; 'In Lively Hope and in Grateful Memory', MERL, SR WFGA/9/5; 'Lady Lumbermen at Lydford', MERL, SR WFGA/9/5.
78. See C. Gowdy-Wygant, *Cultivating Victory: The Women's Land Army and the Victory Garden Movement* (Pittsburg: University of Pittsburg Press, 2013), 37–8.
79. Meriel Talbot to Organising Secretaries, Recruiting, 15 April 1918, MERL, SR WFGA/9/5.
80. N. Joseph and N. Alex, 'The Uniform: A Sociological Perspective', *American Journal of Sociology* 77 (1972): 722–3.
81. D. Thom, *Nice Girls and Rude Girls: Women Workers in World War I* (New York: Tauris & Co., 1998), 178.
82. For more on public perceptions of motherhood, the maternal body, and questions of women's maternal role in wartime, see S. Grayzel, *Women's Identities at War: Gender, Motherhood and Politics in Britain and France during the First World War* (Chapel Hill, NC: University of North Carolina Press, 1999), 50–90.
83. T. McKay, 'The Shortage of Labour: Harvest Work for Women', *Weekly News*, 21 June 1915; 'Women to Work the Land?' *Crediton Chronicle*, 30 December 1916; 'Blackguarded by Farmers', *Western Guardian*, 27 January 1916.
84. National Service, 'Women! Enrol for Service on the Land', 1915, TNA, NATS 1/1308.
85. 'Ready and Capable', no date, WWI: Home Front. Land Girls (Farming MISC), The Women's Library, 10/51; 'The Women's Army', no date, WWI: Home Front. Land Girls (Farming MISC), The Women's Library, 10/51; 'Our Women Foresters', no date, WWI: Home Front. Land Girls (Farming MISC), The Women's Library, 10/51; 'The Foresters' Helpmeets', no date, WWI: Home Front. Land Girls (Farming MISC), The Women's Library, 10/51.
86. 'Daughter of the Soil', no date, WWI: Home Front. Land Girls (Farming MISC), The Women's Library, 10/51; 'The New Pomona', no date, WWI: Home Front. Land Girls (Farming MISC), The Women's Library, 10/51; 'War Service Fashions: How our Women Workers Dress', no date, WWI: Home Front. Land Girls (Farming MISC), The Women's Library, 10/51.
87. In her study of the Women's Land Army of America, Pamela Jo Pierce argues that patriotism and femininity were in conflict due to conflicting public expectations of the war and traditional attitudes about women's work. See P. J. Pierce, *That Dame's Got Grit: Selling the Women's Land Army* (2010). All Graduate Theses and Dissertations. Paper 625. http://digitalcommons.usu.edu/etd/625.
88. Meriel Talbot to Organising Secretaries, 12 March 1917, TNA, MAF 42/2.
89. Braybon, *Women Workers in the First World War*, 166–70; Thom, *Nice Girls and Rude Girls*, 142–53; S. K. Kent, *Making Peace: The Reconstruction of Gender in Interwar Britain* (Princeton, NJ: Princeton University Press, 1993), 34–41; A. Woollacott, '"Khaki Fever" and its Control: Gender, Age and Sexual Morality on the British Homefront in the First World War', *Journal of Contemporary History* 29 (1994): 325–47.
90. Hertfordshire Women's Agricultural Committee to Miss Talbot, 29 August 1918, TNA, MAF 42/8.

91. Rules for members of the Land Army in Devonshire, WWAC, 29 August 1917, DRO, 1262M/L138.
92. '"The Green Armlet", National Service: A Story of Today', TNA, NATS 1/1308, 1–8.
93. Recruiting in Devonshire, Selection of Recruits, Confidential Draft, 15 January 1918, DRO, 1262M/L142; County Executive, conduct and misdemeanors, prepared by the WWAC, Devonshire, 29 May 1918, DRO, 1262M/L142.
94. 'God Speed the Plough and the Woman Who Drives It', National Service, Women's Land Army, poster 1918, TNA MAF 42/8; 'Friends – A Girl War Worker on the Land with her Horse', no date, WWI: Home Front. Land Girls (Farming MISC), The Women's Library, 10/51; 'The Wartime Shepherdess', no date, WWI: Home Front. Land Girls (Farming MISC), The Women's Library, 10/51. See also Clarke, *The Women's Land Army: A Portrait*, 46–9.
95. Food Production Department, Women's Branch, confidential report from travelling inspectors, 7 June 1918, TNA, MAF 42/8; Hepburn to Talbot, 31 May 1918, TNA, MAF 42/8.
96. Food Production Department, Women's Branch, confidential report from travelling inspectors, 7 June 1918, TNA, MAF 42/8; Hepburn to Talbot, 31 May 1918, TNA, MAF 42/8.
97. The Land Army and Need for More Effective Control, 18 June 1918, FPD, TNA, MAF 42/8.
98. Meriel Talbot to Chairman WWACs, Report July 1918, 15 July 1918, FPD, TNA, MAF 42/8.
99. Meeting of Hertfordshire Women's Agricultural Committee and Farmers' Union, 16 August 1918, TNA, MAF 42/8.
100. 'Army of Women on a Military Basis', 18 January 1917, *The Daily Express*; 'Women Mobilising for Land Work', *The Lady's Pictorial,* 10 February 1917; 'The Educated Woman on the Land', *The Common Cause*, 12 January 1917.
101. J. Watson, 'Khaki Girls, VADS, and Tommy's Sisters: Gender and Class in First World War Britain', *International History Review* 19 (1997): 40–41.
102. 'No Land Army: Women's Military Organisation Scheme Given Up', 30 January 1917, *The Evening News*. Despite Talbot's efforts to devoid the Land Army of a military connection, its name invited comparisons until the demobilisation of the WLA. See, Watson, 'Khaki Girls, VADS, and Tommy's Sisters: Gender and Class in First World War Britain', 39–40.
103. 'Armlets for Women', no date, WWI: Home Front. Land Girls (Farming MISC), The Women's Library, 10/51.
104. Women's Land Army, Roll of Honour, 3 August 1917, MERL, SR WFGA/9/5.
105. Edith Lyttelton to Dr Perrie Williams, 3 August 1918, Women's Branch, TNA, MAF 42/8.
106. Memorandum on information for Welfare Officers, FPD, 3 July 1918, TNA, MAF 42/8.
107. 'Report for the Food Production Department for the period up to 1 June 1918', June 1918, TNA, MAF 42/8, 10–12.
108. Meriel Talbot, 'Recruiting and Enrolments for 1918', 14 January 1919, TNA, MAF 42/7.

109. See D. Silbey, *The British Working Class and Enthusiasm for War, 1914–1916* (New York: Frank Cass, 2005), 158.
110. IWM, Sound Recording, Mary Lees, Session 506, 30 November 1974; Alice Mildmay to Meriel Talbot, Devonshire WWAC, 17 August 1917, DRO 1262M/141. Board of Agriculture and Fisheries report from Women's Branch, September 1917, TNA, MAF48/2.
111. P. Dewey, *War and Progress: Britain, 1914–1945* (London: Longman: 1997), 210; A. Offer, *The First World War: An Agrarian Interpretation* (Oxford: Clarendon Press, 1989), 94; Board of Agriculture, speech by Mr Prothero, 18 January 1917, DRO, 1262M/L113. The plough campaign meant that farmers had to increase the percentage of arable land. With the number of men and horses dwindling, the Board of Agriculture recommended that farmers rely more heavily on farm machinery, which until 1917 was in short supply. Report of the Devon War Agricultural Committee, 4 June 1917, DRO, 1262M/L139. For an alternative explanation see Horn, *Rural Life in England*, 81–2, 72–86, 136.
112. 'Women in Agriculture during War-time', *Journal of the Board of Agriculture*, October 1917, Vol. XXV, TNA, MAF 59/2, 802.
113. Meriel Talbot to Chairman WWACs, 15 July 1918, FPD, TNA, MAF 42/8.

4 'The Lasses Are Massing': The Land Army in England and Wales

1. S. Steinbach, *Women in England, 1760–1914: A Social History* (New York: Palgrave, 2004), 16–17.
2. E. Spring, 'Landowners, Lawyers, and Land Law Reform in Nineteenth-Century England', *The American Journal of Legal History* 21 (1977): 43–5.
3. A. Howkins, *The Death of Rural England: A Social History of the Countryside since 1900* (New York: Routledge, 2003), 31–3.
4. See S. Grayzel, *Women and the First World War* (Harlow: Pearson, 2002); J. Watson, *Fighting Different Wars: Experience, Memory, and the First World War in Britain* (Cambridge: Cambridge University Press, 2004), 119–27; P. Horn, *Rural Life in England in the First World War* (London: Palgrave MacMillan), 124–8.
5. B. Ruck, *The Land Girl's Love Story* (New York: Dodd, Mead and Company, 1919), 352.
6. Watson argues that middle-class women, like middle-class men, tended to see their war work in terms of service, whereas working-class men and women tended to see their war work as work. Watson, *Fighting Different Wars*, 118.
7. See J. M. Winter, *The Experience of World War I* (London: Macmillan, 1988), 176; S. Grayzel, 'Nostalgia, Gender and the Countryside: Placing the "Land Girl" in First World War Britain', *Rural History* 10 (1999): 156–7, 159.
8. IWM, Department of Documents, Rosa Freedman, P360.
9. IWM, Department of Documents, Mary Bale, P360.
10. IWM, Sound Recording, Vera Raymond, Session 3079, Reel 1, 1977.
11. IWM, Sound Department. Mary Lees, 3078/1, 30 November 1974.
12. IWM, Department of Documents, Edith Airey, 81/9/1.

13. Report on Training: The Women's Land Army, 29 November 1917, TNA, MAF 59/1.
14. IWM, Sound Recording, Vera Raymond, Session 3079, Reel 1, 1977.
15. IWM, Sound Recording, Eva Marsh, Session 7450, Reel 1, 1983.
16. E. J. T. Collins, 'The Age of Machinery', in *The Victorian Countryside, vol. 1*, ed. G. E. Mingay (London: Routledge & Kegan Paul, 1981), 205; H. Crowe, 'Profitable Ploughing of the Uplands? The Food Production Campaign in the First World War', *Agricultural History Review* 55 (2007): 206–7.
17. Wilfred Denning, 'Devon Farms', *Salcombe Gazette*, 18 October 1916.
18. Letter to Lord Fortescue from Tom Marshall, 4 November 1915, DRO, Lord Lieutenancy Papers, 1262M/L153 Bundle 42; Joseph Keap, 'An Unpatriotic Farmer?' *Bideford Gazette*, 24 July 1915. Huntsham Court is owned by the Williams' Troyte of Huntsham Court, Esq, Bampton; Letter to Lord Fortescue from Tom Marshall, 4 November 1915, DRO, Lord Lieutenancy Papers, 1262M/L153 Bundle 42; Joseph Keap, 'An Unpatriotic Farmer?' *Bideford Gazette*, 24 July 1915, no page number. Huntsham Court is owned by the Williams' Troyte of Huntsham Court, Esq, Bampton (on the edge of Exmoor National Park).
19. See 'War Work for Women', *Western Guardian*, 27 January 1916, 2; 'Farmers Must Try Women', *Teignmouth Post*, 27 October 1916.
20. G. Holloway, *Women and Work in Britain since 1840* (London: Routledge, 2005), 5; K. Sayer, 'Field-faring Women: The Resistance of Women Who Worked in the Fields of Nineteenth-century England', *Women's History Review*, 2 (1993): 186.
21. Thom, *Nice Girls and Rude Girls*, 26–9, 28.
22. IWM, Department of Documents, W. M. Bennett, 01/19/1.
23. O. Hockin, *Two Girls on the Land: Wartime on a Dartmoore Farm* (London: Arnold, 1918), 10. Olive Hockin was a member of the Women's Social and Political Union and was thought to be one of the perpetrators in the attack on Lloyd George's house in February 1913. After a police raid on her home, Hockin was arrested and sentenced to four months' imprisonment. She enlisted in the WLA in early 1917. See E. Crawford, *Women's Suffrage Movement: A Reference Guide, 1866–1928* (London: Routledge, 2001), 287–8.
24. H. Bentwich, *If I Forget Thee: Some Chapters of Autobiography, 1912–1920* (London: Elk, 1973), 113.
25. Hockin, *Two Girls on the Land*, 10. It is difficult to uncover farm workers' attitudes toward Land Girls due to a lack of sources. Some insights can be found in the accounts of Land Girls, but the conclusions would be responsive and potentially biased.
26. IWM, Department of Documents, W. M. Bennett, 01/19/1; IWM, Sound Recording, Mary Lees, Session 506, 30 November 1974.
27. For more on the motivations of the English agricultural workforce see N. Mansfield, *English Farmworkers and Local Patriotism, 1900–1930* (Farnham: Ashgate, 2001).
28. IWM, Department of Documents, W.M. Bennett, 01/19/1.
29. See Margaret R. Higonnet and Patrice L. R. Hogonnet, 'The Double Helix', in *Behind the Lines: Gender and the Two World Wars*, ed. Margaret Randolph Higonnet et al. (New Haven: Yale University Press, 1987), 41–2.
30. Hockin, *Two Girls on the Land*, 137–8.

31. IWM, Sound Recording, Marjorie Stone, Session 7455, July 1983.
32. IWM, Sound Recording, Mary Lees, Session 506, 30 November 1974.
33. IWM, Department of Documents, Mary Bale, P360.
34. IWM, Department of Documents, Edith Airey, 81/9/1.
35. Braybon, *Women Workers in the First World War*, 53–7. See also D. Thom, 'The Bundle of Sticks: Women, Trade Unionists and Collective Organisation before 1918', in *Unequal Opportunities: Women's Employment in England, 1800–1918*, ed. Angela V. John (New York: Basil Blackwell, 1986), 261–85.
36. IWM, Department of Documents, W.M. Bennett, 01/19/1.
37. Bentwich, *If I Forget Thee*, 110.
38. IWM, Department of Documents, Mary Bale, P360.
39. IWM, Sound Recording, Mary Lees, Session 506, 30 November 1974.
40. IWM, Department of Documents, Rosa Freedman, P360.
41. IWM, Department of Documents, Minnie Harrold, 86/20/1.
42. Hockin, *Two Girls on the Land*, 18.
43. Hockin, *Two Girls on the Land*, 38.
44. Meriel Talbot to Organising Secretaries, 3 July 1918, TNA, MAF 42/8.
45. Meriel Talbot to Organising Secretaries, 3 July 1918, TNA, MAF 42/8.
46. H.L. French to Meriel Talbot, Appointment of Welfare Officers, Women's Land Army, 23 October 1918, TNA, MAF 42/8; H.L. French to Meriel Talbot, Report of Welfare Officers for L.A.A.S, 13 November 1918, TNA, MAF 42/8.
47. IWM, Department of Documents, F. Westlake, 88/1/1.
48. Welfare Officers' Appointments, 6 November 1918, TNA, MAF 42/8.
49. Meriel Talbot to Organising Secretaries, 1 November 1918, TNA, MAF 42/8.
50. Meriel Talbot to Organising Secretaries, 6 November 1918, TNA, MAF 42/8.
51. Essex War Agricultural Committee to Meriel Talbot, 19 September 1918, TNA, MAF 42/8.
52. Report on Welfare Officers and Labour Exchanges, Monmouthshire, 1 November 1918, TNA, MAF 42/8.
53. Edith Lyttleton to Meriel Talbot, Report on Welfare Officers, Kent, 15 October 1918, TNA, MAF 42/8.
54. Edith Lyttleton to Organising Secretaries, 7 November 1918, TNA, MAF 42/8.
55. Report of the Brechnockshire Agricultural Committee, 7 June 1918, TNA, MAF 42/8.
56. Miss Wright to Edith Lyttleton, 25 September 1918, TNA, MAF 4/8; Edith Lyttleton to Miss Wright, 2 October 1918, TNA, MAF 42/8.
57. Meriel Talbot to Miss Crowdy, 21 January 1918, TNA, MAF 42/8.
58. IWM, Sound Recording, Beatrice Gilbert, Session 3076, Reel 1, 1977.
59. IWM, Department of Documents, Rosa Freedman, P360, 1978.
60. See the wartime accounts of Dorothea Cross, Swardeston, Norfolk and Dora Brazil, Seaton, Devon in C. Twinch, *Women on the Land: Their Story during Two World Wars* (Cambridge: Lutterworth Press, 1990), 41–6.
61. IWM, Sound Recording, Vera Raymond, Session 3079, Reel 1, 1977.
62. IWM, Department of Documents, Miss A. Watkins, 87/5/1; IWM, Sound Recording, Marjorie Stone, Session 7455, July 1983.
63. The need to connect with family and loved ones was also part of the trench experience of the war. See M. Roper, *The Secret Battle: Emotional Survival in the Great War* (Manchester: Manchester University Press, 2009), 51–9.
64. IWM, Department of Documents, F. Westlake, 88/1/1.

65. IWM, Sound Recording, Beatrice Gilbert, Session 3076, Reel 1, 1977; IWM, Sound Recording, Kathleen Gilbert, Session 9105, Reel 3, 1985.
66. IWM, Sound Recording, Mary Lees, Session 506, 30 November 1974.
67. Hockin, *Two Girls on the Land*, 21, 34.
68. IWM, Department of Documents, Minnie Harrold, 86/20/1.
69. B. White, 'Remembrance, Retrospection, and the Women's Land Army in First World War Britain', *Journal of the Canadian Historical Association* 22 (2011): 162–94.
70. P. James, *Picture This: World War I Posters and Visual Culture* (Lincoln, NE: University of Nebraska Press, 2010), 2–3.
71. Questions related to patriotism are difficult for the historian to assess because the concept of patriotism is subjective and constantly changing. One's understanding of patriotism also changes based on changing perspectives and circumstances. See A. Gregory, *The Last Great War: British Society and the First World War* (New York: Cambridge University Press, 2008), 3 and A. Thomson, 'Memory as a Battlefield: Personal and Political Investments in the National Military Past', *Oral History Review* 22 (1995): 65.
72. IWM, Sound Recording, Helen Beatrice Poulter, Session 727, Reel 4, 1975; IWM, Sound Recording, Annie Sarah Edwards, Session 740, Reel 6, 1976; IWM, Sound Recording, Doris Robinson, Session 12582, Reel 1, 1992; IWM, Sound Recording, Olive Crosswell, Session 7482, Reels 1 & 2; IWM, Sound Recording, Vyvyan Garstang, Session 3077, Reel 1, 1977.

5 'Respectable Women': The Land Army in Scotland

1. G. F. B. Houston, 'Agriculture', in *The Scottish Economy: A Statistical Account of Scottish Life*, ed. A. K. Cairncross (Cambridge: Cambridge University Press, 1954), 85–7.
2. Houston, 'Agriculture', 104. In the decades before the First World War, a sizeable portion of the one million acres of mountain was converted for raising sheep (and deer forests), which were also kept in large numbers in the south. While arable farming remained fruitful in the east, in the west the land was primarily given over to grasslands, and ultimately dairy production. T. M. Devine, C. H. Lee and G. C. Peden, *The Transformation of Scotland: The Economy since 1700* (Edinburgh: Edinburgh University Press, 2005), 186–7.
3 See L. Jamieson and C. Toynbee, *Country Bairns: Growing Up 1900–1930* (Edinburgh: Edinburgh University Press, 1992), 68.
4. D. T. Jones, F. Duncan, H. M. Conacher and W. R. Scott, *Rural Scotland during the War* (New Haven: Yale University Press, 1926), 130–3.
5. Jones et al., *Rural Scotland*, 134–5.
6. Devine et al., *Transformation of Scotland*, 192–3.
7. Jones et al., *Rural Scotland*, 138–9.
8. The Lowlands experienced depopulation as well, but at a loss of 16 per cent over 40 years, compared to 26 per cent in the Highlands over the same period. T. C. Smout, *A Century of the Scottish People, 1830–1950* (New Haven: Yale University Press, 1986), 60.
9. Smout, *Century of the Scottish People*, 60.
10. Jones et al., *Rural Scotland*, 211. See Smout, *Century of the Scottish People*, 60.

11. Small Landholders (Scotland) Act 1911, 16 December 1911, TNA.
12. This was part of Gladstone's approach to land ownership in Scotland. Common pasturage had been in place for centuries and had been abandoned as the commercialisation of the land increased. Past precedent, Gladstone argued, granted rights to the people, protecting them against eviction and the further consolidation of estate farms. Smout, *Century of the Scottish People*, 72–5.
13. The Boards were under-funded and under-manned leading to congestion and delays.
14. T. M. Devine, *The Scottish Nation: A History, 1700–2000* (New York: Viking, 1999), 461. The decline in the number of women and children in agriculture can also be traced to the introduction of compulsory education in 1872 and rising wages for men, which negated the need to have wives and daughters included in the labour contract. Smout, *A Century of the Scottish People*, 79–80.
15. H. Crowe, 'Keeping the Wheels of the Far in Motion: Labour Shortages in the Uplands during the Great War', *Rural History* 19 (2008): 201–16; Lord Ernle, *The Land and its People* (London: Hutchinson, 1923), 165.
16. Devine, *The Scottish Nation*, 462.
17. Smout, *A Century of the Scottish People*, 81.
18. Jamieson and Toynbee, *Country Bairns*, 68–9. Wheat required far fewer labourers and the corn harvest with sickle required three or four labourers.
19. T. M. Devine, *Exploring the Scottish Past: Themes in the History of Scottish Society* (East Linton: Tuckwell Press, 1995), 216.
20. E. Cameron, 'Settling the Heather on Fire: The Land Question in Scotland, 1850–1914', in *The Land Question in Britain, 1750–1950*, ed. M. Cragoe and P. Readman (New York: Palgrave Macmillan, 2010), 109–16.
21. For a look at Scotland during the First World War see Jones et al., *Rural Scotland*; J. A. Kerr, *Scotland and the Impact of the Great War, 1914–1928* (London: Hodder Gibson, 2010).
22. The Board of Agriculture was divided into ministerial branches with separate committees appointed for Scotland and Ireland. Despite the division, the English committee was most important for developing policies and decisions reached here tended to be reproduced in Scotland with some modifications to suit local needs and conditions.
23. John Keith, 'The War and the Agriculturalist: II, the Farmer', *Scottish Journal of Agriculture* 25 (1944): 193–8.
24. Jones et al., *Rural Scotland*, 207–8.
25. R. Anthony, 'The Scottish Agricultural Labour Market, 1900–1939', *Economic History Review* 46 (1993): 562.
26. T. M. Devine, 'Scottish Farm Labour in the Era of Agricultural Depression, 1875–1900', in *Farm Servants and Labour in Lowland Scotland, 1770–1914*, ed. T. M. Devine (Edinburgh: John Milner Associates, 1984), 245–50. The rush to colours may have been a sign of patriotism among Scottish workers, but it was also likely connected to the servicemen resettlement scheme adopted in 1916, whereby the Duke of Sutherland, and other landed families, allocated land to help motivate men to enlistment.
27. While wheat production increased nominally, the yields for oats and potatoes nearly doubled between 1916 and 1919. Charles Douglas, 'Scottish Agriculture during the War', *Transaction of the Highland and Agricultural Society for Scotland* 31 (1919): 46–9.

28. Jones et al., *Rural Scotland*, 205.
29. The farmers were represented by the National Farmers' Union formed in 1913 and farm workers were represented by the Scottish Farm Servants' Union formed in 1912. Between 1916 and 1919 the membership for the FSU increased from 6,000 to more than 23,000. One-twelfth of the members were women. The Corn Production Act remained in place until it was repealed in 1921. Jones et al., *Rural Scotland*, 208–10. The National Federation of Women Workers increased its membership from 10,000 to 60,000 between 1914 and 1919, although most members worked in munitions, transportation, and manufacturing. C. M. M. Macdonald and E. W. McFarland, *Scotland and the Great War* (East Linton: Tuckwell Press, 1999), 24.
30. Anthony, 'Scottish Agricultural Labour Market', 563.
31. E. Cameron, *Impaled upon a Thistle: Scotland since 1880* (Edinburgh: Edinburgh University Press, 2010), 119.
32. While the WNSS worked to place both men and women, its primary function was to promote the employment of women in agriculture and only assumed responsibility for training female applicants. Women's National Service Scheme, Scotland, 22 June 1916, TNA, NATS 1/560.
33. 'Extract from Report on the Increased Employment of Women during the War, for April 1918', April 1918, TNA, LAB 2/271/LE1823/81/1915.
34. 'The Prime Minister, National Service Department, Report 22, 21 June 1917, TNA, CAB 24/17.
35. 'Interim Report on Women in Industry during the War (Scotland only), for October 1917', October 1917, TNA, LAB 2/271/LE1823/81/1915.
36. Women's National Service Scheme, Scotland, 27 August 1916, TNA, NATS 1/560.
37. Report on Agricultural Wages, Scotland, National Register 1915, 27 January 1916, The National Archives of Scotland, GR05/1944..
38. Report on Women's Occupations (Agriculture) for August 1916, 8 August 1916, The National Archives of Scotland, GR05/1944.
39. Scottish Women's Land Army Scheme, January 1917, TNA, NATS 1/560.
40. Scottish Women's Land Army Scheme, Scotland, 12 July 1918, TNA, LAB 2/172/LE 1823/81/1915; 'Women's National Service Scheme: The Scottish Women's Land Army', 17 March 1917, TNA, LAB 2/172/LE 1823/81/1915.
41. Scottish Women's Land Army, 5 May 1918, TNA, LAB 2/171/ED29202/5/1918.
42. It is important to note that the financial responsibilities of these three bodies was debated and disputed over the course of the war and at times responsibility for various aspects of the SWLA transferred hands, often more than once.
43. Women's Land Army Scheme (Scotland only), 25 January 1917, TNA, LAB 2/271/LE1823/81/1915.
44. 'Employment of Women in Agriculture', Board of Agriculture for Scotland, 21 May 1917, TNA, CAB 24/14/23.
45. Instruction to Employment Exchange Managers and Agricultural Cooperating Officers (Scotland only) Regarding the Enrolment and Placing of Members of the Scottish Women's Land Army, 21 March 1917, Board of Agriculture, TNA, LAB 21/172/LE1823/81/1915.
46. Instruction to Employment Exchange Managers and Agricultural Cooperating Officers (Scotland only) Regarding the Enrolment and Placing of Members of the Scottish Women's Land Army, 21 March 1917, Board of Agriculture, TNA, LAB 21/172/LE1823/81/1915.

47. Instruction to Employment Exchange Managers and Agricultural Cooperating Officers (Scotland only) Regarding the Enrolment and Placing of Members of the Scottish Women's Land Army, 21 March 1917, Board of Agriculture, TNA, LAB 21/172/LE1823/81/1915.
48. Training Centre Scheme (Scotland only), Board of Agriculture (Scotland), The National Archives of Scotland, 28 March 1917, GR05/1944.
49. Enrolment in Scottish Women's Land Army, April 1917, Board of Agriculture for Scotland, TNA, LAB 21/172/LE1823/81/1915.
50. Special Need for the Supply of Women Labour, 11 October 1918, TNA, LAB 2/172/LE1823/81/1915.
51. Enrolment in Scottish Women's Land Army, April 1917, Board of Agriculture for Scotland, TNA, LAB 21/172/LE1823/81/1915.
52. Douglas, 'Scottish Agriculture during the War', 46–7; E. A. Cameron, *Land for the People? The British Government and the Scottish Highlands, c. 1880–1925* (East Linton: Tuckwell Press, 1996), 199–200.
53. 'Programme for the Work of Dealing with Women in Agriculture: Scottish Division', March 1917, TNA, LAB 2/172/LE1823/81/1915.
54. 'Women in Agriculture: Scottish Division', 19 September 1918, TNA, LAB 2/172/LE1823/81/1915.
55. E. Gordon and E. Brietenbach, *The World Is Ill Divided: Women's Work in Scotland in the Late Nineteenth and Early Twentieth Centuries* (Edinburgh: Edinburgh University Press, 1990), 31, 33.
56. Smout, *A Century of the Scottish People*, 80.
57. In-and-out girls tended to be single women and were not necessarily related to the farmer or his workers. This position was increasingly uncommon and most often only used on very small farms. Jamieson and Toynbee, *Country Bairns*, 70–1.
58. Ledgard to Dunham, 13 May 1918, TNA, NATS 1/560.
59. See Reports of Women's Employment in Industry (Scotland), March 1917–November 1918, TNA, LAB 2/172/LE1823/81/1915.
60. Instructions to Employment Exchange Managers and to the Women's County Committees for Agriculture (Scotland only) regarding the Scottish Women's Land Army, 4 October 1918, TNA, NATS 1/560.
61. See Reports on Women's Committees, November 1915–August 1916, TNA, LAB 2/172/LE1823/81/1915.
62. Board of Agriculture Interim-Report on Highland Dairy Farms, Labour (Scotland), 9 August 1917, TNA, LAB 2/172/LE1823/81/1915.
63. Closure of the Kilmarnock Training Facility, WNSS, 16 May 1918, TNA, LAB 2/172/LE1823/81/1915.
64. Report on Training Facilities in Kilmarnock, Inverness, Stirling, Fife (Scotland), 20 May 1918, TNA, LAB 2/172/LE1823/81/1915.
65. Joint Meeting of Board of Agriculture (Scotland), Ministry of Labour, and Women's Land Army Scheme (Scotland), 27 September 1917, TNA, LAB 2/172/LE1823/81/1915.
66. 'Enrolment of Women for Work on the Land', 18 September 1918, TNA, LAB 2/172/LE1823/81/1915.
67. 'Interview between Mr. Weatherhill and Mr. Caie', 20 September 1918, TNA, LAB 2/172/LE1823/81/1915.
68. Dunham to Ledgard, 27 June 1918, TNA, NATS 1 560; T. L. Heath to Sheriff McClure, 7 September 1918, TNA, NATS 1/560; Scottish Women's Land Army Scheme, 16 September 1918, TNA, NATS 1/560.

69. Summary of Recommendations of the Royal Commission on housing in Scotland (Cd. 8731/1917), TNA, RECO 1/473. Scotland had some of the worst housing conditions in Britain in the first decade of the twentieth century. Overcrowding was especially prevalent in crofting districts and while these areas were among the first to see reform, significant progress was not made until the early 1950s. See L. Abrams and C. G. Brown, *A History of Everyday Life in Twentieth Century Scotland* (Edinburgh: Edinburgh University Press, 2010), 34.
70. The Women's Land Army, Scotland. Report on Housing and Care for Land Girls, 23 November 1917, The National Archives of Scotland, Board of Agriculture (Scotland) E824/245.
71. Improvements for Women's Land Army (Scotland) Enrolment Scheme, 18 October 1917, TNA, LAB 2/172/LE1823/81/1915.
72. Scottish Women's Land Army, Training Facilities, 13 August 1918, TNA, LAB 2/172/LE1823/81/1915.
73. Women's County Committee, Scottish Women's Land Army, Joint meeting of the Perth, Stirling, Fife, Forfar, and Kinross Women's County Agricultural Committee, 8 October 1918, TNA, LAB 2/172/LE1823/81/1915.
74. Miss Strange to G. Gerrald, 20 August 1918, TNA, LAB 2/172/LE1823/81/1915.
75. Proposed Farm Instructional and Training Centre at Rossie, Auchtermuchty, 17 August 1918, TNA, NATS 1/561; Proposed Farm Instructional and Training Centre at Rossie, Auchtermuchty, 31 August 1918, TNA, NATS 1/561.
76. Minutes of the Joint Advisory Committee, 17 September 1918, TNA, NATS 1/560.
77. Scottish Women's Land Army, Beechwood Training Centre, Inverness, 31 October 1918, TNA, NATS 1/562; Scottish Women's Land Army, Beechwood, Inverness, 21 September 1918, TNA, NATS 1/562.
78. Letters and Extracts from letters on file L3A/1903. Meeting of Joint Advisory Committee, 21 September 1918 and 21 October 1918, TNA, NATS 1/562.
79. Scottish Women's Land Army, Beechwood Training Centre, Inverness, 21 September 1918, TNA, NATS 1/562.
80. Mr Weatherhill to Mr Caie, 30 November 1918, TNA, LAB 2/172/LE1823/81/1915.
81. Enrolment Scottish Women's Land Army, Report for December 1918, TNA, LAB 2/172/LE1823/81/1915.
82. Heath to Ciad, Report on Financial Report for SWLA Year Ending 1917, 28 May 1918, TNA, NATS 1/560; Report on performance of Scottish Women's Land Army 1917 by J. Reid Hyde, 12 June 1918, TNA, NATS 1 560.
83. Reorganisation of Scottish Women's Land Army for the Purpose of Ending Volunteer Schemes under the National Service Scheme, April 1918, TNA, NATS 1/560.
84. Integration of Volunteer Schemes under Scottish Women's Land Army, 12 July 1918, TNA, NATS 1/560.
85. Meeting of Scottish Women's Land Army, 11 October 1918, TNA, LAB 2/172/LE1823/81/1915.
86. The Scottish Women's Land Army, Notes for Organisers, 21 January 1917, TNA, NATS 1/560.
87. Mrs Ferguson to Miss Talbot, Conditions for Land Service in Scotland, 2 February 1918, TNA, LAB 2/172/LE1823/81/1915.

88. Scottish Women's Land Army – Revised Scheme (L3A/1903), 31 October 1918, TNA, NATS 1/560.
89. Training and Uniforms, Women's Land Army, Scotland, 11 June 1918, The National Archives of Scotland, Board of Agriculture (Scotland) E824/252.
90. Scottish Women's Land Army – Revised Scheme (L3A/1903), 31 October 1918, TNA, NATS 1/560; Women's Work on the Land, Uniforms, Report 1918, The National Archives of Scotland, Ministry of Labour, E824/214.
91. Request for the Extension of Training Period, Women's Land Army of Scotland, 22 May 1919, The National Archives of Scotland, Board of Agriculture (Scotland) E824/286.
92. Supplementary Report from Joint Meeting 23 October 1918, 31 October 1918, TNA, LAB 2/172/LE1823/81/1915. Report issued to the Ministry of Labour and the English Women's Land Army on the proceedings of the Joint Meeting in Edinburgh.
93. Margaret Ellis to Alice Younger, 22 October 1918, TNA, LAB 2/172/LE1823/81/1915.
94. Instruction to Employment Exchange Managers and Agricultural Co-Operating Officers, 1917, TNA, LAB 2/171/ED29202/5/1918; Scottish Women's Land Army. Travel and Accommodation Allowances, 22 November 1918, TNA, LAB 2/172/LE1823/81/1915.
95. Mrs Younger to Mr Caie, 12 August 1918, TNA, LAB 2/172/LE1823/81/1915; J. B. Adams to E. Sandford Fawcett, 9August 1918, TNA, NATS 1/560.
96. Alice Younger to Sheriff McClure, Deputy of Labour Sub-Committee (A3/332), 8 August 1918, TNA, NATS 1/560.
97. Minutes Scottish Women's Land Army, 21 October 1918, Letter 17A Treasury Correspondence, June–October 1918, TNA, NATS 1/560.
98. Travel Warrants. Scottish Women's Land Army, 7 November 1918, TNA, NATS 1/560.
99. Leave and Travel Warrants for Scottish Women's Land Army Scheme, 17 September 1918, TNA, NATS 1/560.
100. Minutes Scottish Women's Land Army, 21 October 1918, Letter 17A Treasury Correspondence, June–October 1918, TNA, NATS 1/560.
101. Interdepartmental Committee Report. Scottish Women's Land Army, Scot.L/3610.DNS, 31 October 1918, TNA, NATS 1/560.
102. Scottish Women's Land Army Scheme. Revised Instructions to Employment Exchanges regarding Enrolment, Placing, etc., 8 October 1918, TNA, NATS 1/560; Instruction and Training Scottish Women's Land Army, 28 October 1918, TNA, NATS 1/560; Expansion of Scottish Land Service Training Scheme, 22 November 1918, TNA, LAB 2/172/LE1823/81/1915.
103. Ministry of National Service report on Interdepartmental Committee Recommendations for Scottish Women's Land Army Scheme from 31 October 1918, 8 November 1918, TNA, NATS 1/560.

6 Back to the Land: The Land Army after 1918

1. See S. Ouditt, *Fighting Forces, Writing Women: Identity and Ideology in the First World War* (New York: Routledge, 1994), 50–1; G. E. Mingay, *A Social History of the English Countryside* (London: Routledge, 1990), 177–85, 200, 202.

2. 'Best Women in the World', *The Daily Express*, 15 November 1918; 'What to Do with the Girls', *The Daily Mail*, 15 November 1918.
3. 'Rural Romances: Will Returning Farm Hands Marry the Land Girls!', *The Daily Express*, 19 November 1918.
4. 'The Land Girl's Problem', *The Nottingham Evening News*, 5 December 1918; 'What Will Become of the Land Army', *The Nottingham Weekly Journal*, December 1918; MERL, SR WFGA/F/10/U54/370; 'Women's Work in the Future', *The Northampton Echo*, 30 November 1918.
5. Ministry of Reconstruction report on Interdepartmental Meeting for Agriculture, 20 November 1918, TNA, NATS 1/560.
6. Board of Agriculture and Fisheries, Report Ending, 7 October 1919, Training Branch, Disabled Men, October 1919, TNA, CAB 24/89.
7. Ministry of Reconstruction report on Interdepartmental Meeting for Agriculture, 20 November 1918, TNA, NATS 1/560.
8. Ministry of Reconstruction report on Interdepartmental Meeting for Agriculture, 20 November 1918, TNA, NATS 1/560; National Service Department, Labour Exchanges and Scottish Women's Land Army, Council Minutes, 27 November 1918, TNA, NATS 1/560.
9. 'Women in Agriculture: Scottish Women's Land Army Scheme', 19 November 1918, TNA, LAB 2/172/LE1823/81/1915.
10. Board of Agriculture and Fisheries, Food Production Department, 20 November 1918, TNA, CAB 24/70.
11. Meriel Talbot to Organising Secretaries, 25 November 1918, TNA, LAB 2/172/LE1823/81/1915.
12. Employment on the Land, Agricultural Section, Food Production Department, 15 January 1919, TNA, CAB 42/6; Alice Younger to Meriel Talbot, 17 January 1919, TNA, LAB 2/172/LE1823/81/1915.
13. Mrs Fielden to Mrs Bridgeman, 18 November 1918, Shropshire Archives, 4629/1/1918/81; Mrs Maud Alexander to Meriel Talbot, no date, Shropshire Archives, 4629/1/1918/80.
14. War Agricultural Committee, Women's Organising Office, 14 December 1918, Berkshire Record Office, D/EX 438/3/2.
15. Report on Women's War Agricultural Committees (Scotland), November 1918, TNA, LAB 2/172/LE1823/81/1915.
16. Meriel Talbot to Organising Secretaries, Circular, 14 March 1918, TNA, MAF 42/3; Meriel Talbot to Organising Secretaries, Circular, 11 March 1918, TNA, MAF 42/3; Scottish Women's Land Army – Publicity, 18 June 1918, TNA, LAB 2/171/Ed29202/5/1918; Division Office, Scotland and North of England, Director, 6 May 1918, TNA, LAB 2/171/Ed29202/5/1918.
17. Meriel Talbot to Organising Secretaries, Circular, 28 March 1918, TNA, MAF 42/3.
18. Memorandum on Women's Help on the Land, Publicity and Recruitment, 23 April 1918, TNA, MAF 42/3; Circular Letter to Agricultural Executive Committees, The Programme for 1919, 15 August 1918, TNA, MAF 42/4. See Peter Dewey, *British Agriculture in the First World War* (London: Routledge, 1989), 101–2.
19. Scottish Women's Land Army – Publicity, Labour Employment Department, 19 October 1918, TNA, LAB 2/171/Ed29202/5/1918; Meriel Talbot to Publicity Office, 23 October 1918, TNA, LAB 2/171/Ed29202/5/1918.

20. Meeting of the Devon Farmers' Union, 13 May 1919, DRO, Fortescue of Castle Hill, 1262L/L14; Executive Meeting of National Farmers' Union, May 1919, MERL, U352/319; General Meeting of National Farmers' Union, May 1919, MERL, U352/319.

21. Ministry of Labour Agriculture Employment, Meeting with Representatives of National Farmers' Union, 29 May 1919, TNA, LAB 2/172/LE1823/81/1915.

22. The focus on farming as a professional pursuit for women pre-dated the war, as did a focus on scientific studies rather than field training. See D. L. Opitz, '"A Triumph of Brains over Brute": Women and Science at the Horticultural College, Swanley, 1890–1910', *Isis*, 104.1 (March 2013): 31–2; D. M. Turner, *The History of Science Teaching in England* (London: Chapman & Hall, 1927), 119–20.

23. In the 1920s countless cottages in Britain and Wales were without gas, electricity, or main water, and many cottages that were unfit for human habitation were rented to working-class families. Alun Howkins, *The Death of Rural England: A Social History of the Countryside since 1900* (New York: Routledge, 2003), 86–7.

24. Howkins, *The Death of Rural England*, 38. Rents in England had not increased since 1917, and even then, had not risen much above their pre-war numbers. The demand for land during the war years, the land's potential for profit, and renewed government interest in agriculture meant that the immediate post-war period was a prime time to sell. See D. Cannadine, *The Decline and Fall of the British Aristocracy* (New York: Vintage Books, 1990).

25. Royal Commission on Agriculture, Minutes of Evidence, 14 October 1919 to 29 October 1919, Volume IV, TNA, Cmd. 445.

26. Due to slumping world markets the Agriculture Act was repealed in 1921. British markets were flooded with foreign products and unable to compete internationally, British agricultural wages began to decline in 1921 leading to labour unrest in the countryside and outmigration from rural areas. G. E. Cherry and A. Rogers, *Rural Change and Planning: England and Wales in the Twentieth Century* (London: E. & F. N. Spon, 1996), 46–7.

27. F. M. L. Thompson, *English Landed Society in the Nineteenth Century* (London: Routledge & Kegan Paul, 1963), 327–35; J. V. Beckett, *The Aristocracy in England* (London: Blackwell, 1986), 475; B. A. Holderness, 'The Victorian Farmer', in *The Victorian Countryside, vol. 1*, ed. G. E. Mingay (London: Routledge & Kegan Paul, 1981), 227–32; T. W. Beastall, 'Landlords and Tenants', in *The Victorian Countryside vol. II*, ed. G. E. Mingay (London: Routledge & Kegan Paul, 1981), 428; J. Winter and A. Prost, *The Great War in History* (Cambridge: Cambridge University Press, 2005), 166. For a revisionist interpretation see J. Beckett and M. Turner, 'End of the Old Order? F. M. L. Thompson, the Land Question, and the Burden of Ownership in England, c. 1880–c.1925', *Agricultural History Review*, 55 (2007): 275–6.

28. C. R. Williams to Meriel Talbot, 16 November 1918, TNA, NATS 1/560; C. R. Williams to Meriel Talbot, 26 November 1918, TNA, NATS 1/560.

29. 'Women and the Land', *The Daily Telegraph*, 16 June 1919; 'Women's Land Army, A New Class', *The Globe*, 29 October 1919; 'Women's Farm Experiment', *The East Cumberland News*, 16 September 1919.

30. 'The Wives of To-Morrow', *Royal Magazine*, November 1918, 39. This article was first printed in November 1916. See D. Beddoe, *Back to Home and Duty: Women between the Wars, 1918–1939* (London: Pandora Press, 1989); A. Light, *Forever England: Femininity, Literature and Conservatism between*

the Wars (London: Routledge, 1991); S. Kingsley Kent, *Making Peace: The Reconstruction of Gender in Interwar Britain* (Princeton, NJ: Princeton University Press, 1993). See also A. Bingham, 'An Era of Domesticity? Histories of Women and Gender in Interwar Britain', *Cultural and Social History* 1 (2004): 225–53.

31. See Gail Braybon, *Women Workers in the First World War* (London: Routledge, 1981), 105–9, 148–9; S. Boston, *Women Workers and the Trade Union Movement* (London: Davis-Poynter, 1981), 96–130, 132–4; Jane Lewis, *Women in England* (London: Wheatsheaf, 1984), 145–58; Gail Braybon and Penny Summerfield, *Out of the Cage: Women's Experiences in Two World Wars* (London: Routledge, 1987), 1–7, 77–8, 111–13, 129; A. Woollacott, *On Her their Lives Depend: Munitions Workers in the Great War* (Berkeley, CA: University of California Press, 1994), 1–14, 188–92, 214–16; D. Thom, *Nice Girls and Rude Girls: Women Workers in World War I* (London: I. B. Tauris, 1998), 53–74, 203–6; C. Culleton, *Working Class Culture, Women, and Britain, 1914–1921* (London: St Martin's Press, 1999), 4–5, 51–75.

32. 'Women in Workshop and Office: Land Girls' Work', *The Times*, 6 March 1919; 'Women as Farm Labourers, Better than Men at Milking', *The Times*, 16 May 1919; 'The Women's Tractor Record', *The Daily Express*, 7 December 1918.

33. Meriel Talbot to Women's Committees, 7 March 1919, TNA, MAF 42/8; Meriel Talbot to Lord Clinton, 25 February 1919, TNA, MAF 42/8.

34. 'The Queen and Women Workers', *The Morning Post*, 2 December 1918; 'Women and the Land', *The Gentlewoman*, 30 November 1918; 'Women Land Workers: Gaps to be Filled', *The Times*, 4 December 1918; 'Next Year's Food: Great Preparation', *The Daily Mail*, 20 November 1918; 'Function of the Land Army', *Liverpool Evening Courier*, 18 November 1918.

35. Meriel Talbot to County Organising Secretaries, 'Land Army Books and Outfits', 3 March 1919, TNA, MAF 42/6; Lawrence Weaver to Horticultural Sub-Committee, 24 February 1919, TNA, MAF 42/5.

36. 'The Organisation of the Women's War Agricultural Committees', July 1919, TNA, MAF 42/7; Edith Lyttleton to Organising Secretaries of WWAC, 11 July 1919, TNA, MAF 42/7; 'Reorganisation of Women's War Agricultural Committees', 17 March 1919, TNA, MAF 42/6; 'Circular Letter to Chairmen of Horticultural Sub-Committee: Future Organisation', 13 March 1919, TNA, MAF 42/6; 'Reorganisation of Horticultural Instruction', 10 March 1919, TNA, MAF 42/6.

37. 'Future Organisation of Agricultural Executive Committees', 1 February 1919, TNA MAF 42/6; 'Memorandum to Agricultural Executive Committees', April–September 1919, 8 March 1919, TNA, MAF 42/6. Changes to the Board of Agriculture and Fisheries had already been recommended in February 1919. Under the Land Settlement Act 1916 the Board of Agriculture was to remain in place for two years after the end of the war. Its reorganisation began in 1919 when it was renamed the Ministry of Agriculture and Fisheries. 'Future of the Board of Agriculture and Fisheries', 8 February 1918, TNA, MAF 42/6.

38. 'Reorganisation of Women's Committees. Scotland Only', 29 August 1919, TNA, LAB 2/172/LE1823/81/1915. In December 1919 the Board of Agriculture for Scotland assumed control of the WACs for Scotland. The

WACs became an advisory board for agricultural education and agricultural training schemes that were not carried out by the agricultural colleges. 'War Agricultural Committees, Scotland Only', 19 December 1919, TNA, LAB 2/172/LE1823/81/1915; 'Extract from Report on Agriculture or the Month Ending 6 February 1920 (Scotland)', February 1920, TNA, LAB 2/172/LE1823/81/1915.

39. L. M. Oramond to Local Officers, 'Women in Agriculture', 31 December 1919, TNA, LAB 2/172/LE1823/81/1915.
40. C. L. Mowat, *Britain between the Wars, 1918–1940* (Chicago: University of Chicago Press, 1955), 22; S. R. Graubard, 'Demobilisation in Great Britain Following the First World War', *Journal of Modern History* 19 (1947), 297–300; Speech by Lord Milner, Progress of Demobilisation, December 1918, TNA, PRO 30/30/8.
41. Woollacott, *On Her their Lives Depend*, 105–6.
42. See J. Watson, *Fighting Different Wars: Experience, Memory, and the First World War in Britain* (Cambridge: Cambridge University Press, 2004), 118–20.
43. F. W. Hirst, *The Consequences of the War to Great Britain* (London: Oxford University Press, 1934), 82.
44. L. Noakes, 'From War Service to Domestic Service: Ex-servicewomen and the Free Passage Scheme, 1919–1922', *Twentieth Century British History* 22 (2011): 20. Woollacott notes that although Armistice Day was a day of jubilation, for many women their happiness was fleeting and ultimately marked their displacement from the workforce. Woollacott, *On Her their Lives Depend*, 106.
45. 'Enrolment of Women for Work on the Land (England, Scotland and Wales)', Board of Agriculture Circular, 18 November 1918, TNA, LAB 2/172/LE1823/81/1915; 'Instructions to Employment Exchange Managers and Agricultural Cooperating Officers (Scotland Only)', 21 March 1919, TNA, LAB 2/172/LE1823/81/1915; Meriel Talbot to Organising Secretaries, 24 June 1919, TNA, MAF 42/6; 'Domestic Training Scheme, Land Army and Horticultural Sub-Committee', 9 July 1919, TNA, MAF 42/6; 'Training and Outfits for Land Army', 21 August 1919, TNA, MAF 42/8; Meriel Talbot to Organising Secretaries, 10 September 1919, TNA, MAF 42/8.
46. Meriel Talbot to Chairmen of WWACs, 20 August 1919, TNA, MAF 42/7; Meriel Talbot to Chairmen of WWACs, 30 August 1919, TNA, MAF 42/7.
47. Meriel Talbot to Chairmen of WWACs, 'Northampton Rally', 6 September 1919, TNA, MAF 42/7; Meriel Talbot to Organising Secretaries, 'Northampton Rally', 6 September 1919, TNA, MAF 42/7.
48. The major change being that the Women's Committees were instructed to target smallholdings rather than the larger estate farms. The estate farms would be most likely to receive the assistance of demobilised service men, leaving the smaller farms in needs of substitute workers.
49. Gifts for Land Settlement Act 1916, Section (1) Power to accept or administer gifts for settlement of ex-sailors or servicemen on land, 1916 Chapter 60 6 and 7 GEO 5.
50. Board of Agriculture. Agricultural Training for Officers, Board of Agriculture Grants, 13 June 1919; Ministry of Labour Application for Training and Grants. Cooperation with the Board of Agriculture, 7 August 1919, TNA, LAB 2/1516/DRA1287/1918; 'Draft Statement of the Fact by the Board of Agriculture,' 7 August 1919, TNA, LAB 2/1516/DRA1287/1918; 'Training of

Officers and Men of Like Standing in Agriculture, 24 May 1919, TNA, LAB 2/1516/DRA1287/1918; M.E. Glyn to Weston Priestly, 10 March 1919, TNA, MAF 42/8; M. E. Glyn to A. W. Priestly, 14 March 1919, TNA, MAF 42/8; Weston Priestly to Miss Glyn, 23 March 1919, TNA, MAF 42/8.

51. 'Demobilisation of the Land Army', 8 February 1919, TNA, MAF 42/6.

52. 'Resettlement Scheme for Ex-servicemen and Women', 19 July 1920, TNA, LAB 2/1516/DRA1287/1918; 'Demobilisation of the Women's Land Army, Land Settlement Scheme', 11 February 1919, TNA, MAF 42/6; 'Report of the Executive Committee for Council, 6 July 1920', Minute Books, Women's Library, SOSWB 1/202/1. See Noakes, 'From War Service to Domestic Service', 16–17.

53. Noakes, 'From War Service to Domestic Service', 1–2.

54. A. D. Hall to Agricultural Executive Committees in England and Wales, Cuts in Expenditures, 9 September 1919, TNA, MAF 42/7; Meriel Talbot to Organising Secretaries, 23 September 1919, TNA, MAF 42/7.

55. Meriel Talbot to Organising Secretaries, 12 August 1919, TNA, MAF 42/7; Report on Enrolments from Organising Secretaries to Women's Branch, 20 August 1919, TNA, MAF 42/7.

56. Meriel Talbot to Organising Secretaries, 14 October 1919, TNA, MAF 2/7.

57. Meriel Talbot to Organising Secretaries, 14 October 1919, TNA, MAF 2/7.

58. Meriel Talbot to Organising Secretaries, 'Release on Demobilisation', 13 November 1919, TNA, MAF 42/7; Memorandum to District Commissioners, Board of Agriculture, Applications received from Women for acceptance on the Board's Farm Settlements, 26 November 1919, TNA, MAF 42/7.

59. Meriel Talbot to Organising Secretaries, 17 November 1919, TNA, MAF 42/7.

60. Meriel Talbot to Women's Organising Secretaries, 18 November 1919, TNA, MAF 42/7.

61. 'Land Army and Rural Life', *Western Daily Mercury*, 24 November 1919.

62. Meriel Talbot to Women's Sub-Committees, 'National Association of Landswomen', 22 November 1919, TNA, MAF 42/7.

63. Meriel Talbot to Women's Sub-Committees, 'National Association of Landswomen', 22 November 1919, TNA, MAF 42/7; Meriel Talbot to Organising Secretaries, 'National Association of Landswomen', 25 November 1919, TNA, MAF 47/2; Meriel Talbot to Organising Secretaries, 'The Women's Land Army', 2 October 1919, TNA, MAF 42/7.

64. Meriel Talbot to Women's Sub-Committees, 'National Association of Landswomen', 22 November 1919, TNA, MAF 42/7; Meriel Talbot to Organising Secretaries, 'National Association of Landswomen', 25 November 1919, TNA, MAF 47/2; Meriel Talbot to Organising Secretaries, 'The Women's Land Army', 2 October 1919, TNA, MAF 42/7.

65. Meriel Talbot to Organising Secretaries, 'The Good Work of the Land Army', 22 November 1919, TNA, MAF 42/7.

66. Meriel Talbot to Organising Secretaries, 'Certificate of Discharge on Demobilisation', 22 November 1919, TNA, MAF 42/7.

67. 'Queen of Hearts – And Spades!', no date, WWI: Home Front. Land Girls (Farming MISC), The Women's Library, 10/51; 'Farwell Rally: Princess Mary's Investiture', no date, WWI: Home Front. Land Girls (Farming MISC), The Women's Library, 10/51.

68. Meriel Talbot to Organising Secretaries, 6 December 1919, TNA, MAF 42/7.

69. Organising Secretaries to Meriel Talbot, 'Work of the Organising Secretaries, Outfits and Demobilisation', 23 December 1919, TNA, MAF 42/7; Meriel Talbot to Organising Secretaries, 'Termination of World in the Counties', December 1919, TNA, MAF 42/7; Meriel Talbot to Organising Secretaries, 'Termination of work in the Counties, 30 December 1919, TNA, MAF 42/7.
70. Meriel Talbot to Organising Secretaries, 'The National Association of Landswomen', 17 December 1919, TNA, MAF 42/7.
71. Organising Secretaries to Meriel Talbot, 'Work of the Organising Secretaries, Outfits and Demobilisation', 23 December 1919, TNA, MAF 42/7; Meriel Talbot to Organising Secretaries, 'Termination of World in the Counties', December 1919, TNA, MAF 42/7; Meriel Talbot to Organising Secretaries, 'Termination of work in the Counties', 30 December 1919, TNA, MAF 42/7.
72. *The Landswoman*, December 1919.

Conclusion

1. Berta Ruck, *A Land Girl's Love Story* (New York: Dodd, Mead and Company, 1919), 17.
2. Ruck, *A Land Girl's Love Story*, 352.
3. The 1919 American film *Little Comrade* and the 1921 operetta *The Farmerette* were propaganda pieces aimed at reasserting the femininity of female land workers in the United States. This image of the WLA has proven to be remarkably resilient. See A. Huth, *Land Girls* (London: Constable, 2012); A. Huth, *Once a Land Girl* (London: Constable, 2010). See also *Land Girls*, Series 1–3, BBC, 30 October 2012.
4. For more on the 'enclosure' of women's experiences see D. R. Cohen, *Remapping the Home Front: Locating Citizenship in British Women's Great War Fiction* (Boston: Northeastern University Press, 2002), 8, 85.
5. Extending the 'men's story' beyond soldiers and the soldier's role. See R. Wohl, *The Generation of 1914* (New Haven: Harvard University Press, 1979), 1–4.
6. Ruck, *A Land Girl's Love Story*, 35, 63.
7. Ruck, *A Land Girl's Love Story*, 85.
8. Cecilia Gowdy-Wygant, *Cultivating Victory: The Women's Land Army and the Victory Garden Movement* (Pittsburgh: University of Pittsburgh Press, 2013), 184.
9. See M. R. Higonnet and P. L. R. Higonnet, 'The Double Helix', in *Behind the Lines: Gender and the Two World Wars*, ed. M. R. Higonnet et al. (New Haven: Yale University Press, 1987), 33–4.

Select Bibliography

Archives

Bedfordshire and Luton Archives, Bedford
Berkshire Record Office, Reading
Bodleian Library, Oxford
British Library, London
Colindale Newspaper Library, London
Churchill College Archive Centre, Cambridge
Devon Record Office, Exeter
Essex Record Office, Chelmsford
Glamorgan Archives, Cardiff
Imperial War Museum, London
Kent Archives, Maidstone
Museum of English Rural Life, Reading
The National Archives, Kew
National Archives of Scotland, Edinburgh
North Devon Record Office, Barnstaple
Oxfordshire Record Office, Cowley
Plymouth and South Devon Record Office, Plymouth
Wiltshire and Swindon Archives, Chippenham
The Women's Library, London
Worcestershire Archive and Archeology Service, Worcester

Newspapers and journals

The Auckland Chronicle
The Bideford Gazette
The Birmingham Mercury
The Birmingham Dispatch
The Bristol Evening Times
Casswell's Saturday Journal
The Crediton Chronicle
The Common Cause
The Daily News and Leader
The Daily Express
The Daily Mail
The Daily News
The Daily News and Leader
The Daily Sketch
The Daily Telegraph
The Dartmouth & South Hans Chronicle
The Dundee Advertiser

The East Cumberland News
The Eastern Daily
The Evening Standard and Chronicle
The Englishwoman
The Express and Echo
The Glasgow Weekly
The Globe
The Graphic
The Hereford Times
Journal of the Board of Agriculture
The Ladies' Field
The Landswoman
The Mark Lane Express
The Mercury
The Morning Post
The North Devon Herald
The Northern Echo
The Northampton Echo
The Nottingham Evening News
The Nottingham Weekly Journal
The Pall Mall Gazette
The Pictorial
The Salcombe Gazette
The Sheffield Telegraph and Dispatch
The Standard
The Sunday Pictorial
The Sunday Times
The Teignmouth Post
The Times
The Standard
The Sheffield Daily Telegraph
The Western Independent
The Western Morning News
The Western Times

Dissertation/theses

Pierce, P. J., *That Dame's Got Grit: Selling the Women's Land Army* (2010). All Graduate Theses and Dissertations. Paper 625. http://digitalcommons.usu.edu/etd/625.

Secondary sources and printed material

Abrams, L. and C. G. Brown, *A History of Everyday Life in Twentieth Century Scotland.* Edinburgh: Edinburgh University Press, 2010.
Anthony, R., 'The Scottish Agricultural Labour Market, 1900–1939'. *Economic History Review* 46 (1993): 558–74.
Augé-Laribé, M. and P. Pinot, *Agriculture and Food Policy in France during the War.* New Haven, CT: Yale University Press, 1927.

Barnett, M., *British Food Policy During the First World War.* Boston: George Allen & Unwin, 1985.

Beastall, T. W., 'Landlords and Tenants', in *The Victorian Countryside vol. II*, ed. G. E. Mingay, 428–438. London: Routledge & Kegan Paul, 1981.

Beckett, J. V., *The Aristocracy in England.* London: Blackwell, 1986.

Beckett, J. and M. Turner, 'End of the Old Order? F.M.L. Thompson, the Land Question, and the Burden of Ownership in England, c. 1880–c.1925', *Agricultural History Review*, 55 (2007): 269–88.

Beddoe, D., *Back to Home and Duty: Women between the Wars, 1918–1939.* London: Pandora Press, 1989.

Bentwich, H., *If I Forget Thee: Some Chapters of Autobiography, 1912–1920.* London: Elek, 1973.

Bingham, A., 'An Era of Domesticity? Histories of Women and Gender in Interwar Britain', *Cultural and Social History* 1 (2004): 225–33.

Boston, S., *Women Workers and the Trade Union Movement.* London: Davis-Poynter, 1981.

Bourne, J. M., *Britain and the Great War, 1914–1918.* London: Edward Arnold, 1989.

Braybon, G., *Women Workers in the First World War.* London: Routledge, 1981.

Braybon, G. and P. Summerfield, *Out of the Cage: Women's Experiences in Two World Wars.* London: Routledge, 1987.

Brown, C. G., *A History of Everyday Life in Twentieth Century Scotland.* Edinburgh: Edinburgh University Press, 2010.

Brown, J., 'Agricultural Policy and the National Farmers' Union, 1908–1939', in *Agriculture and Politics in England, 1815–1939*, ed. J. R. Wordie, 178–98. New York: St Martin's Press, 2000.

Bush, J., *Edwardian Ladies and Imperial Power.* London: Leicester University Press, 2000.

Cameron, E., *Impaled upon a Thistle: Scotland since 1880.* Edinburgh: Edinburgh University Press, 2010.

——— *Land for the People? The British Government and the Scottish Highlands, c. 1880–1925.* East Linton: Tuckwell Press, 1996.

——— 'Setting the Heather on Fire: The Land Question in Scotland, 1850–1914', in *The Land Question in Britain, 1750–1950*, ed. M. Cragoe and P. Readman, 109–25. New York: Palgrave Macmillan, 2010.

Cannadine, D., *The Decline and Fall of the British Aristocracy.* New Haven: Yale University Press, 1990.

Chambers, I., *The Chamberlains, the Churchills and Ireland, 1874–1922.* London: Cambria Press, 2006.

Cherry, G. E. and A. Rogers, *Rural Change and Planning: England and Wales in the Twentieth Century.* London: E. & F. N. Spon, 1996.

Clarke, G., *The Women's Land Army: A Portrait.* Bristol: Sansome & Company, 2008.

Cohen, D. R., *Remapping the Home Front: Locating Citizenship in British Women's Great War Fiction.* Boston: Northeastern University Press, 2002.

Collins, E. J. T., 'The Age of Machinery', in *The Victorian Countryside, Vol. I*, ed. G. E. Mingay, 200–13. London: Routledge & Kegan Paul, 1981.

Cooper, A. F., *British Agricultural Policy, 1912–1936: A Study in Conservative Politics.* Manchester: Manchester University Press, 1989.

Crawford, E., *Women's Suffrage Movement: A Reference Guide, 1866–1928*. London: Routledge, 2001.

Crowe, H., 'Keeping the Wheels of the Form in Motion: Labour Shortages in the Uplands during the Great War', *Rural History* 19 (2008): 201–16.

Crowe, H., 'Profitable Ploughing of the Uplands? The Food Production Campaign in the First World War', *Agricultural History Review* 55 (2007): 205–28.

Culleton, C., *Working Class Culture, Women, and Britain, 1914–1921*. London: St Martin's Press, 1999.

Cummins, I. A., 'The Woman Engineer', *The Englishwoman* 46 (April 1920): 38.

Dakers, C., *The Countryside at War, 1914–1918*. London: Constable and Company Limited, 1987.

Darrow, M. H., *French Women and the First World War: War Stories of the Home Front*. New York: Berg, 2000.

DeGroot, G., *Blighty: British Society in the Era of the Great War*. London: Longman, 1996.

Devine, T. M., *The Scottish Nation: A History, 1700–2000*. New York: Viking, 1999.

—— *Exploring the Scottish Past: Themes in the History of Scottish Society*. East Linton: Tuckwell Press, 1995.

—— 'Scottish Farm Labour in the Era of Agricultural Depression, 1875–1900', in *Farm Servants and Labour in Lowland Scotland, 1770–1914*, ed. T. M. Devine, 243–55. Edinburgh: John Milner Associates, 1984.

Devine, T. M., C. H. Lee and G. C. Peden, *The Transformation of Scotland: The Economy since 1700*. Edinburgh: Edinburgh University Press, 2005.

Dewey, P., *British Agriculture in the First World War*. London: Routledge, 1989.

——*War and Progress: Britain, 1914–1945*. London: Longman, 1997.

—— 'Nutrition and Living Standards in Wartime Britain', in *The Upheaval of War: Family, Work and Welfare in Europe, 1914–1918*, ed. R. Wall and J. Winter, 199–220. Cambridge: Cambridge University Press, 1988.

Douglas, C., 'Scottish Agriculture during the War', *Transaction of the Highland and Agricultural Society for Scotland*, 31 (1919): 46–9.

Ernle, Lord, *English Farming: Past and Present*. London: Frank Cass & Co., 1961.

—— *The Land and its People: Chapters in Rural Life and History*. London: Hutchinson, 1923.

—— 'The Food Campaign of 1916–18', *Journal of the Royal Agricultural Society* 82 (1921): 1–48.

Fussell, P., *The Great War and Modern Memory*. Oxford: Oxford University Press, 1976.

Gilbert, B., *British Social Policy, 1914–1939*. New York: Cornell University Press, 1970.

Goodwin, A., 'Early Years of the Trade Unions', in *Women in the Labour Movement: The British Experience*, ed. L. Middleton, 94–112. London: Croom Helm, 1977.

Gordon, E. and E. Brietenbach, *The World Is Ill Divided: Women's Work in Scotland in the Late Nineteenth and Early Twentieth Centuries*. Edinburgh: Edinburgh University Press, 1990.

Gowdy-Wygant, C., *Cultivating Victory: The Women's Land Army and the Victory Garden Movement*. Pittsburgh: University of Pittsburgh Press, 2013.

Graubard, S. R., 'Demobilisation in Great Britain Following the First World War', *Journal of Modern History* 19(1947): 297–311.

Grayzel, S., 'Nostalgia, Gender and the Countryside: Placing the "Land Girl" in First World War Britain', *Rural History* 10.2 (1999): 155–70.

————— *Women's Identities at War: Gender, Motherhood and Politics in Britain and France during the First World War*. Chapel Hill, NC: University of North Carolina Press, 1999.

————— *Women and the First World War*. London: Longman, 2002.

Gregory, A., *The Last Great War: British Society and the First World War*. Cambridge: Cambridge University Press, 2008.

Grieves, K., *The Politics of Manpower, 1914–18*. Manchester: Manchester University Press, 1988.

Grigg, J., *Lloyd George: War Leader 1916–1918*. London: Penguin, 2005.

Harris, J., *Private Lives, Public Spirit: A Social History of Britain, 1870–1914*. Oxford: Oxford University Press, 1993.

Hibbard, B., *Effects of the Great War upon Agriculture in the United States and Great Britain*. New York: Oxford University Press, 1919.

Higonnet, M. R. and P. L. R. Higonnet, 'The Double Helix', in *Behind the Lines: Gender and the Two World Wars*, ed. M. R. Higonnet, J. Jenson, S. Michel and M. Collins Weitz, 31–47. New Haven: Yale University Press, 1987.

Hirst, F. W., *The Consequences of the War to Great Britain*. London: Oxford University Press, 1934.

Hockin, O., *Two Girls on the Land: Wartime on a Dartmoore Farm*. London: Arnold, 1918.

Holderness, B. A., 'The Victorian Farmer', in *The Victorian Countryside Vol. 1*, ed. G. E. Mingay, 227–44. London: Routledge & Kegan Paul, 1981.

Hollis, P., *Ladies Elect: Women in English Local Government, 1865–1914*. Oxford: Clarendon Press, 1987.

Holloway, G., *Women and Work in Britain since 1840*. London: Routledge, 2005.

Horn, P., *Rural Life in England in the First World War*. New York: St Martin's Press, 1984.

————— *The Rural World, 1750–1850: Social Change in the English Countryside*. New York: St Martin's Press, 1980.

Horne, J. N., *Labour at War: France and Britain, 1914–1918*. Oxford: Oxford University Press, 1991.

Houh, R., *The Great War at Sea, 1914–1918*. Oxford: Oxford University Press, 1984.

Houston, G. F. B., 'Agriculture', in *The Scottish Economy: A Statistical Account of Scottish Life*, ed. A. K. Cairncross, 84–108. Cambridge: Cambridge University Press, 1954.

Howkins, A., *Poor Labouring Men: Rural Radicalism in Norfolk*. London: Routledge, 1985.

————— *The Death of Rural England: A Social History of the Countryside since 1900*. New York: Routledge, 2003.

Hunt, E. H., 'Labour Productivity in English Agriculture, 1850–1914', *The Economic History Review*, 20 (August 1967): 280–92.

Huth, A., *Once a Land Girl* (London: Constable, 2010).

————— *Land Girls* (London: Constable, 2012).

Hynes, S., *A War Imagined: The First World War and English Culture*. London: Bodley Head, 1990.

James, P., *Picture This: World War I Posters and Visual Culture*. Lincoln, NE: University of Nebraska Press, 2010.

Jamieson, L. and C. Toynbee, *Country Bairns: Growing Up 1900–1930*. Edinburgh: Edinburgh University Press, 1992.

Jones, D. T., J. F. Duncan, H. M. Conacher and W. R. Scott, *Rural Scotland during the War*. New Haven: Yale University Press, 1926.

Joseph, N. and N. Alex, 'The Uniform: A Sociological Perspective', *American Journal of Sociology* 77 (1972): 19–30.

Keith, J., 'The War and the Agriculturalist: II, the Farmer', *Scottish Journal of Agriculture*, 25(1944): 193–8.

Kendle, J., *Ireland and the Federal Solution: The Debate over the United Kingdom Constitution, 1870–1921*. Kingston: McGill-Queen's Press, 1989.

Kent, S. K., *Making Peace: The Reconstruction of Gender in Interwar Britain*. Princeton, NJ: Princeton University Press, 1993.

Kerr, J. A., *Scotland and the Impact of the Great War, 1914–1928*. London: Hodder Gibson, 2010.

Kirby, M., 'Industry, Agriculture and Trade Unions', in *The First World War in British History*, ed. S. Constantine, M. Kirby and M. Rose, 51–80. New York: St Martin's Press, 1995.

Lewis, J., *Women in England*. London: Wheatsheaf, 1984.

Light, A., *Forever England: Femininity, Literature and Conservatism between the Wars*. London: Routledge, 1991.

Love, D., *Ayrshire: Discovering a County*. Ayr: Fort Publishing, 2003.

MacDonald, C. M. M. and E. W. McFarland, *Scotland and the Great War*. East Linton: Tuckwell Press, 1999.

Mansfield, N., *English Farmworkers and Local Patriotism, 1900–1930*. Farnham: Ashgate, 2001.

Marwick, A., *The Deluge: British Society and the First World War*. London: Norton, 1970.

—— *Women at War*. London: Fontana, 1977.

Middleton, T. H., *Food Production in War*. London: Oxford Clarendon Press, 1923.

Mingay, G. E., *A Social History of the English Countryside*. London: Routledge, 1990.

Money, A. L., *History of the Girls' Friendly Society*. London: Wells Gardner & Company, 1911.

Morgan, M., 'The Women's Institutes Movement: The Acceptable Face of Feminism', in *This Working-Day World: Women's Lives and Culture(s) in Britain*, ed. S. Oldfield, 29–39. Bristol: Taylor & Francis, 1994.

Morgan, V., 'Agricultural Wage Rates in Late Eighteenth-Century Scotland', *The Economic History Review* 24 (1971): 181–201.

Morris, J., 'Skilled Workers and the Politics of "Red" Clyde: A Discussion Paper', *Journal of Scottish Labour History Society* 19 (1984): 6–17.

Mowat, C. L., *Britain between the Wars, 1918–1940*. Chicago: University of Chicago Press, 1955.

Noakes, L., 'From War Service to Domestic Service: Ex-servicewomen and the Free Passage Scheme, 1919–1922', *Twentieth Century British History* 22 (2011): 1–27.

Offer, A., *The First World War: An Agrarian Interpretation*. Oxford: Clarendon Press, 1989.

Olson, M., *The Economics of the Wartime Shortage: A History of British Food Supplies in the Napoleonic War and in World Wars I and II*. Durham, NC: Duke University Press, 1963.

Opitz, D. L., '"A Triumph of Brains over Brute": Women and Science at the Horticultural College, Swanley, 1890–1910', *Isis* 104 (2013): 30–62.

Orwin, C. S. and E. H. Whetham, *History of British Agriculture, 1846–1914*. Newton Abbot: David & Charles, 1971.

Ouditt, S., *Fighting Forces, Writing Women: Identity and Ideology in the First World War*. Chapel Hill, NC: University of North Carolina Press, 1999.

Parker, G., *Citizenship, Contingency and the Countryside: Rights, Culture, Land and the Environment*. London: Routledge, 2002.

Pennell, C., *A Kingdom United: Popular Responses to the Outbreak of the First World War in Britain and Ireland*. Oxford: Oxford University Press, 2012.

Prothero, R. E., *Whippingham to Westminster*. London: Murray, 1938.

—— *The Pioneers and Progress of English Farming*. New York: Longmans, 1888.

Pyecroft, S., 'British Working Woman and the First World War', *Historian* 56.4 (1994): 699–710.

Riedl, E., 'Women, Gender and the Promotion of Empire: The Victoria League, 1901–1914', *The Historical Journal* 45 (September 2002): 569–99.

Roper, M., *The Secret Battle: Emotional Survival in the Great War*. Manchester: Manchester University Press, 2009.

Rubin, G., *War, Law, and Labour*. Oxford: Clarendon Press, 1987.

Ruck, B., *A Land Girl's Love Story*. New York: Dodd, Mead and Company, 1919.

Sayer, K., 'Field-faring Women: The Resistance of Women Who Worked in the Fields of Nineteenth-century England', *Women's History Review*, 2 (1993): 185–98.

Sheail, J., 'Land Improvement and Reclamation: The Experiences of the First World War in England and Wales', *Agricultural History Review* 24.2 (1976): 110–25.

—— 'The Role of the War Agricultural and Executive Committees in the Food Production Campaign of 1915–1918 in England and Wales', *Agricultural Administration* 1 (1974): 141–54.

Shewell-Cooper, W. E., *Land Girl: A Handbook for the Women's Land Army*. London: English University Press, 1942.

Silbey, D., *The British Working Class and Enthusiasm for War, 1914–1916*. New York: Frank Cass, 2005.

Smout, T. C., *A Century of the Scottish People, 1830–1950*. New Haven: Yale University Press, 1986.

Spring, E., 'Landowners, Lawyers, and Land Law Reform in Nineteenth-Century England', *The American Journal of Legal History* 21 (1977): 40–59.

Steinbach, S., *Women in England, 1760–1914: A Social History*. New York: Palgrave, 2004.

Story, M. and P. Childs, *British Cultural Identities*. London: Routledge, 2002.

Thom, D., *Nice Girls and Rude Girls: Women Workers in World War I*. London: I.B. Tauris, 1998.

Thom, D., 'The Bundle of Sticks: Women, Trade Unionists and Collective Organisation before 1918', in *Unequal Opportunities: Women's Employment in England, 1800–1918*, ed. A. V. John, 261–285. New York: Basil Blackwell, 1986.

Thompson, F. M. L., *English Landed Society in the Nineteenth Century*. London: Routledge & Kegan Paul, 1963.

Thomson, A., 'Memory as a Battlefield: Personal and Political Investments in the National Military Past', *Oral History Review* 22 (1995): 55–73.

Turner, D. M., *The History of Science Teaching in England*. London: Chapman & Hall, 1927.

Twinch, C., *Women on the Land: Their Story during Two World Wars*. Cambridge: Lutterworth Press, 1991.

Verdon, N., *Rural Women Workers in Nineteenth-Century England: Gender, Work, Wages*. New York: Boydell Press, 2002.

Waites, B., *A Class Society at War: England 1914–1918*. New York: St Martin's Press, 1987.

Watson, J., 'Khaki Girls, VADS, and Tommy's Sisters: Gender and Class in First World War Britain', *International History Review* 19 (1997): 32–51.

—— *Fighting Different Wars: Experience, Memory, and the First World War in Britain*. Cambridge: Cambridge University Press, 2004.

Weiss, E., *Fruits of Victory: The Women's Land Army of America in the Great War*. Washington: Potomac Books, 2008.

White, B., 'Feeding the War Effort: Agricultural Experiences in First World War Devon', *Agricultural History Review* 58 (2010): 95–112.

—— 'Remembrance, Retrospection, and the Women's Land Army in First World War Britain', *Journal of the Canadian Historical Association* 22 (2011): 162–94.

—— 'Sowing the Seeds of Patriotism: The Women's Land Army in First World War Devon', *The Local Historian* 41 (2011): 13–27.

—— 'Volunteerism and Early Recruitment Strategies in Devonshire, August 1914–December 1915', *Historical Journal* 53 (2009): 621–66.

Wilson, T., *The Myriad Faces of War: Britain and the Great War, 1914–1918*. Cambridge: Polity Press, 1986.

Winter, M., *Rural Politics: Policies for Agriculture, Forestry, and the Environment*. New York: Routledge, 1996.

—— *The Great War and the British People*. London: Macmillan, 1985.

—— *Sites of Memory, Sites of Mourning*. Cambridge: Cambridge University Press, 1995.

Winter J. and A. Prost, *The Great War in History*. Cambridge: Cambridge University Press, 2005.

Wohl, R., *The Generation of 1914*. New Haven: Harvard University Press, 1979.

Woollacott, A., '"Khaki Fever" and its Control: Gender, Age and Sexual Morality on the British Homefront in the First World War', *Journal of Contemporary History* 29 (1994): 325–47.

—— *On Her their Lives Depend: Munitions Workers in the Great War*. Berkeley, CA: University of California Press, 1994.

Yeandle, S., *Women's Working Lives: Patterns and Strategies*. London: Tavistock Publications, 1984.

Index

Printed and bound by CPI Group (UK) Ltd, Croydon, CR0 4YY